AMERICA AND BRITAIN

GUY ARNOLD

America and Britain

Was There Ever a Special Relationship?

HURST & COMPANY, LONDON

First published in the United Kingdom in 2014 by
C.Hurst & Co. (Publishers) Ltd.,
41 Great Russell Street, London, WC1B 3PL
© Guy Arnold, 2014
All rights reserved.
Printed in India

Distributed in the United States, Canada and Latin America by
Oxford University Press, 198 Madison Avenue, New York, NY 10016,
United States of America.

A Cataloguing-in-Publication data record for this book
is available from the British Library.

ISBN: 978-1-84904-328-1

www.hurstpublishers.com

This book is printed on paper from registered sustainable
and managed sources.

CONTENTS

INTRODUCTION

COLLAPSE OF POWER

At the beginning of the twentieth century internal upheavals in Venezuela led to attacks upon foreigners and their assets, with the result that Britain, Germany and Italy blockaded the country to enforce reparations. This action was strongly opposed by the United States, which invoked the Monroe Doctrine, and Britain (followed by the other two powers) backed down. What later came to be described as the 'American disease' at the heart of the British establishment dates from this confrontation over Venezuela between Britain and the United States. Ever since the Venezuelan crisis of 1902 it became a dogma of British foreign policy that nothing should be done to offend the United States and from this confrontation, through to Prime Minister David Cameron's assertion in 2010 that Britain was the 'junior partner', the special relationship has been entrenched in British political thinking. This did not mean that the relationship was necessarily amicable and in 1939, for example, the British politician 'RAB' Butler was to say, dismissively, 'In my political life I have always been convinced that we can no more count on America than Brazil.'

When the Second World War came to an end in 1945, Britain faced the monumental task of rebuilding a society whose economic and power base had been deeply eroded if not destroyed. John Stuart Mill, in another era, had said, 'When society requires to be rebuilt there is no use in attempting to rebuild it on the old plan.' Sadly, Britain did not take this advice but instead attempted to restore the imperial myth and worldwide role it had maintained, if fictionally, up to the war. The basis of a great power is a great and thriving economy. In the years 1945–1951 Britain ought to have put all its effort into rejuvenating and modernising its economy. This it failed to do, instead using the American loan and subsequent Marshall aid to implement the welfare state (the New Jerusalem) that the Labour party had promised to create. Meanwhile, Britain faced a deliberate and sustained US policy of undermining British power, which was the price that Britain had to pay for US assistance during the war. The expectation in London that, somehow, the United States would assist Britain to remain a great power was a political absurdity, a contradiction of the reality of US aims, which were to downsize Britain and replace it as the sole great power of the West. A. F. K. Organski, writing in 1958 at the height of the Cold War and just after the Suez debacle, provides us with a precise run-down of US/UK relations at that time: 'We have encouraged the dissolution of her empire, taken over much of her trade, and given her aid on condition that she follows our lead in dealing with other nations. When it came to a showdown over the Suez Canal, we humiliated the British and forced them to retreat militarily because we were not pleased with their seizure of the Canal. England's dependence upon the United States grows daily. There is no doubt that she is pleased to have the most powerful nation in the world for her friend rather than her enemy, but her lot is by no means as happy as it was when England was second to none.'[1]

The great mistake from 1945 onwards was perpetual regret for an empire that was about to disintegrate, and world influence that could only be sustained by an economic base that did not exist. All British efforts, whether under Labour or Tory governments, were geared to regaining a position that was lost instead of planning in terms of the country's true capacity. No leader, whatever rhetoric he employed, came to terms with the real changes that had occurred to acknowledge that Britain had to go down a different road to the one it had followed up to the triumph of 1945. Ernest Bevin, Attlee's foreign secretary, understood clearly what constituted power in the new world order when he insisted that Britain should have its own nuclear bombs, but his position was to be subverted by Attlee (as well as by Bevin himself) through to Macmillan when they sought American assistance with the

British nuclear deterrent. This defied logic. Britain could only be a great power if it had its own bomb and means of delivery not in any way dependent upon US input. Moreover, the expectation of American help presupposed the readiness to depend. A great power does not depend upon another great power. There is an almost inexplicable problem here. Perceptive British leaders from Attlee to Macmillan who clearly understood the sources of British weakness nonetheless contrived to ignore the logic of what they understood and continued to pursue policies that the country could not sustain. Lionel Gelber, a sympathetic Anglophile American, described the British dilemma as, 'A struggle to maintain an identity of her own is what Britain's crisis is all about.'[2]

Much soul searching about Britain's position in the world took place during the 1960s. In 1960, four years after the debacle of Suez, Sir William Hayter, an eminent British diplomat but by then Warden of New College, Oxford, wrote an elegant monograph, *The Diplomacy of the Great Powers*, in which he compared the diplomacy of the USA, the USSR, France and Britain. At a time when Britain grasped at straws to re-establish some of the worldwide influence that Suez had destroyed, Hayter pointed out, almost pleadingly, that whatever else we had lost of our great power status, we were still at the top of the ladder as far as diplomacy was concerned. One gem in his appraisal that reeks of Oxbridge superiority is the statement, 'The American's distrust of foreigners is compounded of suspicion that they are inevitably after his dollars and a fear that they may be smart enough to get them.' Towards the end he says, 'All I am claiming for British diplomacy is that it is better than American, Soviet or French.' Any crumb to shore up British morale.[3]

Macmillan spent an inordinate amount of his premiership (1957–1963) restoring and shoring up the special relationship that Eden with his Suez adventure had all but shattered. He knew, from his experience in the Second World War at the centre of strategic decisions, that Britain could never recover her position as a great power and so turned to cultivating the United States although he must also have known that there were other policies that Britain could have adopted with greater success and more pride than acting as a US satellite. Michael Shanks, in his best-selling book *The Stagnant Society* (1961), was concerned with economic issues; however, he excoriated the mood of nostalgia for past greatness that Macmillan constantly invoked. 'We should move forward,' he wrote. 'A society which loses interest in material progress is a society on its way to the embalming chamber. The petals which fall on it are romantic, but they are suffocating. This is the great psychological danger facing the British people today—that we may bury ourselves under the rose petals of a vast collective nostalgia, lost in a sweet sad love affair with our own past.'[4] Shanks portrays a class-bound society stagnating in nostalgia and class warfare that is more concerned to maintain a moribund social status than to move forward. The ambition of too many industrial tycoons, he argues, is to buy a plot of land and set up as a tax-loss farmer and bring up their sons to be intellectuals, civil servants or 'something in the city'. 'Not since Marie Antoinette milked cows in the Trianon has there been a ruling class in Europe with such an urge to play the peasant.'

Defence of the West throughout the Cold War, always spearheaded by the United States, made defence a top priority in both Britain and Europe. And this remained the case after the Cold War had come to an end and the Soviet threat, real or assumed, had passed. Britain, as Tony Benn pointed out, had allowed itself to become an offshore military base for the United States and its willing military satellite. Two-thirds of a century after the end of the Second World War and twenty years after the end of the Cold War, Britain remained a military outpost for the spread of American worldwide hegemony, a state of affairs that few people would have thought possible in 1945. But, as another ancient, Plutarch, pointed out: 'He who wants a defender is naturally a subject to him who can defend.' Writing in the 1990s, the Tory politician Norman Fowler recalled a trip he had made to the United States in 1976. 'The Americans were friendly and polite, but there was no mistaking their view that Britain had gone downhill to the point that we had become an irrelevance.'[5]

Anglo-American relations from the late 1940s onwards have been about the ways in which Britain has adjusted to the lopsidedness of the special relationship, while its prime ministers, one after another, have sought excuses to cross the Atlantic and pay court to whoever was the incumbent in the White House. Churchill, in his last period as prime minister (1951–55), always wanted to visit America and see its president as did Macmillan and Wilson, whether they were truly welcome or not. With the single exception of Edward Heath who took Britain into the European Economic Community (EEC) in 1973, every British prime minister from Churchill to Brown regarded the special relationship as the cornerstone of British foreign policy. This was always a fallacy: the relationship was never more than peripheral to American interests even when they recognised its existence. The importance of the special relationship to Britain, however, was in direct proportion to its real decline in power after 1945 and it was to become a constant of post-war politics to persuade Washington of Britain's unique value as a peacetime ally. By the time (May 2010) that a coalition government under David Cameron had been formed, reliance upon, and subservience to the Americans had become deeply embedded in British political calculations and was taken for granted like the monarchy. The political elite, almost without exception, has assumed that the American relationship was a 'given' and that all other policies were subordinate to it. They need not have been.

Writing towards the end of his long life in his book *The Culture of Contentment*, Kenneth Galbraith argues that in a democracy the contented majority do not wish to be disturbed by changes or 'revolutionary' action that will upset their lifestyle.[6] A change of policy away from the special relationship in Britain would certainly upset the lifestyle of a political elite that has settled for the predictable role of the faithful US satellite state and this may well explain why British leaders, no matter what other policies occur to them, always return to the safe if demeaning role of number two in the American alliance. Resistance to change plays a greater part in this British choice than the merits or demerits of the choice may suggest.

At the centre of the British problem of government is the dilemma: how much does Britain originate policy and how much does it accept and implement policies coming from outside? Writing in his diary for the period 1977–80, Tony Benn blames the Foreign Office: 'The extent to which the treachery of our senior officials in the FO has grown is astonishing. It prevents us in many ways from developing our potential and influence to the full. Just as we never wanted to upset the Americans during the days of the special relationship, now we never want to upset the Germans or the French.'—'In a curious way, we are led by a group of people who have a conception of Britain as a governed colony of some international organisation. The Treasury doesn't want to upset the IMF, and the FO doesn't want to upset the EEC and the Ministry of Defence doesn't want to upset NATO. These are the organisations that govern affairs in Britain.'[7]

Henry Kissinger at this time said, 'British statesmen were content to act as honorary consultants to our (US) decisions.' Indeed, ongoing belief in the special relationship has become a sickness in the body pol-itic of Britain that needs to be flushed out if the country is ever again to stand on its own feet. Peter Riddell, writing in the new century, described the special relationship as 'an emotional blanket for a declin-ing power'[8] with the traffic all one way. The United States has rarely adapted to accommodate the British. American international policies are conceived in the interests of the United States and should not be resented. Britain, however, should not adopt or defend them yet it does so under the cover of the special relationship. Now if Britain is ever to bring an end to the special relationship and embark upon its own pol-icies it is necessary to ask who benefits from maintaining this asymmet-rical alliance. Although the US political hierarchy apparently has little time for it they would not like to see it pass if only because that would mean the loss of a valuable satellite. Michael Heseltine (Secretary of Defence under Margaret Thatcher) described the special relationship as 'the most naïve delusion fostered on this side of the Atlantic, and hardly ever referred to on the other side of the Atlantic. The only real special relationship for the United States is that with Israel.' At the heart of the British determination to cling to the special relationship is the collapse of British power, which may be traced back to develop-ments in the nineteenth century.

The collapse of British power

In 1995 *Our Global Neighbourhood, The Report of the Commission on Global Governance*[9] was published. It was a painstaking piece of work and presented all the arguments for producing a better world. It is worth examining two or three of its recommendations to compare these with the kind of unilateralist actions pursued by the United States and too readily supported by its special ally, Britain.

Democracy provides the environment with which the fundamental rights of cit-izens are best safeguarded and offers the most favourable foundation for peace and stability. The world needs, however, to ensure the rights of minorities, and to guard against the ascendance of the military and corruption. Democracy is more than just the right to vote in regular elections. And as within nations, so globally, the democratic principle must be ascendant.

This is very much what might be described as UN-speak, or going back to 1920, League-speak. The report went on to discuss the reform of the Security Council. It suggested that permanent membership of the

Security Council, which was limited to five countries (the United States, the USSR, Britain, France and China) that derived their primacy from events (then) fifty years in the past, was no longer acceptable as was their possession of the veto. It argued for a widening of the permanent members from five to nine and the phasing out of the veto by 2005. Sixteen years later nothing had changed. *Our Global Neighbourhood* is a fine, aspirational but ultimately forlorn document, rendered irrelevant by the five powers determined not to surrender the veto and only prepared to support a weak United Nations whose proposals they can always ignore or veto. The failure of the United Nations to develop into the world's governing body simply represents the realities of power. US President Woodrow Wilson, whose fourteen points became the blueprint for the League of Nations, was repudiated by the US Senate which made plain it would not endorse US membership of any organisation that had the power to tell the USA what to do. Only the weak pursue world government, the strong aim for hegemony.

Following the defeat of Napoleon at Waterloo in 1815, Britain emerged as the world's leading power, a position she maintained from 1815 to 1914. However, increasingly through this century Britain rested on her laurels while rivals sought to overtake her, the two leading contenders being the United States and Germany. Moreover, secure in her empire, which was guarded by the world's greatest naval fleet or fleets, and living off the results of her industrial revolution that had given her pre-eminence as a trading nation, she enjoyed delusions of grandeur as her young men were trained in the Greek and Roman classics at the new public schools before they went overseas to police an empire that was seen increasingly as a blessing to the world, while her rivals meanwhile geared their educational systems to industrial growth.

Correlli Barnett, in his book *The Collapse of British Power*, advances a devastating thesis to explain how the greatest imperial power in the world in 1900 was reduced in all but name to a satellite of the United States after 1945. During the seventeenth and eighteenth centuries Britain had been a robust power fighting its peer nations in Europe to emerge as the world's leading power in 1815, a position it maintained for a century. But the motivation of the ruling elite changed during the period of British predominance from empire building to empire maintenance while liberals and humanitarians began to dominate foreign policy as the British gloried in their empire and increasingly came to persuade themselves that they were superior to other nations and that their imperial spread gave them a unique role to ben-efit the rest of the world. Palmerston, who at his death in 1865 was out of fashion, had said that you should knock down an opponent first and then if necessary apologise afterwards to assuage his feelings but by then the humanitarians were taking over. The Eastern Question, which meant the declining Ottoman Empire, was regarded in terms of *Realpolitik* by Disraeli but in humanitarian or moral terms by his great political rival Gladstone, whose name became synonymous with a moral approach to international problems. But times were changing: 'For after 1870 Britain was back where she had been in the centuries before Waterloo—struggling against powerful rivals, struggling eco-nomically, strategically, diplomatically.'—'Moralising internationalism, born out of liberalism by evangelical faith, was therefore an unsuitable guide to British policy.'[10]

In 1921 Field Marshal Jan Smuts (an anglophile imperialist) described the British Empire that had emerged from the First World War as the greatest power in the world—only unsound policy could rob her of that position. What Smuts failed to note or, perhaps, under-stand was the reality that brute force rather than humanitarian ideal-ism usually won international arguments. During the 1920s and 1930s Britain failed to develop its strength to defend or empower its empire so as to keep pace with the post-war recovery and subsequent milita-risation of its main European rival, Germany. A fundamental problem for Britain was an educational system (the public schools) geared to ruling an empire rather than producing the industrial skills essential to economic growth while European (German) and American education embraced technology, science and engineering. The British political elite as well as ordinary Britons loved the empire upon which the sun never set but did not question what value it would be to Britain in times of trouble. India was the key. Lord Curzon, the Viceroy of India from 1899 to 1905 famously said, 'As long as we rule India we are the greatest power in the world. If we lose it we shall drop straight away to a third-rate power.' The knowledge that possession of India so empowered Britain may have been comforting but what Curzon did not examine was the cost to Britain of defending India on the one hand and just what contribution India could and would make to British power in the event of a war that through the 1930s became ever more certain. In essence, the cohesion of the Commonwealth in war depended upon British naval power and between the wars—with the naval agreement with the United States, constant demands at home for disarmament and faltering British finances—it became increasingly obvious that Britain could not develop its naval power to the extent that would be essential if it was to face an attack upon the empire on two fronts: Germany in Europe and Japan in Asia.[11] 'And lastly there was the huge and rapid expansion of a United States Navy. This was aimed specifically, like the Imperial German High Seas Fleet, against England.'—'There was therefore every strategic, economic and psychological justification for England to see in the United States the successor to Germany, France, Spain—as an overwhelming super-power dangerous to English prosperity and independence.'[12] The extraordinary aspect of this development was the wilful blindness of the British establishment. It was always American policy to destroy the British Empire and downsize Britain so that the United States could take its place—as it did after 1945.

The British, despite evidence to the contrary (that the United States was always intent upon cutting down British power and replacing it with their own) nonetheless appeared to accept that a strong United States, including one much stronger than Britain, would somehow act in support of the old imperial power. This was manifestly not the case. Britain did not have the same delusions about Germany, which it saw as a threat although the way it tackled the German threat was often absurd. In the years leading up to the Second World War Britain tried repeatedly and unsuccessfully to persuade Germany to act through, and according to, the precepts of the League of Nations. 'For during the three years when England was casting away the opportunity of dealing effectively with Nazi Germany from a position of combined British and French military superiority, she had also allowed herself to suffer another defeat with no less catastrophic consequences: she had lost the re-armament race with Germany, especially in the air.'[13]

In the years ending with Neville Chamberlain's premiership, Britain had lost the art of acting as a great power: it compromised with Italian aggression in Abyssinia and then tried moral arguments to dissuade Hitler from the course he had set himself in Europe. As Harold Macmillan was to say twenty years later, 'he left moral questions to the bishops.' Not so Chamberlain. A great power defends its interests by the use of *Realpolitik* and, ultimately, by possessing the strength to withstand attacks. British moral authority meant nothing to Hitler.

The Empire in which the British took so much pride unwittingly assisted in the disaster of British decline. Bismarck took the view that

Germany's strength lay in German industry and power in Europe and though he became a participant in the Scramble for Africa this was more designed to create a confrontation between Britain and France than to add to German power. And to quote Corelli Barnett once more:

'British governing-class education was really appropriate to a moment in history that had already vanished—that of mid-Victorian prosperity and security—they left their universities unaware that that unique moment had passed away. They took it for granted that the British Empire was the greatest and richest power in the world, indeed in history.'[14]

By the mid-1930s collective security, the Covenant of the League of Nations, disarmament and non-aggression—approaches loftily adopted by a superior but weak political elite—were the weapons of diplomacy that Britain adopted in place of economic and military power. A civilised approach to problems is more than counter-productive when dealing with an opponent whose natural approach is that of a pirate. Throughout the inter-war years the British policy of supporting the League of Nations and believing in the inherent goodness of mankind went against the necessary regard that ought to have been paid to the harsher *Realpolitik* of the balance of power. But Britain also made another fateful decision during these years and that was to choose America rather than Japan as an ally in the line-up that was inexorably forming for the Second World War. The continuance of the alliance with Japan that had survived the First World War would have safeguarded Britain's Asian Empire while allowing Britain to concentrate its strength in Europe. But the pull of America was too strong. 'Yet although the British Government did not acknowledge it, even to themselves, they were already in the process of making their choice between Japan and America, for it was America's displeasure which they shrank from incurring.'[15] When in 1940 Britain faced the ultimate test of war with Germany the Empire proved to be a liability, looking to London for defence that Britain was unable to provide. Instead, it had to turn to the United States for assistance and in the end the price of this assistance was the undermining and destruction of the Empire that Churchill had worked so hard to save.

2

1940–1945

US POLICIES, BRITISH RESPONSES

There was a developing confrontation between the United States and Britain over trade practices in the 1930s which appeared to be coming to a head before the Second World War as America pushed to gain entry to British imperial markets. Neville Chamberlain had little love for Americans, but he felt their support was essential in the appeasement of Europe. The situation, therefore, was tailor-made for Roosevelt's secretary of state, Cordell Hull, whom Leo Amery (Secretary of State for India) considered a major threat to the economic unity of the Empire with his doctrinaire insistence on free trade. He sought a trade treaty with Britain in order to break open the Ottawa system and create a stampede towards economic liberalism in which the Germans also could be persuaded to abandon their pursuit of autarky. In return, Hull offered American support and co-operation in dealing with the increasingly dangerous situation in which Britain found herself. Chamberlain was sceptical while his chief economic adviser, Leith Ross, was fearful of American domination if Britain was forced to co-operate on American terms. There was a widespread belief that American commercial policy was one of the major causes of economic strain, and it was pointed out that her own tariffs at their most liberal were more severe than anything imposed by Britain.[1] Anthony Eden, the foreign secretary in 1937, was in favour of a trade treaty with the

11

United States, 'partly because of the need to create either the appearance, or better still the reality, of Anglo-American solidarity in order to deter the dictators, and partly because such an agreement might neutralise isolationism in the middle west.' Thus, as early as 1937 Britain was looking for an alliance with the USA for the coming conflict with the dictators. It is characteristic of British attitudes at this time that finding allies to stand up to the dictators took precedence over trying to make the country strong enough to do so on its own account.

'By April 1937 Chamberlain had come to believe that "world economic stability" rested on Anglo-American co-operation. However, he was unwilling to sacrifice the Empire for American friendship, and the American department in the Foreign Office agreed: '"We cannot destroy the Commonwealth for the beaux yeux of the Middle West".'[2] As he writes in his memoirs *My Political Life* Amery challenged the whole idea of whittling away the Ottawa settlement in order to appease the United States. It is at this time that two clear themes central to the early period of what became the special relationship emerge: The need to appease the Americans; and the determination to defend the Empire from their hostility and desire to dismantle it. Amery, a dedicated Empire man, wrote to Australia's Robert Menzies, 8 April 1941, (by which time American pressures upon Britain were intense): 'No-one can be more convinced than I am that the future peace of the world depends largely on co-operation between the United States and the British Empire. But, to my mind, that just does mean that the British Empire should first co-operate in such a fashion as to be able to deal as a unit with the United States. Nothing could be more disastrous in its effect upon Empire development than any scheme which is based on the United States with its immense export power dealing with each of us singly.'[3]

This trade conflict between the two powers continued well into the war and was resurrected by the terms of the American loan in 1946.

At the congressional hearing on the renewal of the reciprocal trade agreements in 1940, Hull described the Ottawa agreements as 'the greatest injury, in a commercial way that has been inflicted on this country since I have been in public life.' This was an exaggeration but the conflict was never far below the surface.

In 1940, as the war got underway, the chiefs of staff were gloomy about holding the Eastern Empire, for Britain was almost powerless in the area. 'As Britain's strategic position collapsed, the only chance of defending the Empire was to turn to the Americans. As early as May the chiefs of staff told the war cabinet, "We must rely on the United States of America to safeguard our interests in the Far East."[4] The situation might have been very different had Britain opted to maintain its alliance with Japan in 1922 and so risk incurring the anger of the United States—but of course it did nothing of the kind. Once he had become prime minister, Churchill discovered that he did not have at his disposal the means to solve Britain's strategic problems: the country had too many commitments and too few resources to meet them successfully. The United States now began to build up its forces rapidly but this was neither to help Britain nor to rescue Europe but to defend the United States.

'American actions throughout 1940 were based on the policy of self-interest. At the best, if Britain and France could be kept going through US arms supplies and moral support, they might defeat Hitler without the need for American military intervention.'—thus 'in the month after the start of the German attack the Americans were able to supply the British with 250,000 rifles, 130 million rounds of ammunition (a quarter of the US stocks) and 80,000 machine guns'.[5] Churchill, meanwhile, had to work very hard to establish a working 'friendship' with Roosevelt. In the grim British summer of 1940 the Americans wanted a collapsing Britain to send the fleet to North America to which Churchill would give no undertaking.

'The President's reaction was to ask the Canadians to send an envoy secretly to Washington for staff talks about the future defence of North America. At the meeting that followed Roosevelt suggested that Britain and France were finished and that the Canadians should put pressure on the British to sail the fleet to safety in North America. The Canadians refused.'[6] At the meeting of the War Cabinet on 24 May, Roosevelt was described as 'taking the view that it would be nice of him to pick up the bits of the British Empire if this country was overrun'.

Meanwhile negotiations were taking place for the exchange of fifty US destroyers (First World War vintage) in return for bases in Newfoundland and the Caribbean. One of the problems Britain faced was that both Roosevelt and his advisers took the British Empire at face value, believing that a country which controlled a quarter of the world must have the resources to match the spread. They discovered quickly enough that this was not the case. A Churchill letter to Roosevelt (8 December 1940) detailed British weakness—where help was needed—that Churchill tried to disguise by writing about the identity of British and American interests and common purpose.[7] However, the United States soon realised just how weak was the British position. An official in the US Embassy in London reported: 'Willy-nilly the United States holds one end of the Scales of Fate on which balances precariously the future of the British Empire—The British Government is aware that it is not in a position to resist quid pro quo demands from the United States—The British are not ready givers—But the fact remains that they will in the last analysis stand and deliver.'[8] Early in December 1940 the British sought US financial assistance to find that the Americans wanted to look in detail at the British 'balance sheet' and, as the British negotiator Sir Frederick Phillips pointed out to London, 'It would be for them [the Americans] to allow us to keep our assets, not for us to withhold them.' Thus, as a result of neglect, the refusal to rearm and the replacement of Realpolitik by moral persuasion that manifestly did not work, the Ramsay Macdonald—Chamberlain—Baldwin years had reduced British capacity so that in its darkest hour it became a suppliant in Washington where the anti-imperial lobby was only too ready to take advantage of Britain's weakness.

As far as the much-vaunted 'Lend Lease' was concerned, the United States decided unilaterally what it was prepared to do. The Bill, entitled 'An Act to promote the defence of the United States' and numbered 1776 as a deliberate snub to Britain and a symbol of the new relationship was published in early January 1941. In mid-January Henry Morgenthau, Secretary to the Treasury, told Congress: 'Every dollar of property or securities that any English citizen owns in the United States, they have agreed to sell during the next twelve months, in order to raise money to pay for the orders they have already placed, they are going to sell—every dollar of it.'

The following March Morgenthau gave the British Ambassador, Lord Halifax, an ultimatum. An important British company was to be sold within a week in order to demonstrate good faith. Britain had no choice but to obey and the America Viscose Corporation, a subsidiary of the British firm Courtaulds, the largest remaining British holding in the USA, was sold. It was bought by an American consortium at half its market value.[9] Meanwhile, in December 1940 Roosevelt informed the British that a US warship had been despatched to Cape Town to pick up £50 million of gold, one of Britain's last tangible assets. These American activities and demands at the onset of Britain's desperate situation were not the response to a friend in distress but rather represented an almost gloating American seizure of the opportunity to do Britain down when it was least able to resist. Right through the war (understandably) but non-stop after the war (not understandably) Churchill worked to create and maintain the myth of American 'unsordid' generosity in helping Britain. The opposite was the case. These financial transactions represented the collapse of Britain as an independent power and the reduction of Britain to the status of an American satellite.

On 3 December 1941, the United States informed both Britain and the Dutch that it would fight if Japan attacked either British territories in Asia or the Dutch East Indies. 'It was the Japanese attack on Pearl Harbor four days later that finally transformed a European war into a world war and ensured the eventual defeat of Germany, Italy and Japan.'[10] Shortly after Pearl Harbor Churchill described Britain's relationship with the United States as a client receiving help from a generous patron. Churchill flattered America when its actual treatment of its client was less than friendly.

Britain's dependence upon Lend Lease through the war made it possible for the United States to control Britain's economic policy and so ensure British acquiescence in post-war American aims while conditions attached to Lend Lease allowed the Americans to take over British markets, especially in Latin America. In February 1942 Britain was obliged to agree that it would end 'discriminatory' trade and finance systems after the war. Although Britain was to emerge from the war on the side of the victors it had also undergone five years of economic dependence upon the United States. Crucial decisions by the Attlee government in 1945–46 to maintain Britain's role as a world power meant, in the circumstances, adherence to the American alliance that committed Britain to the special relationship. A more realistic assessment of the country's capacities at the time could have led to policies that were to be less grandiose but more suited to Britain's real power. This first opportunity to break free of US tutelage was ignored.

Douglas (Lord) Hurd explains the British dilemma of the declining power of the Empire as follows: 'The longer the war went on, the more the problem developed—for the first time since the end of the sixteenth century, British commitments outweighed resources. As a consequence of this, success in both efforts, winning the war and building the peace, came to depend on a vigorous "Anglo-American alliance".' Hurd then comments upon Churchill's performance: 'As Churchill fashioned the rhetoric of the special Anglo-American relationship, he was learning painfully and as privately as possible the humbler techniques of operating as the junior partner of the United States.'[11] And then, as soon as the war had come to an end, the new American President, Harry Truman, ended Lend Lease without warning and thereby presented Britain's new Labour government with the painful task of rebuilding a relationship that was fraught with new strains while the British economic guru John Maynard Keynes described Britain's plight as 'a financial Dunkirk'. Attlee sent Keynes to America to seek a loan. 'The Americans dismantled his appeals systematically. A grant-in-aid would be impossible, and there was no chance of an interest-free loan.' Keynes and the British Ambassador Lord Halifax were advised that their success (in obtaining a loan) would depend on liberalising imperial trade. Arguments about Britain's past sacrifices should be avoided. A loan of $3,750 million was agreed: it was to be repaid over fifty years at 2 per cent interest. Lend Lease was to be settled by Britain paying $620 million, which was to be added to the loan repayments. In addition, Britain was to reduce imperial preferences and free up its trade while sterling was to be made convertible in a year.[12]

Beggars cannot be choosers and Britain by its own defaults had been reduced to desperate begging in 1940. In 1945 Britain went cap in hand to America for a financial bail-out, originally arguing that her ally, the United States, somehow owed her the aid she sought because of her efforts during the war. When the loan terms were known, Jennie Lee (the wife of Aneurin Bevan who could match her husband in rhetoric) told the House of Commons that the terms were 'niggardly, barbaric and antediluvian'. In fact they were nothing of the kind. The Americans, in pursuit of their own interests, in terms of *Realpolitik*, were taking every advantage they could of Britain's reduced state. They did not owe Britain anything, despite Jennie Lee's outrage and as one Congressman demanded, why should America provide money, which would only go towards 'too much damned socialism at home and too much damned imperialism abroad'.[13] Here was a situation that cried out for a British break with the United States and a resolve—however hard it might prove—to find another way out of its financial problems. Instead, as Averell Harriman said: 'England is so weak she must follow our leadership. She will do anything that we insist upon and she won't go out on a limb.' The mere fact that Harriman could make such a statement and not have it repudiated by Britain is an indication of the depths of dependence to which Britain had sunk.

3

THE ATTLEE YEARS, 1945–1951

'Attlee was always a reluctant cold warrior. He infuriated his chiefs of staff as late as the last months of 1946 and the first days of 1947 by refusing to accept '"a strategy of despair"' whereby '"we are persuaded that the USSR is irrevocably committed to a policy of world domination and that there is no possibility of her alteration".—It was the bomb, however, which caused him his greatest anxiety then in his first days as premier.'[1] Ironically, it was to be the Americans who sought world domination. There was a contradiction in terms for the Labour government to keep faith with the expectations of the party for social reform but then to pay for it with US money instead of the sweat of the workers' brows. Once Britain took the loan from the United States a dependence relationship was established as with all aid. During Attlee's premiership he had to deal with post-war recovery, the use of Marshall aid, the creation of the North Atlantic Treaty Organisation (NATO) and thereby the acceptance of the Cold War and he did this while also trying to maintain Britain's role as a major power—one of the Big Three—when in fact the country was bankrupt. The result: Britain became a Cold War warrior, junior partner to the United States.

He faced a major setback within days of taking office when on 21 August 1945, seven days after the surrender of Japan, 'President Truman cancelled at a stroke the Lend Lease arrangements with America which had provided Britain with the materials to keep fighting when we stood alone in 1940 and enabled us to become a key arsenal of the allies when America joined the war. Not only were outstanding contracts cancelled but supplies of raw materials and food on their way to us on the high seas became immediately payable either by cash or by credits to be negotiated.'[2] Reporting the end of Lend Lease on 24 August to a 'stunned' House of Commons, Attlee said that Britain had been encouraged to spend money abroad on the joint war effort without bothering about exports, since our imports of food and raw materials would be provided under Lend Lease, with repayment terms to be settled after the war. 'If the role assigned to us had been to expand our exports—we should, of course, be in an immeasurably stronger position than we are today,' Attlee said. Churchill said: 'I cannot believe that it is the last word of the United States. I cannot believe that so great a nation, whose Lend-Lease policy was described by me as "the most unsordid act in the history of the world", would proceed in a rough and harsh manner to hamper a faithful ally—who held the fort while their own American armaments were preparing.' Privately, Churchill resented the terms of Lend Lease that in the post-war world would shackle and subordinate the British economy to Wall Street, which indeed occurred. In response to the end of Lend Lease Attlee despatched Foreign Office experts to Washington headed by Maynard Keynes.[3]

Other reflections upon Lend Lease came later. Macmillan, departing from the generally pro-American tone of his memoirs, records that 'many ministers were disturbed—and even disgusted—by the harshness of the terms and the arrogant tone of the American Administration.'[4] James Callaghan, writing in his autobiography, *Time and Chance*, says, 'The record shows that American opposition to the continuation of Lend Lease had been building up steadily in Congress. Just two days before Roosevelt's death a measure to kill its use for post-war reconstruction had resulted in a tied vote in the Senate and was defeated only by the casting vote of Vice-President Truman. So the subject was known to him and it seems more likely that Truman allowed his many domestic difficulties with Congress to outweigh the serious effects on Britain of his decision.'[5] It is an irony as well as an unintended consequence that the more successfully Britain had mobilised for all-out war from 1940 onwards the more it laid the groundwork for financial disaster after 1945. Views about the acceptance of the US loan are almost all positive in the sense that there was not seen to be any alternative. There were alternatives but the British refused to contemplate them. Peter Clarke, writing nearly half a century after the event, argues, 'There was little real alternative to seeking a subvention from North America as the only means of avoiding not only an abrupt run-down of all external commitments but also an unparallel degree of austerity at home. The option of simply relinquishing Great Power status looks more feasible and attractive in hindsight than it did at the time. It is easier now to see that Britain was ultimately weakened by her post imperial pretensions; but these were defended after 1945 with the same bloody-minded stubbornness, which had been vindicated in 1940. Keynes was to point out in February 1946 that '"it comes out in the wash that the American loan is primarily required to meet the political and military expenditure overseas".'[6] The US loan of $3,750 million and the Canadian loan of $1,250 million were jointly meant to tide Britain over from war to peace. Without the loan Britain could not have built the welfare state. This may be true but should Britain have embarked upon building a welfare state at that time?

A consequence of Britain's huge war effort was that post-1945 she had no overseas assets and that in 1951 (after some substantial recovery) her total real wealth was no greater than in 1913. The British government in 1945 thought it had an unanswerable case for serious US assistance as an ally since it was assumed there was a unique special relationship. The Americans did not see it this way and were not prepared even to consider a grant or an interest-free loan. Instead, they insisted that sterling should become convertible into dollars a year after the loan agreement had come into force. By commercial standards the loan eventually agreed at 2 per cent over fifty years was generous. As far as the Americans were concerned the wartime partnership had not been a commercial one. The Labour government, in desperate financial straits, swallowed its pride and accepted the loan on US terms. Despite her huge empire, Britain was no longer a great power in the sense that America was and while the British regarded their relationship with the United States as unique the Americans did not see it in that light.[7] This was a key turning point. The British made great play about 'standing alone' in 1940; they should have considered standing alone to recover in 1945 rather than accepting American terms. Keynes, generally regarded as one of the most brilliant intellectuals of his generation, had described Truman's termination of Lend Lease as 'without exaggeration a financial Dunkirk'. Subsequently, he was chosen by Attlee to lead the British team sent to Washington to negotiate a loan. He hoped that Britain's standing alone ought to have produced an interest-free loan but this did not happen. However, the idea that Britain was owed something became embedded in the post-war national psyche. Thus, 'Washington's blunt determination to impose a free-trading multi-sided system which would benefit US industry caused shock and anger throughout the British establishment. It was a moment of national trauma, when the country confronted the penalties of its long history of economic weakness more clearly than ever before, and the expressions of outrage ran from City Conservatives to intellectual socialists like Michael Foot.'[8] What in retrospect is extraordinary is the way that this and other subsequent instances of American bullying never persuaded the British establishment to discard a special relationship that was so obviously one-sided, instead of which they clung to the American alliance like faithful dogs. As early as 14 August 1945, Keynes had pointed out the economic position that Britain was in at the end of the war and though it could record victories round the world these were not the manifestations of great power status but illusions of it. Recovery was the task that had to be tackled. Following Truman's abrupt termination of Lend Lease, 'A predicament unique in British peace time history now abruptly confronted the new Labour government: national bankruptcy. Yet imperial and world commitments (were) at their grandest and most costly ever.'[9] Britain had so impoverished itself by its war effort that it was soon to find it was losing what it had fought hard to safeguard—its Empire.

The terms of the loan were debated in the House of Commons on 13 December 1945. Bob Boothby, a leading Tory, delivered a memorable speech against accepting the loan, arguing that Britain could not carry out the obligations she had undertaken. The agreement would prise open the markets of the world for the benefit of the United States. He did not want to see the world divided into two opposing systems. An alternative existed—the Sterling Bloc, based upon the British Empire and fortified by the countries of Western Europe. In his peroration Boothby said: 'We have heard a lot about mandates recently. It may be that the Government have a mandate to nationalise the gas works. I do not deny it—But there is one mandate which His Majesty's Government never got from the people of this country and that was to sell the British Empire for a packet of cigarettes.'[10] Voting by the Tory opposition was as follows: 119 members abstained (the official party line), eight voted for the loan and seventy-eight against it while 345 Labour MPs voted for the loan.

'Even with the advocacy of the formidable Keynes—the British were appalled by the American positions. There was a mood of something close to betrayal, that the loyal British ally was being plundered while she was down, among both Churchill's government and the Labour government under Attlee which replaced it after the general election in July.' As Will Clayton, the American negotiator said, 'We loaded the British loan negotiations with all the traffic the market could bear.'[11] As *The Economist* pointed out, 'It is aggravating to find that the reward for losing a quarter of our national wealth in the common cause is to pay tribute for half a century to those who have been enriched by the war.' Writing about Lend Lease, Keynes talked of the futility of seeking 'to appease' the Americans. 'What will arouse suspicion will be our agreeing to unreasonable demands against our better judgement and then inevitably having to find some way of slipping out of our ill-advised words.'

Acceptance of the loan on American terms was to be endlessly debated thereafter but the process of surrendering economic control to the United States had been underway ever since 1940. 'It was Churchill and Roosevelt who, between them, had been largely responsible for putting Britain's financial fate into American hands.'—'Lend Lease, the solution to Britain's crisis in 1940–41, had thus become the prime cause of Britain's crisis in 1945.'[12] Near the end of his life, Keynes said, 'England is sticky with self-pity and not prepared to accept peacefully and wisely the fact that her position and her resources are not what they once were.' This British attitude—perhaps the result of exhaustion—was in total contrast to that of 1940. The ruthless battering at Britain's weakness by the Americans ought to have warned the political leadership not to trust or rely upon the Americans as an ally; instead, both then and later, the British clung to the special relationship as though it was the only policy available for a weakened Britain. This was not the case.

Denis Healey, who came straight into politics from war service, said, 'We had exhausted ourselves economically to win the war. Having spent most of our sterling balances to finance the war effort, we faced appalling difficulties simply in paying for the imports we needed for our post-war reconstruction. Meanwhile the British Empire was seething with revolt, encouraged by our wartime ally, the United States. And the moment the war ended, Washington broke its wartime agreement to continue nuclear cooperation with London.'[13] Like many other political figures Healey saw how American policies were undermining Britain's position yet throughout his political life remained a staunch adherent of the special relationship. The *Sunday Pictorial* of 10 November 1946 editorialised, 'America may not be politically isolationist today, but she is economically isolationist. We in Britain should be foolish to count on any understanding or co-operation from this post-war America in facing our own difficulties. America believes in free for all internally and externally. That means that we must look after ourselves and forget for all time the era of Roosevelt and Lend Lease.'

Britain's ruling elite, born and brought up in late Victorian or Edwardian times when Britain's imperial spread was at its zenith, probably found it impossible to come to terms with the country's catastrophic power collapse and so, to quote Correlli Barnett, the policy was, 'To persist in the ruinous make-believe that the United Kingdom was a first-class world power, and at the same time pursue the dream of New Jerusalem: a double burden of costs to be loaded on the back of a war-impoverished, obsolescent and second rank industrial economy.'[14] Insisting upon its big power status had become a political obsession. Thus, when in 1946 Attlee questioned the size of the Pacific Fleet, the first sea lord, Admiral of the Fleet Lord Cunningham, said the object of keeping the fleet there at its present strength was to show the flag while in the Mediterranean twelve squadrons of bombers were stationed as a striking force in case trouble arose in Palestine or Greece or Italy. Britain also had forces in French Indo-China and the Dutch East Indies to hold the fort until those two European imperial powers could send their own troops to resume control. 'In more Anglophobe US circles, SEAC (South East Asia Command) was said to stand for "Save England's Asian Colonies".' A big question at this time was whether, had Britain rejected American tutelage, it would have been able to persuade its people to accept another five years of deep austerity and a postponement of the promised New Jerusalem while it put all its energies and finances into rebuilding the economy.

On 5 March 1946, at Fulton, Missouri, Churchill gave his 'Iron Curtain' speech that signalled that there should be no appeasement of the USSR; the speech may be taken as the starting point of the Cold War. To combat Soviet 'aggression' Churchill called for a special relationship between Britain and the United States. He appealed for 'the fraternal association of the English-speaking peoples—the special relationship between the British Commonwealth and Empire and the

United States'. Truman, who shared the platform with Churchill, nodded his assent. 'It was Fulton that made "special relationship" into a term of art: the first time that the phrase had been specifically applied in this sense.'[15] Hanging over all other decisions at this time was the question of the 'bomb': was Britain going to have a nuclear deterrent of its own or not? Ernest Bevin, despite his Labour and trade union background, was as much of an imperialist as Churchill and was not prepared to have Britain pushed around by the United States. At this time there was mutual distrust between Britain and the United States as well as the lack of any empathy between Bevin and the US Secretary of State James Byrnes. Secrecy about the bomb was essential and the news that Britain was making its own bomb was only given to the House of Commons in May 1948. Attlee, reflecting in his retirement, said: 'We had to hold up our position vis-à-vis the Americans. We couldn't allow ourselves to be wholly in their hands—we had to bear in mind that there was always the possibility of their withdrawing and becoming isolationist once again.' It was for this reason that the bomb had become essential.[16] For Attlee the British bomb was a diplomatic tool against the Americans. In any case, British and refugee scientists in Britain had invented the bomb and against this background the American attempt to monopolise it was perhaps more deeply resented than anything else they did at this time. When at the end of 1950 Chinese volunteers crossed the Yalu River, which formed the border between China and North Korea, to drive American forces back from China's border, President Truman told a press conference that the US would take whatever measures were necessary, including consideration of using atomic bombs. Attlee then requested a meeting with Truman, arguing that there had to be prior consultation about the use of the bomb. 'Thus Attlee could find considerable justification for his view that, while he was Prime Minister, making a British bomb became diplomatically necessary. Nor would he neglect the opportunity for nuclear power that the production of fissile material represented.'[17] Debate about the bomb, and whether Britain should have it at all as a mark of great power status, would soon be widespread to become a theme of constant concern in the Labour party. Professor P.M.S. Blackett, who had been a government adviser since 1941, proposed in a paper of 1947 that Britain should renounce atomic bombs and weapons of mass destruction and, instead, redesign its forces on defensive lines and adopt a policy of neutrality between America and Russia.

Then in 1949, the government's chief scientific adviser to the Ministry of Defence, Sir Henry Tizard, argued that Britain should not be making atomic bombs and in a memorable statement said: 'We persist in regarding ourselves as a Great Power, capable of everything and only temporarily handicapped by economic difficulties. We are not a Great Power and never will be again. We are a great nation, but if we continue to behave like a Great Power we shall soon cease to be a great nation.' Tizard's warning was ignored. Having a British 'bomb' posed the crucial question as to what real power Britain commanded.

Many developments during Attlee's premiership can be seen in the light of a changing world that resulted from the upheavals of the war: these included the Atlantic Alliance; imperial questions; independence for India; Palestine; the Cold War; and entrance into the nuclear age, and Britain met all of them from the standpoint of a Great Power even as her resources in relation to her policies were visibly shrinking. At home, with these international changes acting as a backdrop, the government pursued full employment while creating a large public sector and its promised welfare state. Indian independence in 1947, meanwhile, reduced Britain to the second rank in power terms. One intractable problem with roots going back to the First World War came to the forefront of foreign policy even as Britain was negotiating the American loan and that was Palestine. Truman tried to force Attlee's hand on this issue, which had great significance for American politics. As Attlee's biographer claims, 'The vital negotiations for the US loan were scarcely underway and he had to reckon with, on the one hand, what he considered to be irresponsible American tactics on Palestine and, on the other, what he considered British delusions of grandeur about the Middle East in general.'[18] The mandate over Palestine, which was approved by the League of Nations on 24 July 1922 committed Britain to secure the establishment of a Jewish national home in Palestine, 'provided it did not prejudice the civil and religious rights of non-Jewish communities'—a condition that was clearly unworkable. By 1945 Britain had come to accept that a compromise between the Jews and Arabs in Palestine was not possible: terrorism was increasing rapidly and pressures from the USA were mounting to persuade Britain to permit unfettered Jewish immigration into Palestine. From a British point of view it was a no-win situation. The creation of a national state for the Jews in Palestine could only be achieved by overriding the rights of the Arabs who lived there and this is what was done. Churchill, who at the time of the mandate was both a strong Zionist and an even stronger imperialist, had always looked upon the creation of a Jewish state by means of massive immigration as the righting of a wrong that had been done to the Jews over the centuries and an addition to Empire—he assumed that the Jewish state would become a member of the Commonwealth and an additional source of strength to Britain. Churchill could not accept that his scenario for immigration 'numbered by millions' implied injustice for the Arabs. 'Why' he asked 'is there harsh injustice done if people come in and make a livelihood for more and make the desert into palm groves and orange groves?'[19] This was Churchill at his most hypocritically romantic. More realistically, as he thought, British strategic needs would be well served by the establishment of a Zionist idyll. Attlee, at the height of the crisis, remarked crisply, 'that he could not understand how two thousand years of absence constituted a claim'. Few of the non-Jewish players understood the depths and compulsions of Zionism. The creation of a Jewish homeland could only be achieved by allowing Jewish immigrants to swamp the tiny state until they became the majority and this in effect was what Truman, the new United Nations that had taken on responsibility for the League mandates and much of world opinion, which was spurred on by the horrific revelations of the Nazi programme to annihilate the Jews entirely, wanted. Hugh Dalton, then chancellor of the exchequer in Attlee's government, said, 'Let the Arabs be encouraged to move out as the Jews move in.' Richard Crossman at least put his finger on the moral dilemma that creating a new state for the Jews implied when he wrote in his diary, 'In my view we cannot assist the Jews in Palestine in any way they would call assistance without violating Arab rights. We must in fact either accept or reject Zionism as such, putting the awkward, incomparable alternatives clearly before our governments.' The issue of Palestine created much ill feeling between Britain and the United States. As Dean Acheson recalls in his memoirs, on 12 June 1946, Bevin made ill-feeling unanimous by stating to the Bournemouth meeting of the Labour party, 'I hope it will not be misunderstood in America if I say with the purest of motives, [that US policy towards Jewish immigration into Palestine] was because they did not want too many of them in New York.'[20] In fact, the world had decided to support the Jewish case and ignore the Arab rights. Few issues at that time led to such angry exchanges between Britain—saddled with a mandate it simply wished to get rid of—and a

United States determined to support the Zionist cause in such a way that it would not be obliged to receive large numbers of Jewish migrants itself. The creation of the State of Israel is a perfect example of righting one wrong and by so doing creating another (and the result is with us still).

Denis Healey, always an Atlanticist, also claimed for Britain greater influence with or over the Americans at this time than was the case. He argues, on the one hand, that 'Strategically Britain needs America even more than America needs Britain,' and 'Morally, as a progressive democracy America is far closer to Britain than is Western Europe, southern Asia, or, of course, the Soviet Union. Anglo-American unity is indeed a condition of Britain's survival.' From 1947 onwards, when America began to use her power in Europe and other parts of the vacuums, she did so mainly as a result of British diplomacy, and her policies were fully compatible if not identical with Britain's. 'Except in Palestine, any American irruption into Eurasian affairs up to the middle of 1956 was coordinated with British policy.'[21] Healey at this time is creating the British myth of the clever Greeks advising the American 'Romans', a myth later to be propagated by Harold Macmillan.

The Labour government's inheritance in 1945 was laid out in the *Chicago Tribune* of 27 July 1945: 'This task will be undertaken at a moment when there is a shortage of houses, food, clothing, and almost everything else that enters into the standard of living; when Britain's industrial plant is in need of immense capital investment; when her domestic debt is greater than ever; and when Britain owes more money abroad and has less coming in from foreign debtors than at any time in her modern history.'[22]

Richard Crossman, who had been very critical of the American role towards Britain, changed his mind when Marshall aid was debated in the House of Commons. 'I will be frank. My own views about America have changed a great deal in the last six months. Many members have had a similar experience. I could not have believed six months ago that a plan of the sort would have been worked out in this detail with as few political conditions. It is an amazing tribute to Mr. Marshall's personality that he has disciplined all the forces against him in America itself and has at least got the policy presented to Congress in a form as acceptable as it is to Western Europe.'[23] This was an unusual public change of mind from a left-wing Labour MP.

As Peter Shore argues,

'In the post-war period, the call for a "socialist" foreign policy was based on deep suspicion of the United States as the leading capitalist power—and a matching tolerance and sympathy for the "socialist" Soviet Union. Thus, in the 1945–51 Parliaments, the Keep Left group strenuously opposed the American Loan, the Marshall plan, the North Atlantic Treaty and the Government's resistance to North Korean aggression against the South in 1950.'[24]

Even as the government demobilised it was still allocating something like 40 per cent of the budget to defence. While Attlee tried to find ways to cut down Britain's overseas commitments, he could also say of the Americans, 'There is a tendency in America to regard us as an outpost, but an outpost that they will not have to defend.' Both Attlee and Bevin were aware of the country's growing dependence on the United States, so why did they accept it? The need to fulfil the socialist programme and the pressures of the party led them to believe that aid from the United States was the only way to meet these party expectations though there were alternative policies they might have adopted. American attitudes towards Britain during the crucial years 1945–47 ought to have persuaded both Attlee and Bevin to face the reality of the country's severely reduced power; instead they continued to act as the leaders of a Great Power but one that could only function adequately with an American input, a policy that did not make sense. However, as Healey pointed out, 'But for the first few years Britain's weakness was masked by the prestige of victory, by the even greater decline of other European states, by Russia's exhaustion and by America's readiness to accept Britain's advice until she found her feet.'[25] The masking of British weakness allowed her, for a few short years, to masquerade as one of the Big Three but she did so as a consequence of prestige and diplomatic skill rather than power.

Apart from independence for India in 1947 that Attlee regarded as his greatest achievement, the rapid disappearance of the British Empire, as colony after colony achieved independence lay ten years in the future. Despite India and Churchill's wrath against a policy of 'scuttle' both Bevin and Attlee were imperialists. Bevin wanted the Empire to become a single defence and economic unit with its own customs union. He thought instinctively in geopolitical terms and made huge efforts to prop up Britain's system of informal empire in the Middle East and keep the lifeline of Middle East oil in good repair. This was one of his prime concerns.[26] When Attlee was in Washington in December 1950 in connection with the Korean War, alone with his entourage, he turned to Field Marshal Sir William Slim, Chief of the Imperial General Staff, and asked 'how long it would take him to create from the African colonies an army comparable in size and quality with the Indian Army, an army which we could use to support our foreign policy just as the Indian Army had done. Slim, who had spent his life in the Indian Army, said he could do something in eight or ten years, but to do anything really worthwhile would take at least twenty or probably more.'[27] This was not the inquiry of a prime minister contemplating imperial scuttle.

An internal State Department memorandum of March 1950 stated: 'Certainly the UK is our closest friend and strongest and most dependable ally.' The Korean War was soon to put this judgement to the test. When the Korean War began in June 1950, the Americans at once exerted pressure upon Britain to increase its defence spending. Barbara Castle, who saw everything from a left-wing perspective, said how Bevin rejected the US attempt to brand China as an aggressor in Korea (Chinese forces had swept into North Korea when the Americans reached the Yalu River) while rather scornfully she said, 'Attlee, too, showed some independence of spirit and was cheered to the echo by our backbenchers when he announced he was flying to Washington to check up on the rumour that America was about to use the atom bomb against North Korea. Even the hostile press applauded what it called Attlee's attempt to "stop a third world war".' There was a split in the Labour party and 'Once again, the argument was about the government's subservience to American policy.' The Korean War—which to begin with was seen as clear aggression by North Korea against South Korea—appeared in a different light when General MacArthur swept north of the 38th parallel far in excess of his UN remit and provoked a reluctant China into entering the war, and the mood changed.[28]

Dean Acheson, President Truman's anglophile secretary of state, provides a different perspective. 'Immediately after the June 27 resolution of the Security Council, the British Government helpfully and loyally put British warships in Japanese waters at General MacArthur's disposal as the quickest method of furnishing help to Korea.' Even this friend of Britain could not restrain his condescension when he spoke of Britain 'loyally' putting its warships at General MacArthur's disposal. The assumption clearly was that loyalty to the United States should override any other British policy.[29] Later, he wrote, 'In Britain Mr. Churchill, of all people, was criticising Mr. Attlee for overstressing the military programme; and in April (1951), Aneurin Bevan resigned as Minister of Health in the Labour Government, protesting against cuts in his programme to find funds for rearmament.' The situation for the Americans was desperate once the Chinese had intervened in November. 'The situation was so desperate that President Truman incautiously suggested to a press conference that the atom bomb might have to be used. This sent Prime Minister Attlee flying across from Britain to seek assurance that the United States would not go nuclear without at least consulting its allies. Truman blithely agreed to do so, until Dean Acheson discreetly reminded him that this would be illegal under US law.'[30] A final comment from a Tory politician, Ian Gilmour, is revealing: 'The strength of Britain's response to North Korea's aggression depended more on her wish to please the United States than on a sober assessment of foreign and domestic needs. The British Ambassador in Washington urged Attlee to send troops to Korea in order to confirm Britain's position as "first in the queue in Washington", and the Labour Chancellor Hugh Gaitskell's highest priority in deciding upon the scale of rearmament was "to show that Britain was America's best and firmest ally".'[31]

On 15 June 1943 Attlee sent a letter to his cabinet colleagues in which he argued, 'I take it to be a fundamental assumption that whatever post-war international organisation is established, it will be our aim to maintain the British Commonwealth as an international entity, recognised as such by foreign countries, in particular by the US and the Soviet Union.' There is the suggestion behind this statement that Attlee was wary of Churchill's too obvious support for an Atlantic Alliance, which was bound to be dominated by the United States. As Attlee's biographer puts it: 'During the war it had become apparent that Washington intended to increase the US share of Middle East oil, gain access to British colonial markets, and break the sterling area—and that there was nothing the British could do about it.'[32] By 1945 this probability was assured as Britain emerged from the war as the world's largest debtor nation. As the Big Three met to arrange the post-war world, 'The prospect of Allied disagreements was of more consequence to Britain than either of her Allies since it was already clear—to the Americans and Russians as well as to her own leaders—that she would have the greatest difficulty in pursuing a policy of her own, without the support of at least one of the other two.'[33] At this time, in the immediate aftermath of the war, Attlee became increasingly wary of American policies in relation to the loan, Palestine and the bomb since the American approach in each case emphasised diminishing British influence. Given the relentless way the United States was 'downsizing' British power, perhaps Britain was lucky that two US secretaries of state, George Marshall and Dean Acheson, were anglophiles or the process might well have been harsher and less disguised.

Ernest Bevin as foreign secretary was the most powerful figure in Attlee's government. He was always sceptical of American intentions though he was to work closely with George Marshall, first over Marshall aid and then over the formation of NATO. At the time of negotiations for the loan he reacted furiously to Americans calling the British 'cry-babies' and writing to Stafford Cripps, he said: 'I should hate any rudeness or anything undignified—but I do think the time has come when the world must realise that though we have paid such a terrible price in this war we are not down and out. We shall survive.' Bevin's attitude towards the Americans came out clearly over the 1946 decision of Britain to go ahead producing its own atomic bomb. Under Truman the Americans halted their wartime co-operation with Britain on nuclear weapons. Attlee decided to go ahead. The process remained hidden from public view but as steps towards making the bomb were taken so the question of cost arose and Dalton and Cripps wanted to halt proceedings but Bevin overrode them. He arrived late for a cabinet meeting in 1946 and was told the programme should be delayed because of finances. He told the meeting: 'That won't do at all, we've got to have this. I don't mind for myself; but I don't want any other Foreign Secretary of this country to be talked at by a Secretary of State in the United States as I have just had in my discussions with Mr. Byrnes. We have got to have this thing over here whatever it costs—We've got to have the bloody Union Jack flying on top of it.'[34]

At the end of 1946 as the economic situation deteriorated, Attlee wrote to Bevin suggesting Britain would have to retrench in its support with troops and money for Greece. The big freeze of 1947 settled the argument: the Thames froze, coal stocks ran out, most British industry had to close for three weeks and unemployment rose from 400,000 to 2.3 million. Attlee then appealed to Truman to replace Britain in providing economic and military support for Greece and Turkey and Truman convinced Congress of the need to replace the British in support of the two countries and so the Truman Doctrine was born. Bevin, however, was unhappy at the turn of events and did not see relying on America as a long-term solution for Britain.[35]

As the Cold War got under way Bevin still hoped that Britain could lead a third force consisting of the Commonwealth that included the development of Africa's resources and closer relations with Europe. In the face of Soviet pressures in East Europe that included the Communist coup in Czechoslovakia, however, Bevin initiated discussions with the United States and then worked closely with the US Secretary of State George Marshall to create what became NATO. Then on 18 June 1948, the Russians launched a land blockade of Berlin, which lay 100 miles inside the Soviet zone of Germany. On 26 June the Anglo-American airlift was launched: it lasted 324 days and successfully supplied two and a quarter million Berliners with the essentials to keep them independent of any Soviet takeover. In October 1949 Bevin reviewed for the Cabinet the options that were open to Britain. He argued that the Commonwealth alone could not act as a third force between the USA and the USSR; that to strengthen Western Europe it would be necessary to remilitarise Germany; and that the best hope for the security of Western Europe lay in the consolidation of a Western alliance so that over ten to twenty years Europe could become economically and perhaps militarily independent of the United States.[36] Bevin, despite what he saw as the necessity for NATO and working closely together with the Americans, was at the same time determined to be as independent as possible and, for example, infuriated Washington when he recognised the new regime in China. The United States was not to do so until the 1970s under President Nixon. Although the Atlantic Alliance and NATO have been described as Bevin's greatest achievement they delivered Europe into the hands of the rising American hegemonic state and that was not something Bevin wanted. British economic weakness always meant that the country was liable to American pressures it would find hard to resist.

Alan Bullock describes how at the end of the war the Americans wanted to disengage from the close wartime ties with Britain. 'Once the armistice was signed, the United States, under a new president, proceeded to disengage itself from the special relationship with the United Kingdom and re-assert the independence of American policy.' The process was already underway when the Labour government came to power in Britain and Bevin was to find himself torn between his desire to have a fully independent British foreign policy and the need, as he saw it, to work closely with Washington as the Cold War created new dangers that could only be dealt with in alliance with the United States.

'The American Administration, however, had ideas of its own and although many of its members were personally friendly to the British, was determined not to let American post-war policy be shaped by Britain. Although the alliance held firm to the end of the war, the Americans chafed at the need always to pay attention to British views, particularly after the scale of the United States' contributions to the war outstripped their partner's. They had no intention of putting themselves in the same position after the fighting ended.'[37]

The end of the war should have meant the parting of the ways and it did mean it in terms of the loan to Britain that Keynes expected to be free to an ally, while the Americans saw it—and Britain's plight—in commercial terms that should be manipulated to their advantage. The coming of the Cold War, however, forced the two countries to come together in a new version of the old alliance.

Even so, throughout his five years as foreign secretary, Bevin was torn between his determination to restore Britain's position as an independent Great Power and his awareness of the country's fundamental weakness in relation to the United States, whether they were on good or antagonistic terms. This emerges in a letter Bevin wrote to Sir Stafford Cripps on 20 September 1945: 'There does seem to be an assumption that Britain is down and out because of what she has done in this war. When the P.M. made his statement in the House on Lend Lease, we were met with headlines in the U.S.calling us "Cry Babies"— I cannot help feeling that Britain has got to stand up for herself—and the world must realise that though we have paid such a terrible price in this war we are not down and out. We shall survive.'[38]

In 1948 the American Ambassador to Britain, Lew Douglas, wrote an appraisal of Britain's current position in which he said: 'Britain accepts our assumption of world leadership in face of Russian aggression,—but Britain has never before been in a position where her national security and economic fate are so completely dependent on and at the mercy of another country's decisions—While they do not expect to regain former relative supremacy, with help from US they are confident that in conjunction with British Commonwealth and Empire they will again become a power to be reckoned with, which, associated with the US, can maintain the balance of power in the world.'[39]

Bevin constantly tried to maintain as independent a Britain as was possible under the circumstances of his period as foreign secretary but the facts of power worked against him. In the immediate post-war years the special relationship was at its closest in 1949–50 when Dean Acheson was US secretary of state and NATO was created and put in place. But all the roles Bevin wanted Britain to play always exceeded the nation's means.

4

CHURCHILL AND THE ATLANTIC ALLIANCE

The concept of an Atlantic Alliance, which later developed into the Special Relationship, was the brainchild of a desperate Churchill seeking the support of the United States to ensure Britain's survival from Hitler's onslaught. After Dunkirk, Churchill in one of his exuberant moods, declared, 'Give us the tools and we will finish the job.' That was an exaggeration, of course: Britain could not finish the job on its own. One of Churchill's most famous wartime speeches—'we will fight on the beaches'—was aimed as much at the Americans as at the British. 'Even if, which I do not for a moment believe, this Island or a large part of it were subjugated and starving, then our Empire beyond the seas, armed and guarded by the British Fleet, would carry on the struggle, until, in God's good time, the New World, with all its power and might, steps forth to the rescue and the liberation of the old.' Churchill always gave the impression that he had a much closer relationship with President Roosevelt than was the case. Roosevelt, for his part, was careful to keep his distance. By 1944 Churchill knew that 'The British and the Americans were stuck with each other as partners—a junior partner and a senior partner respectively.'[1] Churchill, throughout the war, was determined to preserve the British Empire but the Americans did not want to assist this outcome. They wanted to see the Empire brought to an end. Writing in *The Economist* of 30 December 1944 (pp. 857–8), Barbara Ward asked, 'Just how much British safety can be gambled on American goodwill?' Friendship and goodwill by all means, 'But let an end be put to the policy of appeasement which, at Mr. Churchill's personal bidding has been followed, with all the humiliations and abasements it has brought in its train, even since Pearl Harbor removed the need for it.' Chamberlain has been endlessly blamed for his appeasement of Hitler: Churchill, despite his wartime reputation as the British Bulldog, just as endlessly appeased Roosevelt and, more generally, the Americans, setting the tone for British leaders through to David Cameron acknowledging that Britain was still the 'junior partner' in 2010.

By 1945 the alliance was crumbling, fuelled by deep American suspicion of Britain's motives and a growing tendency in Washington to look to the USSR as a comparable power to itself as British relative weakness became ever more apparent. Isaiah Berlin was in Washington, a first secretary in the British Embassy, from 1942 to 1945 with the job of sending weekly reports to London (via the ambassador) on US attitudes towards Britain, the Alliance and the war. As Berlin's biographer reports, 'The voracious appetite for Washington political intelligence was one indication of the increasing subservience of the British towards American opinion. It now became a crucial factor to be weighed, investigated and reported on, before decisions could be made, and Isaiah had become its chief British purveyor.—He himself was scathing about the new British tendency to wait until it was known which way the American cat would jump.' Berlin insisted that the British should make policy, whether or not the Americans could be counted on to support it.[2]

There was however a residue of American belief in the superiority of the British as Averell Harriman told Hugh Dalton in March 1943: 'Most Americans believe that we are so damned clever that we have already got all our post-war plans worked out to the last dot, and intend to inveigle the Americans into accepting them to their own great disadvantage.' In retrospect one might wish that such had actually been the case but it was not so. The possibility of a trade war between the two countries was never far from the surface and those parts of the Atlantic Charter that concerned trade became a source of tension. Churchill greatly upset India when

'He told the Commons on 9 September 1941 that Article 3 of the Atlantic Charter ("the right of all peoples to choose the form of government under which they will live") applied only to European nations under Nazi rule and not to "the development of constitutional government in India, Burma, or other parts of the Empire".'[3]

Writing in his diary on 17 January 1942 Leo Amery records how Churchill had described his experiences in America: 'he really seems to have got on a footing of complete intimacy and understanding with Roosevelt. We just touched on the Lease Lend and Imperial Preference question and he rather brushed it aside saying that was a fad of Cordell Hull's and that he thought it could be left till after the war.' Did Churchill gild the lily when talking of his relations with Roosevelt? From 1944 onwards, however, trade and preference barriers that inhibited US-UK trade became a major factor of concern as both countries began to plan for the post-war period. Hull advised Roosevelt in September 1944 that the internal pressures on the British not to adopt a liberal commercial policy (which would suit the Americans) were strong and increasing. State department officials urged pinning Britain down and as one observer wrote: 'Everywhere—any discussion of foreign economic policy with the British moved from bad to worse. By the end of 1944, largely as a result of the nearly total collapse of mutual confidence in Anglo-American economic relations, sheer power in hand determined the future course of foreign economic policy.' It was all very well for the Americans to speak of relations turning sour but they enjoyed the whip hand as a result of Lend Lease and their takeover of British markets. The same observer noted that, 'Throughout 1943 and 1944 the United States negotiated and argued with the English, fully aware of the stakes involved as it tailored and controlled British export markets, dollar balances, and even concessions in Middle Eastern oil fields, with a view to implementing American economic objectives.—The British did not respond well to the merciless pressures that the Americans applied in various ways.'[4] During the war Britain concentrated on its war effort and effectively allowed the United States to take over the country's markets—nor did the United States mean Britain to win them back once peace came.

Following Pearl Harbor, American criticisms of British imperialism became muted at least in public while the 1942 Cripps Mission to India, the offer of post-war independence turned down by Gandhi, led to a softening of American criticisms at least for a time. As Clarke recalls, Churchill was always aware of preponderant American power and on one occasion wrote to Roosevelt a letter in which he said, 'The keynote of our relations must surely be equality' but then did not send the letter,[5] a cowardly drawing back that does not fit with his 'Bulldog' image. Churchill was no doubt the essential link that ensured American support when it was most needed but to obtain it he made too many surrenders and he appeared afraid to counter either American animosity to the Empire or its more insidious whittling away at British trade interests. Churchill, whose mother was American, felt far closer to America emotionally than ever he did towards the Empire and Commonwealth (although he felt emotionally about India, though not its people, because of the power it represented) and was the real creator of the special relationship, which meant survival for Britain in the 1940s though it never had any such urgency for the Americans. Indeed, Churchill's 'wooing' of Roosevelt was determined and sustained and it needed to be since there was a significant and influential group in the US establishment that saw no reason why the United States should go to the aid of the British Empire whose demise they would prefer to bring about. Churchill's judgement that the war could only be won if the Americans became fully involved was borne out following the Japanese attack upon Pearl Harbor when he recorded with relief, 'So we had won after all' since the attack brought the Americans into the war and Allied victory was then assured. After Pearl Harbor, the myth of the special relationship with the United States was sedulously cultivated, in part to sustain the British dream of strategic strength but also to disguise Britain's real role as a client of the United States. To look to the future, once it was obvious that Britain could never be an equal partner with the United States, it would have been better had Britain adopted an independent 'Gaullist' policy rather than trying to be a partner at all. Roosevelt made clear his real attitude towards Britain and Europe towards the end of the war: 'When we've won the war, I will work with all my might and main to see to it that the United States is not wheedled into the position of accepting any plan that will further France's imperialistic ambitions, or that will aid or abet the British Empire in its imperial ambitions.'[6] Churchill must have been aware of Roosevelt's attitude towards Britain (as of other members of the US ruling elite) and while it was understandable that he ignored them during the war it is not understandable that he persisted to the end of his life in pursuing a relationship that was to the detriment of Britain's long-term interests and standing in the world, or did he not mind being an American satellite?

At the end of the war Morgenthau was to argue that Britain's plight of dependence upon American aid 'has to be approached from the standpoint that Great Britain made this fight for democracy. Now we have got to help her. She is a good credit risk, and we have got to put her back on her feet.' Churchill said that the safety of the free world depended on Britain and the United States getting 'somewhat mixed up together' and he worked tirelessly to see that the mixing up took place. When in 1946 Churchill gave his 'Iron Curtain' speech at Fulton, Missouri, he said: 'Neither the sure prevention of war nor the continuous use of world organisation will be gained without—the fraternal association of the English speaking peoples. This means a special relationship—.' From this time forward the special relationship became a Cold War alliance. Churchill never lost an opportunity to emphasise the special relationship. Speaking at the annual Conservative party conference in Brighton on 4 October 1947, when he was in opposition, he said: 'We have given a steady support to Mr. Bevin in his conduct of foreign affairs, and especially in maintaining that close and fraternal association with the United States upon which the peace and safety of the modern world depends.' In this instance he was working to ensure that the Labour party and government took the same line towards the United States as he did himself.

The deliberate undermining of Britain's worldwide power and influence was the price to be paid for American assistance during the war; or, rather, the Americans used the drama of the war and their 'unsordid' aid as a cover for downsizing Britain at the same time. Between 1945 and 1956 there was a steady erosion of British power (or, perhaps, a replacement of it by the Americans) and during these years the British establishment—or a large portion of it—accepted the view that if Britain could no longer be the top power then the next best thing was to be the lieutenant of the power that had replaced it. In 1951 Australia and New Zealand entered into the ANZUS Security Pact with the United States much to Churchill's anger that Britain had neither been consulted nor included. The pact was simply a recognition of changing power structures, an acknowledgement that Britain no longer had the military capacity to safeguard these two most loyal of her Dominions. At least in 1952 Britain got the bomb 'alone' while the following year came the last great imperial hurrah with the Queen's coronation. Despite these 'triumphs' the power transfer continued relentlessly until the debacle of Suez, Britain's last attempt at old-fashioned gunboat diplomacy, was stymied humiliatingly by US opposition to it. By that time Churchill had retired from politics though he watched approvingly as Macmillan worked to restore the special relationship. The British constantly bewailed the switch of power to the United States but never looked at the American side in any situation. Instead, Britain tried to hold on and expected the United States to assist whatever its own interests might have been. Lionel Gelber, a sympathetic American Anglophile, argued that psychologically, the British could not relinquish the leadership of the West without a pang. Historically, the manner in which primacy was transferred from Britain to the United States reveals how unique the Anglo-American factor has been. 'Seldom, if ever, can one power take another's place without their relations being warped irreparably.'[7] Gelber makes it sound too easy, for the switch of power, as subsequent years would reveal, had warped the two-way relationship into a demeaning one of British subservience. 'It is not the lack of American involvement which haunts post-war Britain as the chief ally of the United States, but the spectre of over-involvement.' Gelber overdid his apologia for the downsizing of Britain and paid the fading power handsome compliments. 'And as primacy has shifted from Britain to the United States, Americans have learned—though this is still never fully admitted—what the British have long perceived: that it is better to compromise ideologically and lead than not to lead at all.'[8] Gelber titles his book *America in Britain's Place* and his desire to be complimentary persuades him to suggest that Britain had more influence than was the case and, therefore, was of greater value to the United States as its chief ally than the reality while, for its part, Britain desperately needed to reassure itself and saw the special relationship as providing some of that reassurance.

Cultural ties between Britain and America may be said to stretch back to the *Mayflower*. After the 1783 war, 'Most Federalists remained Anglophiles and understood that their own wealth and power depended mainly on trade with their former rulers. As Alexander Hamilton put it: 'I have always preferred a connexion with Great Britain to any other country, we think in English, and have a similarity of prejudices and predilections.'[9] Such views had an attraction and depth that Churchill could relish and part of his success in promoting the special relationship can be seen decades after his death when another proponent of the alliance wrote: 'As the old Anglo-American military alliance of 1941 was self-consciously reforged in the Iraq War of 2003, one usually sober British commentator described America as "the most reliable axis of good in the world for many years".' The commentator he referred to was Gerard Baker writing in the *Financial Times*, 20 March 2003.[10]

The Cold War was to give the special relationship a new lease of life. Those in Washington who wished to put pressures on Britain were restrained by Dean Acheson who said: 'No. We need Britain. She has her commitments, she's a worldwide power. I'm not prepared to try to make her do things, which are against her nature. What we have to do is to find ways of accommodating her and yet getting her into the European payments Union.'[11] As Hennessy also claims, 'With Byrnes (US Secretary of State 1945–1947) gone from the State Department, crude American attempts to destabilise the Empire ceased.' Indeed, 'From the Korean War onwards, the Americans began to appreciate the global role of the British of which the Commonwealth was a symbol.' The CIA *Review of the World Situation* of June 1949 produced an accurate assessment of the importance of the UK for the US as 'its most powerful and important ally' although the report also pointed out the major uncertainty in the relationship because of its inherent economic weakness. At this time the Americans became increasingly ambivalent about the role they would like to see Britain play in Europe. Lionel Gelber, quoted above, writing in the mid-1960s after Britain's failed attempt to join the EEC, argued: 'To debar serious rifts between the United States and a united Europe or heal them when they occur— that is a task for which Britain is peculiarly suited.' Washington was beginning to line up a new role for its satellite to play. Temperamentally, Churchill was not suited to this role as he revealed in 1945 when he told de Gaulle, the then leader of the Free French, 'Each time I must choose between you and Roosevelt, I shall choose Roosevelt.' It is often difficult, as US secretaries of state change and Britain recovers lost ground, to separate myth and reality. As Robert Cooper claims in his short monograph, *The Breaking of Nations*, 'Some have argued, plausibly, that after the fall of France, British interests would have been better served through an accommodation with Hitler.—The decision to continue the war came from an instinct about the sort of country Britain was and the sort of Europe it wanted—or rather, the sort of Europe it did not want.'[12] Churchill would have agreed with that. As Europe recovered after the war the question of Britain's relations with it and the movement towards unity became enmeshed in the British desire to maintain a special relationship with the United States. Gelber[13] advanced an argument that later became central to all Britain's prevarications about Europe when he wrote, 'The annals of the twentieth century, nevertheless, bear witness to the cardinal fact that an Atlantic world in which the United States comes first would be a more tolerable one for Britain and other free peoples than one in which the French and West Germans have the final say.' This is a racist argument—the Anglo-Saxons sticking together—that would certainly appeal to Churchill who, despite his rhetoric about Europe, was always drawn to the Atlantic Alliance, which, for him, meant Britain and the United States. America versus Europe has remained a central theme of British policies ever since, causing Europhiles to lament that Britain is in thrall to the United States.

During the years of Attlee's premiership Churchill, as leader of the opposition, concentrated his attention upon foreign affairs and gave several memorable speeches that had a wide influence upon western policies. There was his Zurich speech of 1946 in which he called upon France and Germany to forgive and forget the past and work towards a united Europe; there was his Fulton, Missouri, speech in which he accused Russia of creating an iron curtain dividing Europe; and there was his 1948 speech in which he argued that Britain was at the centre of three intersecting circles—the Commonwealth and Empire, the Atlantic Alliance and Europe. His Zurich speech encouraged European union without committing Britain. In his Fulton speech of March 1946 he warned of the threat posed by the Soviet Union and accused Russia of creating 'an iron curtain' stretching from 'Stettin in the Baltic to Trieste in the Adriatic'. At the time the speech did not go down well in the United States since many Americans still believed in working with Russia. Nonetheless, the speech was not extreme, as it was regarded by many Americans, but prescient and can be taken as signalling the start of the Cold War. In it Churchill also called for a special relationship between the United States and Britain; thereafter, the term was to be used frequently by British politicians but far less frequently by the Americans who did not want a special relationship while Britain needed it.

During the years 1945–1951 (when in opposition) and 1951–1955 when he was again prime minister, Churchill pursued the idea of Britain acting as a third force or mediator between the United States and the USSR as they came to be regarded as the world's only two super powers. Neither the United States nor the Soviet Union saw any need for Britain to hold the balance between them, however, and Churchill's efforts came to nothing but not for lack of trying. On 9 October 1948, Churchill addressed a mass rally of the Conservative party at Llandudno in north Wales at which he advanced his three circles thesis.

'As I look out upon the future of our country in the changing scene of human destiny I feel the existence of three great circles among the free nations and democracies.—The first circle for us is naturally the British Commonwealth and Empire, with all that that comprises. Then there is also the English-speaking world in which we, Canada, and the other British Dominions and the United States play so important a part. And finally there is United Europe. These three majestic circles are co-existent and if they are linked together there is no force or combination which could overthrow them or even challenge them. Now if you think of the three inter-linked circles you will see that we are the only country which has a great part in every one of them.'

It was a grandiose idea but lacking realism in several respects: first, for Britain to play a leading role it needed to put huge efforts into upgrading its economy, always its weak point in the years after the end of the war. Second, Churchill still assumed British control over the Dominions and Empire at a time when they wanted to develop in their own ways, and this included a newly independent India. Third, an English-speaking Alliance that included the United States meant the surrender to American control, which was not the intention but would have been the outcome. Fourth, as subsequent events were to prove, Churchill's rhetoric about Europe was never to be matched by British leadership: indeed, under Churchill Britain behaved as though it was separate from the continent to which it belonged. The real consequence of this speech was to persuade the British people that they had greater influence and more power than was the case so that for another generation Britain behaved as though it was a world power when in fact this was no longer so.

Meanwhile, Cold War pressures tended almost always to be given priority treatment. 'The secret 1948 UKUSA Agreement had divided up the world between the two countries for eavesdropping purposes.' In July 1948, informally and without a written treaty, US B29s arrived in East Anglia which sent a clear signal that the bombers were within striking distance of Moscow and from 18 July onwards there was to be a permanent US nuclear presence on British soil. It was a huge step for both nations as General Leon Johnson, who led the bombers over, was fully aware. 'Never before in history,' he said later, 'has one first-class Power gone into another first-class Power's country without an agreement. We were just told to come over and "we shall be pleased to have you".' It was subsequently agreed that three American heavy Bomber squadrons then in Britain might continue to be based there more or less indefinitely.[14]

Different American and British approaches to the Soviet 'threat' were emerging. Vice Admiral Eric Longley-Cook, Director of Naval Intelligence, produced a 'think piece' that was seen by both Attlee and Churchill in 1951 in which he stated that the Joint Intelligence Committee (JIC) did not believe that the Russians would pursue an all-out military offensive while the Americans were convinced that war with Russia was inevitable. Longley-Cook had attended the October 1950 US/UK conference in Washington and had been alarmed at the way US assessments—supposedly made on facts—instead tended to fit in with the pre-judged conclusion that a shooting war with the Soviet Union at some time was inevitable.[15]

In 1949 Britain was forced to devalue the pound sterling, then rated at $5.03 to $2.80. This made economic sense but was seen as a disaster, for in that age, though not in later decades, the strength of the pound was equated with the strength of the country and the devaluation was seen as an admission of waning British power in relation to the United States. In mid-1950 a new crisis for the Western Alliance arose when North Korea invaded South Korea to provoke constant worries about the state of Anglo-American relations. Attlee in power showed himself to be every bit as ready to stand with the Americans against the Communist threat as would have been the case with Churchill. He reacted 'with singular courage, introducing legislation to increase defence spending to £3,600 million over three years, thereby creating six to ten new army divisions.—Then, in January 1951, with even greater courage, Attlee raised the ante to £4,700 million.'[16] In this instance, like Australia in 1939, Britain responded 'ready, aye ready' to the United States as it prepared to repulse the North Koreans and it is from this point that Britain became a loyal source of military mercenaries to support American actions.

Churchill and Eden visited the United States together in 1951 and, 'After dinner one night Churchill asked the American Secretary of State, Dean Acheson, if he had not felt that round the table that evening there had been "gathered the governance of the world". Such a thought had not struck Acheson.'[17] At the end of the Truman era, Eden returned from a visit to Washington in January 1952 and shocked the cabinet by his impressions. 'He had been, recorded Macmillan in his diaries, "forcibly struck—indeed horrified at the way we are treated by the Americans today". They are polite; listen to what we have to say, but make (on most issues) their own decisions. Till we can recover our financial and economic independence, this is bound to continue.'[18] In 1952, once more foreign secretary under Churchill, Eden produced a cabinet paper on 'British Overseas Obligations' which contained the theme of 'power by proxy' by attempting to persuade the Americans to take over more and more of Britain's global functions, albeit as unobtrusively as possible, to 'inconspicuously' shore-up Britain's over-stretched reach and influence to avoid an unstoppable slide in Britain's international prestige.[19] As a policy it is surely both weak and uncon-vincing and gives the impression that Eden was more concerned with prestige than reality. How much better would it have been had Eden, in the light of his experience with the Americans, argued for a real break and suggested a policy commensurate with Britain's capacity? But this would not have been acceptable to Churchill.

In 1951 Iran's new Prime Minister, Mohammed Mossadeg, nation-alised his country's oil. At the beginning of what was to be a major Anglo-Iranian dispute the Anglo-Iranian Oil Company (later BP) exer-cised control over 100 per cent of Iran's oil. By 1954, when Britain had been obliged to turn to the United States for assistance—it was largely courtesy of the CIA that Mossadeg had been ousted—the Shah (who at one point in the dispute had fled the country) was restored (after a CIA-inspired counter-revolution) and a new oil consortium created in which the United States had a substantial share. Presumably Eden accepted this outcome as part of his policy of allowing the Americans to shore up Britain's overstretched reach. One of the last major occa-sions when Churchill could expound upon the Atlantic Alliance occurred on 8 June 1954 when he gave a speech in honour of General Gruenther, the NATO Supreme Commander:

'We are entitled to fix our thoughts on the might, and I think I may say maj-esty, of the unwritten alliance which binds the British Commonwealth and Empire to the great Republic of the United States. It is an alliance far closer in fact than many which exist in writing. It is a treaty with more binding elements than clauses and protocols. We have history, law, philosophy and literature; we have language. We are often in agreement on current events and we stand on the same foundation of the supreme realities of the modern world.'

During his last two years of office Churchill became almost obses-sive about the nuclear threat and this nearly brought him into conflict with the Americans. It was the age of 'brinkmanship', a new expression coined by John Foster Dulles, the American secretary of state. In May 1953, two months after the death of Stalin, Churchill delivered a powerful speech in which he called for three-power talks with Stalin's successors (Khruschev and Bulganin), on the basis of the wartime model in an endeavour to remove Russian anxieties. Churchill in fact split the cabinet and most notably found himself opposed by Eden in his search for a three-power summit. The next month Churchill suffered a major stroke. However, he recovered and hosted a conference in Bermuda that December. Churchill pressed for talks with Russia but Eisenhower, Dulles and Eden opposed and this killed dead his drive for tripartite talks. Churchill would have done well to include France in the conference but he still thought in terms of the Big Three. However, despite his earlier, rousing calls for a united Europe, during the ministry of 1951–55, Churchill left Europe to Eden, who did not like it, and came to see European unity as less important than the restoration of the Anglo-American Alliance. In March 1955, close to the end of his ministry, there was a debate in the House of Commons to consider the challenge of the nuclear age. Aneurin Bevan for Labour asked why there had not been a summit with the USSR: 'Why were the negotiations delayed? Could it be that Churchill wanted to meet the Russians but that the United States would not let him—a sombre thing to say and a wicked thing to believe—that we have now reached the situation where Great Britain can, in a few short years, run the risk of the extinction of its civilisation, and we cannot reach the potential enemy in an attempt to arrive at an accommodation with him because we are at the mercy of the United States.' Churchill intervened, the first time in public, to say how his stroke had interfered with his summit hope. He said Britain was taking a risk 'to back an American policy which had ceased to command his confidence'. This represented a huge shift of position on the part of Churchill, who had always been the most fervent upholder of the American Alliance.

Despite his constant upholding of the Atlantic Alliance and his romantic attachment to all things American, Churchill was also acutely aware of the asymmetrical nature of the alliance. This had been driven home to him by Roosevelt during the war and had become even more glaringly apparent in the years after 1945, leading him to search for an alternative policy for Britain. This could either be in the role of a mediator between the two super powers, though when he pushed the idea he soon discovered that neither Washington nor Moscow wanted or needed a middleman to orchestrate their differences; or, he could look to the Commonwealth. At the beginning of June 1953 Churchill told the Commonwealth prime ministers, who had gathered in London for the coronation of Queen Elizabeth II, that he hoped to test the new Soviet leadership's intentions and the possibility of what he called 'settlement' or 'easement' between East and West. The Russians heightened world tensions at this time by announcing that they had a thermonuclear device. Churchill never really came to terms with the Commonwealth concept, always instead wanting to treat Commonwealth countries as imperial subjects that would accept British leadership. The process of ending empire developed during the inter-war years. In 1926 Balfour, in the chair of an imperial conference, defined the relationship of the Dominions to Britain as 'in no way subordinate one to another' and though this was tantamount to complete independence, both Canada and South Africa sought a more precise legal definition; a demand that was satisfied in 1931 by the Statute of Westminster, which recognised the Dominions as internationally independent countries. The decision of the Dominions to go to war with Germany in 1939 was taken individually by them: Canada waited a week while it imported arms from neutral America, before declaring war; in South Africa there was a bitter debate in Parliament in which the Afrikaner Nationalists opposed the idea of fighting for Britain though General Smuts won the day; and Australia and New Zealand declared war at once. Even so, their loyalty to Britain could no longer be taken for granted. In 1914 Britain had automatically declared war on behalf of the whole Empire including the Dominions. The ability of Britain to defend its huge Empire was soon demonstrated to be unequal to the task when Japan took Singapore and threatened Australia. As Corelli Barnet put it, 'To the last, the existence of the empire forced on England a world role she had not the resources to sustain.' That statement related to the war years. After the war, Churchill soon discovered that he could not use the Commonwealth as he had hoped. 'Although India and Pakistan had been kept in the Commonwealth by the device of enabling republics to be members provided they recognised the British monarch as Head of the Commonwealth, the British Empire and Commonwealth was plainly no longer a unit of power in the way it had been in 1914 and 1939.'[20] The global alternative that the Commonwealth represented did prevent Britain from committing itself wholeheartedly to European integration although Michael Shanks was to argue that British policy should be aimed at avoiding a choice between Europe and the Commonwealth, and instead at bringing about a fusion of the two.[21] An event that drove home the limitations of a Commonwealth policy based upon close Dominion support for Britain occurred in 1951 when Australia and New Zealand joined with the United States in the ANZUS defensive treaty. Churchill's anger that the pact had been agreed without British participation simply highlighted the fact that Britain was no longer in a position to defend these most loyal members of the Commonwealth. Some form of middle role, holding the balance between the superpowers, certainly appealed to Churchill but did it make sense? As positions were adopted after the war it soon became apparent that some kind of mediator role for Britain would only make sense had Britain been powerful enough that neither superpower would want to go against it in case it threw its weight on one side to bring about a decisive power change. In fact, sad as it must have seemed to Churchill, in any superpower confrontation Britain would be largely irrelevant except as a US nuclear base to be 'taken out'. On 23 November 1956, in the immediate chaotic aftermath of Eden's Suez adventure, Churchill made his last contribution to the 'special relationship' in a letter to Eisenhower from his retirement at Chartwell. 'There is not much left for me to do in this world,' it began 'and I have neither the wish nor the strength to involve myself in the present political stress and turmoil. But I do believe, with unfaltering conviction, that the theme of the Anglo-American alliance is more important today than at any time since the war.'[22]

For the special relationship to mean a working alliance, as opposed to an asymmetrical arrangement, one power must be able to persuade the other to change or modify its policies. Yet, in the immediate postwar period the Americans ended Lend Lease without consultation, forced a harsh deal on Keynes when he negotiated a loan and aborted the wartime agreement on nuclear exchanges. Britain accepted these actions and still talked of a special relationship. 'It was always an illusion to imagine that, for the sake of some historical sentiment, the United States would be prepared to abandon the tough and unsentimental pursuit of its own interests in the outside world which it had practised since the formation of the Republic.'[23] Dean Acheson, a fair but penetrating critic of British pretensions, said, 'Of course a unique relationship existed between Britain and America—our common language and history ensured that. But unique did not mean affectionate. We had fought England as an enemy as often as we had fought by her side as an ally. The very ease of communication caused as many quarrels as understandings.' A ruthlessly hard-headed approach to the special relationship is revealed in a US State Department Paper: 'Our petroleum policy is predicated on a mutual recognition of a very extensive joint interest and upon control—of the great bulk of the petroleum resources of the world—the United States and Britain agree on this, the paper continues disingenuously. In fact, American policy was to displace Britain at the top of the system, to remake it on American terms, to play Rome to Britain's Athens.'[24]

As far as the Americans were concerned, the special relationship was always expendable though it had its periodic uses. William Clark, who was press officer to Eden and resigned over Suez, said of the special relationship in his book, *Less Than Kin*, that it was fragile: 'In particular, statesmen and the general public should come to realise that the partnership between Britain and America is not a natural and inevitable part of the structure of world politics. It is fragile, delicate and in constant need of careful nurture.' Clark continues that the Americans, having successfully broken away from Britain and the Empire, wanted thereafter to prove to the British that they were right to secede. 'Hence the peculiar American desire, which persists even today, for British appreciation of their feats, and their violent dislike of any British criticism of their achievements.'[25] Later Clark says: 'After the Anglo-American alliance had been cracked by Suez in 1956 it was not long before leaders on both sides of the Atlantic saw that a Royal visit to America was needed, so that Royalty could heal the breaches which politicians had made.' Clark makes a final point that suggests that he wanted the special relationship to continue: 'If Britain is to succeed in making the partnership work she must realise that her status is not determined by the degree of independence she enjoys, but by the contribution she can make to the partnership. This is the real Athenian role which we can play to America's Rome.'

At least from the war to Suez there was a genuinely working special relationship, however one sided it might have been, and it appeared to be accepted on both sides of the British political divide. Hugh Gaitskell, who succeeded Sir Stafford Cripps as chancellor of the exchequer in 1950 was a dedicated Atlanticist and in Labour party terms, very right-wing. 'The left of the Labour Party felt that not enough effort had been made to reach an agreement with the Russians, that Britain was following too closely the Cold War policies of the United States. The American alliance was so central to Gaitskell's world view that it seemed necessary to take a full role in the creation of a rearmed and economically viable West Germany, which would be able in turn to take its place in the reconstructed Europe. This was central to American policy.'[26] As Gaitskell told the journalist Henry Fairlie in 1952, 'There is only one thing we have to do in the next few years and that is keep the Labour party behind the Anglo-American alliance.' The right of the Labour party at this time was in favour of NATO and the need to keep nuclear weapons. In the heyday of the debate about the bomb Gaitskell wondered whether the United States would withdraw from Europe if Britain went neutral. As his biographer Brivati claimed, Gaitskell was a member of the establishment and in many ways more Tory than Labour. He was a passionate Atlanticist and seemed incapable of seeing the harm that close relations with the United States did to long-term British interests.

5

EDEN AND SUEZ

In 1951 Sir Anthony Eden returned to his wartime post of foreign secretary in Churchill's new government. Early in 1952 he prepared a cabinet paper in which he argued, 'The essence of a sound foreign policy is to ensure that a country's strength is equal to its obligations.' He continued, 'It is becoming clear that vigorous maintenance of the presently accepted policies of Her Majesty's Government at home and abroad is placing a burden on the country's economy which is beyond the resources of the country to meet.' Thus, Eden correctly put his finger on the nub of Britain's problem—matching policy to resources—but nowhere in the years up to Suez did he suggest any retraction of Britain's worldwide role though he was prepared to let the Americans do things for which Britain could take the credit. Also, in 1952, like Ernest Bevin before him, Eden told the cabinet how the British were treated as of no account in Washington. In any case, by this time Britain had already begun the process of transferring responsibilities to the United States. In 1947 Attlee had persuaded the Americans to replace Britain as a financial and military backer in both Greece and Turkey, a move that led the American president to enunciate the Truman Doctrine. Iran was to come next. British politicians were too ready to treat American power as though it were a British resource. Thus Eden had written, 'Our aim should be to persuade the United States to assume the real burdens in such organisations (for defence as in NATO), while retaining for ourselves as much political control—and hence prestige and world influence—as we can.' In another age this would have led to Britain being described as 'perfidious Albion'. Such a view was not likely to meet with any favour in Washington since it reduced the special relationship to the level of the British conman manipulating the simple Americans.

Eden, nevertheless, was to earn considerable prestige for his performance up to Suez. His outstanding year was 1954 during which he presided over the resolution of the Trieste question, reassured a France that was worried by the resurgence of West Germany by promising Britain would maintain four divisions of troops on the European mainland for the next fifty years, and presided over the peace agreement that brought an end to the first Vietnam (or Indo-Chinese) war. Always touchy about American attitudes, Eden sent the following instruction to Sir Roger Makins, the British Ambassador in Washington: 'Americans may think the time past when they need consider the feelings or difficulties of their allies. It is the conviction that this tendency becomes more pronounced every week that is creating mounting difficulties for anyone in this country who wants to maintain close Anglo-American relations. We, at least, have constantly to bear in mind all our Commonwealth partners, even if the United States does not like some of them; and I must ask you to keep close watch on this aspect of our affairs, and not hesitate to press it on the U.S.'[1]

British relations with the United States were not going well long before the Suez eruption took place. There was the oil crisis in Iran, a growing divergence of views in relation to the Middle East and the US intervention in the Central American state of Guatemala. As Eden records in his memoirs, 'According to an account which our Embassy thought reliable, the Secretary of State (John Foster Dulles) had declared his conviction that American policy in the Middle East as in Asia, had been badly handicapped by a tendency to support British and French "colonial" views. He was reported to have spoken of his determination to talk bluntly about the Middle East, and of his aim to "shift policies".'[2]

Meanwhile, the American blockade of Guatemala was likely to interfere with British trade with that country and Dulles was not prepared to give an assurance that the US would not intercept British ships going to Guatemala if they thought they bore arms for the regime. Eden found this 'worrying' but he considered (at this point) that Anglo-American solidarity was of overriding importance to

Britain and the West. 'I believed that even if we did not entirely see eye to eye with the United States government in their treatment of the Guatemalan situation, we had an obligation as their principal ally to go as far as we could to help them.' Consequently, 'Her Majesty's Government agreed to cooperate with the United States Government, or at least not to oppose them, taking the view that first priority must be given to the solidarity of the Anglo-American alliance. If allies are to act in concert only when their views are identical, alliances have no meaning.'[3] Eden was prepared forcibly to put Britain's point of view and did not hesitate to protest or object to US decisions. He believed in the alliance.

The Iranian Prime Minister, Mohamed Mossadeg, nationalised the Iranian oil industry in 1951 and it soon became clear that the American interest in developments in that country was not the same as the British interest, which was to maintain its grip on its oil monopoly. Eden was concerned by the extent to which Mossadeg was being aided in the early days of the dispute by the US policy of neutrality. The United States was clearly much more interested in obtaining a share of Iran's oil than simply supporting Britain in its quarrel with Mossadeg and the State Department, for example, held talks with American oil companies at which it had pressed for the formation of an all-American company to buy out Anglo-Iranian. Meanwhile, in the wake of the revolution that had ousted King Farouk and replaced him with General Neguib and then Colonel Nasser, Anglo-American differences about Egyptian policies persisted—Britain still had a huge military base in the Canal Zone that Nasser wanted removed. In a report to Eden, the British Ambassador in Cairo commented that American policy in general seemed to be conditioned by a belief that Egypt was still the victim of British 'colonialism' and as such deserving of American sympathy. The ambassador added that there was an 'apparent disinclination by the United States Government to take second place even in an area where primary responsibility was not theirs'.[4] In truth Britain was indeed behaving like a colonial power in Egypt and what in fact was Britain's primary responsibility in Egypt and on whose account? Although Eden maintained on a number of occasions his belief in and adherence to the Anglo-American alliance, his distrust of the Americans, coupled with his resentment at their greater power, comes across repeatedly in the years leading to Suez. He complains that in recent years the United States has sometimes failed to put its weight behind its friends, in the hope of being popular with their foes. He objected to the Americans taking the lead yet he expected them to support British policies. He claims that allies must be able to disagree with each other yet is outraged when the Americans do not agree with British actions. In his case it was the negative desire not to be tied to the Americans rather than a positive belief in European unity that led Eden to reflect: 'Both for economic and political reasons, the necessary solution [for Britain] is a wide area of trade agreements which comprises the British Commonwealth and Europe. In vitality and variety this has almost limitless possibilities and would be an effective counterpart to the Communist bloc and to the United States.'[5] Here Eden advances a much clearer alternative policy for Britain than the cloying Anglo-American alliance than does Churchill with his hope for a mediating role.

The Suez debacle has been debated from many angles and the vast majority of critics and assessors have concluded that it was a wrong policy morally, politically and economically. Eden, who first made his mark by resigning in 1938 as a protest at Chamberlain's policy of appeasement, had been foreign secretary under Churchill during the war and then from 1951 to 1955, when he became prime minister. He had been highly regarded as foreign secretary and had a number of diplomatic and negotiating successes to his credit. Yet as prime minister he pursued an astonishingly wrong-headed policy with regard to Nasser and thereby destroyed his career. The background to the Suez crisis was entirely 'Cold War'. In 1955 Britain, the United States and the World Bank had agreed to provide a loan of $90 million to finance the Aswan High Dam, which was Nasser's pet development project. In November of that year the Americans discovered that Egypt was importing military equipment from Czechoslovakia, an 'iron curtain' satellite of the USSR. Dulles, the US Secretary of State, took the line that in the Cold war 'you were either with us or against us' and told Nasser to make up his mind as to where he stood. Nasser responded that he would seek arms where he pleased leading first the United States, then Britain and the World Bank to withdraw their offer of aid. Nasser responded by nationalising the Suez Canal (Britain and France between them owned just over 50 per cent of the shares in the Suez Canal Company). In retaliation, worked out between 26 July, the date the canal was nationalised, and the end of October, Britain and France conspired with Israel, which invaded the Sinai Peninsula to give the two European powers a pretext to intervene and occupy the Canal

Zone. The widespread condemnations of this intervention were led by the United States.

A widening gap developed between Britain and France on the one hand and the United States on the other. As Eden queried in his memoirs, 'With the United States announcing in advance that it will not use force, and Soviet Russia backing Egypt with its propaganda, does not that leave all the trump cards in Nasser's hands?' Dulles then proposed the formation of a Suez Canal Users Association, which was agreed to by Britain and France, but later, 'Yet here was the spokesman of the United States saying that each nation must decide for itself and expressing himself as unable to recall what the spokesman of a principal ally had said. Such cynicism towards allies destroys true partnership. It leaves only the choice of parting, or a master and vassal relationship in foreign policy.'[6] (Subsequently Macmillan chose the vassal relationship.) The crisis led to a major rift between Britain and the United States and there could hardly have been a clearer parting of the ways yet Britain failed to use it to adopt an independent policy of its own that did not depend upon so one-sided an alliance. In the United Nations, 'It was not Soviet Russia, or any Arab state, but the Government of the United States which took the lead in the Assembly against Israel, France and Britain. Their Secretary of State said he moved the resolution with a heavy heart.'[7] Richard Nixon, the US vice-president, said in a speech: 'For the first time in history we have shown independence of Anglo-French policies towards Asia and Africa which seemed to us to reflect the colonial tradition. This declaration of independence has had an electrifying effect throughout the world.' Interestingly, there were distinctive echoes of 1776 in Nixon's claim. Part explanation for the American attitude appeared to be that the US president had been slighted because the allies had acted without US permission or endorsement, an attitude that reflected the American view of Europe at that time. As Eden saw it (although passing over the fact that he had been less than communicative with his principal ally) the United States seemed to be governed by only one idea, to harry its allies. It is perfectly true that the United States played a devious role with regard to Britain, and Eden brings this out very clearly in his memoirs—though eliding those aspects of the relationship when Britain was also devious—but none of this exonerates Eden or his government from pursuing a policy, which turned into a disaster. Eden, with his huge experience of foreign affairs should, after his visit to the United States in 1952, have realised where British power lay and what were its limits, yet he embarked upon the Suez adventure without clearing anything with the United States.

Reflections on the Suez Crisis

Speaking to the Tory 1922 Committee on 18 December 1956 in the immediate aftermath of Suez, Eden said: 'As long as I live, I shall never apologise for what we did.—We have been patient with the US over a long time. We might have expected something in return.' He ought to have remembered that in politics there is always a price to pay. In its imperial twilight, after 1920, Britain believed the Arabs wanted to be ruled by the British, which was clearly a myth; years later it was a 'racing certainty' that Eden and Nasser would misunderstand each other. What was worse, in the Suez crisis, Britain misread the United States so badly. 'Suez was a mistake, at least for Britain: it was fought on the basis that Nasser was a new Hitler and a threat to order, but neither the threat nor the order really existed.'[8] Dulles made up policy as he went along and the Suez Canal Users Association was thought up almost on the spur of the moment to meet the strong British demand for economic pressure and to forestall military intervention, but was then gradually modified as events unfolded. Dulles never really let the British and the French know where they stood and Selwyn Lloyd, Eden's foreign secretary, was not alone in mistaking the shadows for the substance.[9] One of the great ironies of the Suez story and especially with regard to Anglo-American relations occurred on 18 November 1956 when Lloyd visited Dulles just after he had had an operation at Bethesda Naval Hospital: Dulles shook his hand and said 'Selwyn, when you started, why didn't you go through with it?' The answer to his question, which tells us as much about Britain as it does about the United States, was that Eden lost his nerve and that America would have accepted a *fait accompli*. In a letter to Lloyd of 27 January 1957, Eden said, 'Meanwhile this incredible US administration seems to think the only two powers in the world worth courting are Nasser and Ibn Saud.' Eden always felt betrayed by the Americans and this comes through repeatedly in his memoirs. Coming nearer home, a major critic of the whole Suez adventure was the Tory Ian Gilmour who thought it was a disaster for Britain, wrapped in deception, hypocrisy and wilful ignoring of international norms. Eden was a disaster, Macmillan devious beyond belief. 'Unfortunately for him [Eden], the State Department told the President that the Egyptians had acted within their rights, while the American Chief of Naval Operations was certain that taking ships through the Suez Canal was not difficult and the Egyptians would be able to do it comfortably enough.'[10] At the height of the crisis, when ships of the American Sixth Fleet were deliberately sailing alongside the British flotilla heading for Suez, Alec Douglas-Home stated his belief, 'I think what really turned the scale and made the Chancellor of the Exchequer [Macmillan] that day so terribly anxious was the American action in putting the Sixth Fleet alongside us in the Mediterranean for all the world to see, and therefore announcing in effect that America was totally against us. The effect on sterling as a result of that was catastrophic. It was the actual effect on sterling rather than the warnings, I think. Perhaps we ought to have taken the warnings more seriously.'[11] This was a curiously exculpatory statement for Macmillan who, having been 'first in' and then 'first out', was to succeed Eden as prime minister. By the end of October any refinements of attitude were swamped by the common-sense fact that everybody else—Commonwealth, United Nations, United States—was against military action. Throughout the crisis Eden never seems to have taken statements by Eisenhower at their face value, as he should. They were always to the effect that any invasion of Egypt would be wrong and would not be supported by Washington. There was a problem, however, between Eden and Dulles. Thus, on 19 July, while Eisenhower was still recuperating (from an operation), and without consulting Eden or even his own staff, Dulles summarily withdrew the US offer to finance the Aswan High Dam. Two days later the British government also withdrew from the project. At the beginning of the Suez crisis Britain and the USA worked together, despite US reservations, as partners dealing with a crisis that was vital and to be solved jointly. By the end of it, the two were at deep odds with each other: the Americans had financially pulled the rug from under the British whose influence in the Middle East had been dealt if not a death blow, one that would prove mortal. Suez, moreover, marked the end of British pretensions to be one of the Big Three. Thereafter it was to be a lieutenant—often unwilling—to the spread of US hegemony. Although in principle supportive of British efforts, the Americans were drawn at critical moments to stressing their own anti-imperialist credentials; to playing, but usually failing to discharge, the role of mediator between the British and the Arabs; and to exploiting British weakness in order to increase their own influence and material holdings, not least in oil.[12]

On 24 November in the General Assembly of the United Nations a relatively mild Afro-Asian motion called upon the British and the French to withdraw their troops forthwith from Egypt—the voting was sixty-three in favour, five against with ten abstentions including the United States. The reaction in Britain was a wave of anti-Americanism that shocked the American Ambassador Winthrop Aldrich. As R.A.Butler told him: if America did not act firmly about the immediate clearance of the Canal Britain might withdraw from the UN and might even ask the US to give up her bases in Britain. 'It is tragic,' cabled Aldrich on 26 November 1956 'to sit here in London and observe the rapidly changing attitude of the British public towards us—where we are thought of by the British public as enemies of Britain.'[13] A special relationship was of little use if it fell into abeyance during a crisis—the Suez debacle represented the post-war turning point for Britain. 'Eden and the bulk of the Conservative Party were taken aback and affronted by American anger at having been double-crossed. When the tap [economic aid] refused to be turned on they decided to kick the tap. One hundred and thirty Conservative MPs signed a Commons motion censuring the United States for "gravely endangering the Atlantic Alliance".'[14] The Suez crisis had reduced Britain from its position as a world power to a European power. Iain MacLeod said, 'The Suez crisis marked the lowest ebb of Anglo-American relations in modern times—the alliance was shaken to its foundations. Having brusquely withdrawn his offer of a loan for the Aswan Dam he [Dulles] failed to put his weight behind the allies when Nasser seized the Canal as a direct tit-for-tat.' The question then was just what would the Anglo-American alliance amount to in the future? Drew Middleton summed up the change of the relationship between the two countries when he wrote: 'For whatever the alliance means to Americans, to Britons it has meant a special relationship between the two countries under which the United Kingdom is entitled to more consideration than she often receives. It was the realisation that the United States did not recognise this special relationship that touched off the wave of criticism and doubt during the Suez crisis.' Later, in his book, *The British*, he refers again to Suez:

'That adventure was the great watershed of Anglo-American relations; not because it found American political resources arranged against its closest ally, but because it demonstrated to all who could see that Britain henceforth would be incapable of independent military action without the support, either moral or material, of the United States.'[15]

The concept of 'responsibility' had long been accepted as part of Britain's imperial heritage, giving it the right and the duty to intervene in problems round the world. It was a question of world leadership. After 1945, however, world leadership had to be shared with the United States and before long it became obvious that such leadership required power, economic and military, to make it effective. One of the many lessons of Suez was that the United States now had the power to allow it to undertake leadership roles even as the shrinking power of Britain meant it could no longer take on such responsibilities by itself but must operate in tandem with the United States. It was a bitter lesson for Britain to learn. Although Eden had often claimed to believe in the Atlantic Alliance he became determined, no matter what the opposition, to act as a great power on his own over Suez, which meant ignoring the special relationship. The major British concern at this time was to perpetuate its influence round the world in the manner to which it had become accustomed though its resources had shrunk. British leaders, mistakenly, came to believe that by nourishing and adhering to the special relationship they would achieve this end. The assumption was that the Americans would be persuaded by superior British wisdom to act as London wanted. Increasingly, Britain discovered that the Americans had plans and policies of their own.

Sir Charles Keightley, the Commander in Chief of the allied forces in the Suez operation, said subsequently, 'The one overriding lesson of the Suez operation is that world opinion is now an absolute principle of war and must be treated as such.' He was correct but it was not only a principle of war but would soon also be a principle of de-colonisation, another area where British power was about to shrink. Eden never tried to understand Eisenhower despite all the lessons his long years as foreign secretary ought to have taught him. In early March 1956 Eden entertained John McCloy and Ambassador Aldrich at Chequers, when he said, 'I never move a step without our American friends.' As he launched his Suez operation, Eden assumed that the Cold War factor would override US doubts about an attack upon Egypt, which he saw as the chosen instrument of Soviet penetration in the Middle East, expecting that Eisenhower would have to support the British and French action. 'So far from falling into line at the last moment, Eisenhower was to interpose the political might of the USA and, if possible, the UN between invaders and invaded in the eastern Mediterranean. He had not been fooled for one second by the Anglo-French cover story of separating the combatants.'[16] In the end it came down to money when the Americans refused any financial help as Britain's reserves of currency as well as its oil supplies ran down at an alarming rate.

There were many lessons to be learnt from Suez. The first, do not embark upon an enterprise that you are unable to carry through alone. The second, do not act against the wishes of your more powerful special ally. The third, do not deceive him. Prime Minister Nehru of India said of Nasser's nationalisation of the Canal that it was 'a sign of the weakening of that European domination of Asia and the Middle East which had lasted more than a hundred years'. John Strachey, a formidable intellectual on the left, analysed the impact of the Suez Crisis and so posed the question: 'What is to be done? We now observe that the question we are really asking is this: what is to be put in the place of Empire?'[17]

Although Suez was a disaster, it did present Britain with the opportunity to reappraise its policies. The opportunity was not embraced. Even though the breach between Britain and the United States was more absolute than any other division since the Second World War, the British under the premiership of Macmillan adopted the line that the breach was a 'hiccup' and that all we had to do was heal the wounds and return to the alliance as it had been before Suez. Macmillan ought to have asked: was the special relationship essential and what did it do for Britain? Why, given the nature of the breach did Macmillan subsequently seek, almost obsessively, to rebuild the alliance? In the aftermath of Suez, with Britain beset by a financial crisis, the Americans clearly wanted Eden to go. Britain faced a choice: Butler or Macmillan for prime minister? The American ambassador, Winthrop Aldrich, said either was required to cover up the acutely embarrassing nakedness of the British government. This 'nakedness' said Macmillan, with undiluted bitterness, had been caused 'by humiliations almost vindictively inflicted upon us at the instance of the United States Government.'

6

MACMILLAN

On the two major issues facing Britain when Macmillan came to power—dealing with the post-Suez crisis with the United States and the question of Britain's relations with Europe—Macmillan was fundamentally negative. He had been a leading advocate of taking control of the Canal and then, as things went wrong, he used his position as chancellor to argue that the pound would collapse and Britain should abandon its invasion for financial reasons, earning as a result of this *volte face* Harold Wilson's famous quip 'first in, first out'. A savage attack upon Macmillan's Suez posturing is described in *Suez*:[1] he first postured as the scourge of Nasser and then became the leader of the bolters while he had been absent from the Treasury where he might otherwise have discovered earlier the damage that the Suez adventure was doing to sterling. He spent his first year as prime minister working to restore the special relationship as it had been prior to the Suez debacle rather than seeking to remodel it on a sounder basis of equality or ditch it for a different policy altogether. As for European Unity, it was under Macmillan that Britain first walked out of the Messina negotiations and then tried to undermine the Common Market of the Six by creating a wider free trade area and when that was turned down, setting up the European free trade association (EFTA). When this was shown to be an inadequate alternative to the Common Market he applied to join the Six. De Gaulle vetoed the 1961 British application on the grounds that Britain did not really believe in the ECM and only wanted to join because it had made a mess of its other policies.

On 10 January 1957 Macmillan succeeded Eden as prime minister. He made the restoration of the special relationship his top priority. On 17 January he made his first television appearance. After referring to Suez, he said: 'The life of the free world depends upon the partnership between us. Any partners are bound to have their differences now and then. I've always found it so.—But true partnership is based on respect. We don't intend to part from the Americans, and we don't intend to be satellites.'[2] Macmillan's political genius, much admired by Harold Wilson, was to hold up the banner of Suez for the party to follow while in practice leading it in the opposite direction. His political shrewdness allowed him to use a nation's pride in itself to ease its transition into a less comfortable world role. He taught the British to accept loss of power—including Empire—but did not go the further essential step and cease being America's loyal lieutenant.[3]

Macmillan is a baffling figure. He saw clearly, for example, in May 1960 when his efforts at a summit collapsed, that Britain no longer had the power it once wielded yet he, like others, went on with the special relationship and still tried to project greater power than was any longer feasible. In part he tried to act according to Churchill's grandiose idea of Britain being at the centre of three intersecting circles and, for example, tried to forge a link—though only half-heartedly—with the EEC but without relinquishing the special relationship with the United States. At a time when Britain needed to make clear choices about its international role he attempted to cling on to too much from the past. The Macmillan generation that had been born when the Empire was at its height, and had lived through the two world wars accepted the special relationship as the best means of prolonging Britain's waning power. Macmillan could see and understand how Britain was losing its place at the 'top table' but could not adjust to it. At Christmas 1960 he produced his 'Grand Design' memorandum in which he acknowledged that Britain, with all its experience had neither the economic nor the military power to take the leading role in the struggle against communism. Nonetheless, he still wanted a leading role for Britain that he must have known in his bones it could not justify in power terms. It was a contradictory attitude shared by other politicians of his generation but it was not going to work.

'But Mr. Macmillan will probably be the last British Prime Minister whose education and statesmanship goes back to World War II and the birth of the

Anglo-American Alliance. Henceforth, whether or not the United Kingdom enters Europe, the United States will have to deal with British leaders less involved emotionally in strengthening and perpetuating the American link and less likely to be guided by the Churchillian precept that the Alliance with Washington comes first.'[4]

In the aftermath of Suez, Macmillan brought all his political skills to bear upon the restoration of the special relationship and in pursuit of this object very obviously relegated Britain's relations with Europe into second place. It remains far from clear half a century after this time why Macmillan felt that the special relationship was so 'absolutely' important to Britain, especially as the Americans had discarded it entirely during the Suez disaster. He claimed that at the beginning of 1957 he found the special relationship virtually destroyed, the European alliance almost shattered, and dismay and uncertainty in the Commonwealth. However, as far as Europe was concerned Britain's relations with it were no better in 1963 when Macmillan's term of office came to an end than in 1957. An examination of Volume Two of Alistair Horne's biography of Macmillan reveals an enormous number of references to Anglo-American relations, a subject that clearly took first place in his priorities. By 1963 Macmillan could reasonably claim to have repaired the damaged special relationship and so was able to draw upon a remarkable personal friendship, which he had established with President Kennedy. Indeed, Macmillan had enjoyed good personal relations with both President Eisenhower and his successor and his diaries reveal how he worked at these personal relationships. As Lionel Gelber tells us, Britain had great difficulty in giving up its leadership of the West but 'historically, the manner in which the primacy was transferred from Britain to the United States reveals how unique the Anglo-American factor has been' and Macmillan can take much of the credit for this. Randolph Churchill described Macmillan's healing of the breach with the United States as a great act of statesmanship. How statesmanlike would Macmillan have appeared if he had used the Suez debacle as the starting point for a new British direction without the slavish adherence to Washington's policies that followed the reconciliation? There was a price to pay: 'Many Americans moreover are gratified by the deference, at times verging on servility, showed to United States interests and policies by Prime Minister Macmillan and the majority of his associates in the cabinet.'[5] Why did Macmillan not see how this subservient approach to Washington damaged Britain's international standing?

It was not all to be subservience, however. Duncan Sandys as minister of defence visited Washington in January 1957 and told Dulles that what Britain most complained of in US behaviour over Suez was being misled by Dulles' scheme for a Suez Canal Users' Association to bring pressure to bear on Nasser. He said that frankly, we felt that we had been 'led up the garden path' and from then onwards the British government had lost all confidence in the friendly intentions of the American government. Dulles was momentarily embarrassed. It was the year of 'sputnik' when Cold War tensions were especially high and there were growing fears in the West that the USSR could move into the power vacuum left in the Middle East by Britain.

Macmillan enjoyed a huge advantage as he began to restore relations with America because he and Eisenhower had worked closely together in North Africa during the war and established a good working relationship with each other at that time. Eisenhower wrote a friendly letter to greet Macmillan's assumption of the premiership. Later, he sent a second letter in which he suggested a March meeting in Bermuda, demonstrating that he and the United States clearly wished to mend the breach. Macmillan was delighted. The Bermuda meeting was to prove a turning point with regard to Europe for, whether by accident or design, Macmillan made plain his preference for a two-way meeting with the American president rather than any broader exchange that would include European partners. Macmillan was to spend twenty minutes alone in a car with Eisenhower when they renewed their close past friendship. However, Eisenhower told Macmillan that he could not dispense with the unpopular Dulles. Macmillan wrote to his deputy, R.A.Butler, 'as far as the President is concerned, there is a genuine desire to forget our differences and to restore our old relationship and cooperation in full measure'. Eisenhower wrote to Captain 'Swede' Hazlett, 'Macmillan is, of course, one of my intimate wartime friends and so it is very easy to talk to him on a very frank, even blunt basis.' Later Eisenhower was to count Bermuda 'the most successful international conference that I had attended since the close of World War II'.[6] Subsequently, 'The Declaration of Common Purpose which Macmillan agreed with Eisenhower in October 1957 must rank as one of his greatest achievements and led directly to the amendment of the McMahon Act in the following summer, thus giving Britain its special place within the nuclear framework of the Atlantic Alliance.'[7]

Always a showman, Macmillan got Eisenhower while on a visit to Britain to appear with him on television having a chat (it was just prior to the 1959 election) and the president announced that Anglo-American relations had never been stronger. At the end of their 'chat' Macmillan said—'and I know I speak on behalf of every man, woman and child in this country—how very glad we are to have you with us and we welcome you here.' Thus Macmillan projected himself as a national leader above politics, on the friendliest first-name terms with the popular American president. Macmillan loved classical references and famously, at this time, suggested it was Britain's historical duty to guide the power of the United States as the ancient Greeks had the Romans. Just how Americans accepted this arrogant assumption is not clear but Macmillan appears to have forgotten that Greece became a Roman colony and a not very important one at that. He pushed the idea of an Atlantic Community and suggested the 'interdependence' of the nations of the free world and the partnership, which had to be maintained between Europe and the United States. He coined the term 'interdependence' as applied to the Atlantic Alliance—it was a term that allowed for the blurring of the edges and suggested a greater role for Britain than was the case. Macmillan may have had good or even close relations with Eisenhower and Kennedy but this often did not extend to top officials in the State Department and for example, reacting to a letter from Macmillan to Kennedy about a meeting with Khruschev, Arthur Schlesinger says the letter received a 'dusty answer' in the State Department, with one high official declaring contemptuously, 'We can't let Macmillan practice emotional blackmail on us.'[8] Like Churchill, Macmillan hankered after summits and hoped to act as a mediator between the two superpowers, a role they neither wanted nor needed. He hoped to persuade the Americans to seek compromises with the USSR while his continued attempts to act alone offended Europe, eliciting from Germany's Chancellor Konrad Adenauer the comment that British policy was 'one big fiddle'.

Britain's effort to be an independent nuclear power became an embarrassing farce once it became clear that the deterrent depended upon an American input, which included the means of delivery. Macmillan suggested that Britain's deterrent force required to be no stronger 'than the minimum necessary to convince the Americans, once they have been made fully aware of our economic difficulties, of our sincerity as allies'.[9] The supposed reason for a British deterrent was to deter a Soviet attack upon Britain rather than to impress the Americans. The 1962 Skybolt crisis demonstrated just how fragile was the

British nuclear accord with the United States. (Skybolt was the missile to deliver nuclear warheads onto their targets—it could be deployed from Britain's V-Bombers.) Kennedy and his Secretary of Defense Robert McNamara, unilaterally cancelled what was a joint project with Britain in December 1962. This left the British deterrent policy in tatters and demonstrated how it was dependent upon American decisions. Immediately, Macmillan arranged a meeting with Kennedy in the Bahamas and after long discussion persuaded Kennedy to supply Britain with the submarine-launched polaris missile. For all practical purposes the British deterrent was an arm of the American defensive screen against the Soviet threat, with the added disadvantage for Britain that if a war did occur the country would be a prime Soviet target.

Meanwhile, the Cuban crisis overshadowed everything else. It was the nearest the world came to a nuclear war throughout the years of the Cold War and all the world had to act as spectators while the United States and the Soviet Union squared up to each other. Macmillan at least was able to act as a close spectator and confidant of Kennedy through their long telephone discussions though he did not influence the American president. 'McGeorge Bundy, assistant to the President for National Security Affairs, said the "Cuba Phone Calls" were "more to touch base than because of a sense that he really wanted to know what Macmillan thought about a thing".' What Kennedy required was 'an assurance that a tough line of interception would—be supported by the British Government'. Douglas-Home claimed that Britain was consulted throughout the crisis to the point of the final decision.[10] As it happened the British Ambassador to the United States, David Ormsby-Gore, enjoyed especially good personal relations with Kennedy. He had come to know the Kennedy family when Joseph P. Kennedy was US Ambassador in London and a solid friendship between the families had developed. Robert Kennedy later recalled that Ormsby-Gore was almost part of the government. 'The president would rather have his judgement, his ideas, his suggestions and recommendations than even anybody in our government. John F. Kennedy felt free to try ideas out on his British friend, knowing also that this would strengthen the ties between the two former wartime allies.' Reporting to London, Ormsby-Gore said of Kennedy's statements, 'In some instances they were so frank that I doubt very much whether he would repeat them to any member of his administration except his brother Bobby.'[11]

This cosy relationship was not accepted elsewhere. According to Noam Chomsky: 'But Europe was kept in the dark and treated with disdain. Kennedy's ExComm "summarily dismissed any idea of sharing with the allies decisions that could have led to the nuclear destruction of Western Europe as well as North America". Kennedy said, "allies must come along or stay behind—we cannot accept a veto from any other power".' And, according to Chomsky, Kennedy's closest ally, British Prime Minister Harold Macmillan, told his associates that Kennedy's actions were 'escalating into war' but we could do nothing 'to stop it': he knew only what he could learn from British intelligence. Washington's perception of the US-UK 'special relationship' was articulated by a senior Kennedy adviser in internal discussion at the peak of the crisis: Britain will 'act as our lieutenant (the fashionable word is partner)'.[12]

Kennedy took decisions without consulting his allies. When the US Ambassador in London, David Bruce, took aerial photographs of the Soviet missile sites in Cuba to show him, 'Macmillan's reaction when he saw the pictures was very interesting. He looked at them for a little while and then said, more to himself than to us, pointing at the missile sites, "Now the Americans will realise what we in England have lived with for the past many years".' Macmillan's role throughout the crisis would appear to have been to provide a highly knowledgeable sympathetic listener to Kennedy who felt free to discuss all the difficulties with him. When Kennedy had prevailed and the Soviet flotilla had turned back, Macmillan wrote to him: 'It was indeed a trial of wills and yours has prevailed. Whatever dangers and difficulties we have to face in the future I am proud to feel that I have so resourceful and so firm a comrade.' Kennedy replied: 'I am grateful for your warm generous words. Your heartening support publicly expressed and our daily conversations have been of inestimable value in these past days.' Ormsby-Gore said of Macmillan's impact on Kennedy: 'I can't honestly think of anything said from London that changed the US action—it was chiefly reassurance to JFK.'[13]

In retrospect Dean Rusk reckoned that 'in terms of motivating the unanimity of NATO; the British attitude had been very important'. One last quote from Ormsby-Gore to Macmillan:

'The President has, I know, already told you how much he appreciated your support and advice during the critical week. In this he was being deeply sincere and has repeatedly said the same thing to his closest friends, adding that he has no similar close contacts with any other ally. He is furious with newspaper commentators who suggest that recent events indicate that there is little value for the US in the special Anglo-American relationship.'

The president may have been angry at such comments, by Michael Foot in *Tribune* for example, but the fact remains that all the decisions were made in Washington without consultation with allies so that in this crisis the special relationship amounted to Macmillan giving Kennedy daily reassurances over the phone. Thus, Macmillan, who always wanted to be at the centre of world decisions, was allowed a special observer status as the crisis proceeded. He was told what was being done, not asked to contribute.

British politicians, during the Macmillan era and later, spent a good deal of their energies explaining Britain to the United States. Thus, in September 1961, the British Foreign Secretary, Alec Douglas-Home, addressed the National Press Club in Washington: 'The first profound conviction which I had on taking up my new office, is that if Britain is to fulfil her role as leader of the Commonwealth, as a reliable ally and as a buttress to the free world, that Britain must be strong; economically strong, because solvency is the essential basis of all national enterprise and of all international influence; physically strong because our island holds a strategic position on the continent of Europe and in the Atlantic—and morally strong because let us have no doubt that in the last analysis communism is going to be beaten by a creed and by principles of living which are demonstrated to be more viable and to be more compelling than their own creed.'[14]

Macmillan never had good relations with France's President Charles de Gaulle, partly because they were too far apart and there was little personal chemistry at work between them but, more importantly, because of British insistence upon being the third nuclear power and sharing nuclear technical cooperation with the United States that was not open to France. De Gaulle saw that the special relationship would always keep Britain a remove from Europe. Henry Kissinger, writing in 1994, said how forty years ago, 'De Gaulle frequently behaved obstreperously in order to make ignoring him painful; Macmillan made it so easy for the United States to solicit Britain's views that ignoring him would have been embarrassing.'[15] In 1957, while the 'Six' were finalising the Treaty of Rome, Macmillan was busy repairing the special relationship. Subsequently he did huge damage to Britain's relations with Europe as he tried to bypass or downgrade the importance of the ECM with his proposal of a free trade area and then the creation of the EFTA so that when he finally sought entry to the ECM de Gaulle used his veto. President Kennedy was in favour of Britain joining the ECM and there was always the fear in London that the United States would see Europe as a more important ally than Britain, certainly as long as the Cold War lasted.

Dean Acheson, the US secretary of state from 1949 to 1951, was a confirmed Anglophile. In his memoirs he tells of his close working relationship with the British Ambassador Sir Oliver Franks: 'I made him an unorthodox proposal. On an experimental basis I suggested that we talk regularly, and in complete personal confidence, about any international problems we saw arising. Neither would report or quote the other unless, thinking that it would be useful in promoting action, he got the other's consent and agreement on the terms of a reporting memorandum or cable. The dangers and difficulties of such a relationship were obvious, but its usefulness proved to be so great that we continued it for four years.'[16]

Speaking of the special relationship, Acheson said: 'Of course a unique relation existed between Britain and America.' However, Acheson was most famous (from a British point of view) for the speech he delivered in December 1962 at West Point when he said: 'Great Britain has lost an empire and has not yet found a role. The attempt to play a separate power role—that is, a role apart from Europe, a role based on a "Special Relationship" with the United States, a role based on being the head of a "Commonwealth" which has no political structure, or unity, or strength and enjoys a fragile and precarious economic relationship by means of the sterling area and preferences in the British market—this role is about played out.'[17]

This passage can be interpreted in two opposing ways: the first, a derogatory attack upon Britain by a leading figure of the US establishment determined to downsize British pretensions to world influence; or second, an exasperated admonition by a friend of Britain to find a role commensurate with its resources, a plea to cut its cloth according to its purse. No leading figure in Britain saw Acheson's remarks in this light, perhaps because the truth of what he said was too hard to bear. Instead, much offence was taken, especially by Macmillan, who made an angry response:

'In so far as he appeared to denigrate the resolution and the will of Britain and the British people, Mr. Acheson has fallen into an error which has been made by quite a lot of people in the course of the last four hundred years, including Philip of Spain, Louis XIV, Napoleon, the Kaiser and Hitler. He also seems to misunderstand the role of the Commonwealth in world affairs. In so far as he referred to Britain's attempt to play a separate power role as about to be played out, this would be acceptable if he had extended this concept to the United States and to every other nation in the Free World. This is the doctrine of interdependence, which must be applied in the world today, if Peace and Prosperity are to be assured. I do not know whether Mr. Acheson would accept the logical sequence of his own argument. I am sure it is fully recognised by the US administration and by the American people.'

Had Acheson's admonition been examined analytically it might have helped Britain understand that a change of both attitudes and objectives was required if she was to adopt policies more suited to her resources but the opportunity was passed. Just before he died Acheson spoke admiringly of Attlee's attempt to achieve the promise (Truman 1950) of consultation over nuclear strikes. He added: 'We had to unachieve that.'

At least up to Macmillan the fixation with the special relationship could be understood to represent the view of his generation who wanted a continuation of the war partnership and could not bear to see the passing of Britain's worldwide influence and power. C.P. Snow in his Rede Lecture of 1959—*The Two Cultures and the Scientific Revolution*—explains the dilemma of Britain's ruling class when he compares Britain's decline with that of the Venetian Republic: 'I can't help thinking of the Venetian Republic in their last half century. Like us, they had once been fabulously lucky. They had become rich, as we did, by accident. They had acquired immense political skill, just as we have. A good many of them were tough-minded, realistic, patriotic men. They knew, just as clearly as we know, that the current of history had begun to flow against them. Many of them gave their minds to working out ways to keep going. It would have meant breaking the pattern into which they had crystallised. They were fond of the pattern, just as we are fond of ours. They never found the will to break it.'

7

THE NUCLEAR QUESTION

The nuclear question—should Britain have its own bomb or rely upon the Americans?—dominates the debates about the special relationship between 1945 and well into the 1960s. Dependence upon the Americans meant subservience or a satellite relationship. An independent British bomb would mean a real measure of independence from American domination. The background to this debate was the Cold War and the assumption that if there were to be a hot war with the USSR, Britain and the United States would necessarily stand together. Margaret Gowing, an expert on matters nuclear, said: 'Had it not been for the brilliant scientific work done in Britain in the early part of the war, by refugee scientists, the Second World War would almost certainly have ended before an atomic bomb was dropped. It had been the cogency and clarity of the British Maud Report in 1941 which had persuaded the Americans of the practical possibility of an atomic bomb and the urgency of making one.'[1]

Throughout most of the Cold War only a handful of nations were members of the so-called 'nuclear club'. The United States and the Soviet Union were charter members. Britain, France, and later China were admitted to 'membership'. Looking back on Macmillan's determination to persuade President Kennedy to supply Polaris for the means of delivery for British bombs, Robert Cooper says:

'From the point of view of "interest", the case for a British deterrent could be argued either way. The question—as Macmillan put it—was not about inter-

71

est, but about Britain's perception of itself, about the kind of country it was and the kind of country it wanted to be.'[2]

In his book, suitably titled *Test of Greatness: Britain's Struggle for the Atom Bomb*, Brian Cathcart says how, 'In 1944, for example, Churchill and Roosevelt had agreed that: Full cooperation between the United States and the British Government in developing Tube Alloys for military and commercial purposes should continue after the defeat of Japan unless and until terminated by joint agreement.' The later misunderstandings arose because the term Tube Alloys was used as a top-secret code to cover this Roosevelt-Churchill agreement about the bomb. Unfortunately, the Tube Alloys file was misfiled and 'lost' so that no record of the 1944 agreement was available when President Truman stopped further Anglo-American collaboration after the war. Indeed, no sooner had the two bombs been dropped on Nagasaki and Hiroshima and the British atomic scientists who had moved to America halfway through the war to take part in the Manhattan Project returned to Britain than collaboration ceased. 'The Anglo-American atomic partnership had always had an on-off air about it; now, with Germany and Japan defeated, the Americans regarded the bomb as their exclusive property.'[3] Indeed, and regardless of Tube Alloys, this might be taken as the point at which the United States began consciously to push the concept of its own world hegemony. The British left-wing intellectual, Raymond Williams, considered the time in the years immediately after the war when only the United States had the bomb: 'We have only to look at the international politics of the mid-late 1940s, when the United States but not the Soviet Union possessed atomic weapons, and when proposals for use of this monopoly to destroy the world centre of Communism while there was still time acquired significant support, over a surprising range, to realise that in this as in so much else a monopoly of such terrible power, in any hands, is profoundly dangerous.'[4]

Even had the Tube Alloys file not been lost there were powerful forces at work in the United States to stop nuclear collaboration with Britain: the Americans wanted to be ahead rather than sharing such knowledge. As Dean Acheson noted dryly: 'The honeymoon of Anglo-American relations existing during the war was clearly coming to an end, and some of the commitments of the marriage seemed to be causing pain to one of the spouses.' Although he always portrayed himself as an Anglophile there is a malicious aspect of superiority in his use of the term spouse. This, surely, was the first occasion when Britain should have accepted the death of the special relationship. Instead, though the Americans quite clearly wanted to follow their own policies, the British began their clinging act, which was to last for decades. On 8 October 1945 President Truman told journalists that any other country wanting to develop the atomic bomb 'will have to get it on their own hook, just as we did'. He no doubt had the British in mind. A month later, however, Attlee flew to Washington for a meeting with Truman and Canada's Prime Minister Mackenzie King at which they entered into a secret agreement: 'We desire that there should be full and effective cooperation in the field of atomic energy between the United States, the United Kingdom and Canada.' The 'desire' was not a clear-cut commitment and in 1946 Congress passed the McMahon Act that prohibited co-operation with any country on nuclear matters. Following the passing of the McMahon Act, 'Mr. Attlee sent a long letter to the President, rehearsing the whole background of our collaboration in the war, and so on, and saying that this was an intolerable situation. A very strong document. He never got an answer.'[5]

Reflecting upon Hiroshima and Nagasaki, Attlee wrote: 'No government has ever been placed in such a position as is ours today. The Governments of the UK and the USA are responsible as never before for the future of the human race.' Britain shared this burden with the United States because it had also shared in the development of the atomic bomb. As the Tory Ian Gilmour was to write decades later: 'Notwithstanding the large British contribution to the invention of the atomic bomb and contrary to the wartime agreement to continue sharing information, America ended nuclear collaboration.'[6] On this issue especially the British felt deeply aggrieved since the Americans were trying to create a monopoly of the bomb based on a very sizeable British input. Britain therefore set out to develop its own nuclear deterrent. Tony Benn has often criticised the extent to which Britain had surrendered 'sovereignty' to the Americans and has consistently resented the commanding position in the deployment of its own nuclear weapons in Britain: the UK of Attlee and Bevin ceded to the USA of Truman and Marshall. This surrender of sovereignty may be seen as the end of an independent Britain in relation to the United States.[7] Even if the Tube Alloys file was lost, the Americans acted very high-handedly over sharing nuclear information. The Quebec Agreement of 1943 paved the way for the two countries plus Canada to develop atomic weapons side by side. The UK handed over vital documents from its Tube Alloys project and sent a delegation to assist in the work of the Manhattan Project. The United States, however, subsequently kept the results of the work to itself under the terms of the MacMahon Act. Only after Britain had developed its own bomb and under great pressure from Macmillan did the United States agree to supply delivery systems.

In the spring of 1946 Britain informed the US government that it was to build an atomic pile and asked for technical information under the terms of the Washington agreement. In April the United States refused. When options with the United States proved not to exist, Britain went ahead on its own. Years later Attlee said: 'It had become essential. We had to hold up our position vis-à-vis the Americans. We couldn't allow ourselves to be wholly in their hands, and their position wasn't awfully clear always.' He went on: 'At that time we had to bear in mind that there was always the possibility of their withdrawing and becoming isolationist once again.'[8] In October of that year the cabinet discussed whether or not to go ahead with the bomb and two members, Hugh Dalton and Stafford Cripps, opposed doing so on grounds of cost. Bevin arrived late and insisted that Britain had to have it. After relating the attitude towards Britain by the US Secretary of State Byrnes, he said: 'We've got to have the bloody Union Jack on top of it.' By 1947 Attlee had accepted that Britain must manufacture its own atomic weapon in a world where Britain had many responsibilities. However strong the conviction of Attlee and Bevin about the need for a British bomb they kept trying to reopen the agreement with the United States. Churchill supported the Attlee decision. 'If we are unable to make the bomb ourselves and have to rely entirely on the American army for this vital weapon we shall sink to the rank of a second class nation, only permitted to supply auxiliary troops like the native levies who were allowed small arms but no artillery.'[9] On 12 May 1948 the Minister of Defence A.V. Alexander announced to the House of Commons that Britain was making its own bomb. In December 1951, back in office, Churchill told Lord Cherwell, his scientific adviser, to proceed with the bomb, which was to be tested in Australia.

In 1947 Ernest Bevin had a wholly British bomb in mind. Subsequently Macmillan, Wilson and Healey were each to argue that possession of the bomb would help Britain restrain America. Healey, who was minister of defence under Wilson, said: 'If you look at the arguments which took place in the Attlee government about whether we should have a nuclear bomb, there is absolutely no doubt at all that Attlee himself and, even more explicitly, Ernest Bevin, wanted the nuclear bomb to show we were a world power equal to the United States, irrespective of any particular function it would have in the military field.'[10] The later story of the bomb reveals the persistence with which both Attlee and Churchill sought American help with the development of Britain's 'independent' deterrent.

Although the exchange of nuclear information had been cut off by the Americans in 1946, the British never abandoned the hope that the exchange could be renewed. In January 1948 Britain agreed to tear up the wartime understanding that required the US government to consult the British government before using the atomic bomb. Such an agreement was never going to be kept once the Americans had realised the huge power gap that existed between them and Britain. Nonetheless, the Americans in a quid pro quo did agree to release to Britain atomic energy information in nine areas though none were pertinent to manufacturing a bomb. At this time the Americans were determined to maintain their monopoly on nuclear power, at least in relation to weapons. In 1951, as a propaganda war was waged between the United States and the Soviet Union over atomic weapons, William Penney (Britain's leading nuclear scientist) argued that either Britain had to make the bomb or admit it could not afford to do so. 'The discriminative test for a first-class power is whether it has made an atomic bomb and we have either got to pass the test or suffer a serious loss in prestige both inside this country and internationally.'[11] Unfortunately, Britain's efforts to secure closer liaison with the United States were dealt a devastating blow when Klaus Fuchs, a refugee scientist who had worked on the British bomb, confessed his treason in supplying nuclear secrets to the Russians. This played into the hands of those Americans who were opposed to sharing any nuclear know-how with the British. When Britain was approaching the point of its first bomb test, the Americans wanted the test to be carried out in America but this was turned down. The closer the British came to testing their bomb the readier the Americans were to resume talks and information exchange. In October 1952, following the successful test of the British bomb, the *Daily Graphic* declared: 'Britain now has what is believed to be the world's most powerful atomic weapon.' By this time prestige appeared to have displaced defence as the primary reason for a British bomb.

Churchill and the Tory party had come back to power in 1951, just as Britain was preparing to test its bomb and the subject was to remain at the top of the agenda for much of his ministry. It was suggested in cabinet that since many defence preparations were based upon the assumption that Britain would only fight another major war alongside the Americans, was there any need for the bomb? Should Britain simply rely upon the Americans? A JIC assessment pointed out, 'The danger the United States might succumb to the temptation of precipitating a "forestalling" war cannot be disregarded. In view of the vulnerability of the United Kingdom we must use all our influence to prevent this.'[12] In 1954 Churchill determined that Britain should develop the 'H' bomb. Through all the debates about sharing nuclear secrets it never seems to have occurred to the British that they had at their disposal a formidable bargaining card and that was the presence of US nuclear bases in Britain. This was never used and Britain remained a frontline target as a result of the US nuclear presence in the country. Britain got the 'H' bomb in 1957, greatly strengthening Macmillan's hand in his talks with Eisenhower. Macmillan's reasons for maintaining an independent deterrent were: 'To retain our special relation with the United States and, through it, our influence in world affairs, and, especially, our right to have a voice in the final issue of peace and war.'[13] On examination, these reasons imply greater dependence upon the United States rather than greater independence for Britain. At a Labour party meeting of April 1955, Aneurin Bevan, the one-time hero of the 'left', became an advocate of the British bomb when he argued that the emasculation of the United Kingdom would simply lead to a further polarisation of the world between the Soviet Union and the United States—both of whom he distrusted. 'We want to have the opportunity of interposing between those two giants, modifying, moderating and mitigating influences.' By that time the Campaign for Nuclear Disarmament (CND) had become a significant political factor in the country and especially in the Labour party. Bevan went on to argue that to renounce unilaterally the UK's nuclear weapons was not an act of statesmanship, it was just 'an emotional spasm'. The left was outraged.[14]

During the defence estimates debate of 9 May 1957, Tony Benn said: 'The Prime Minister has said that he had a better deal than Lord Attlee. I frankly doubt that—The nuclear deterrents cannot be used without the permission of the United States, whereas under the old agreement the American deterrent could not be used without the permission of the United Kingdom.'[15] The following year the Macmillan government signed an agreement with the United States, which overruled the MacMahon Act of 1946 and so permitted the exchange of nuclear information. Britain wanted to develop its own nuclear arsenal but also needed the means of delivery. The United States, therefore, agreed to provide Britain with the Skybolt missile but in exchange for a deepwater base for US Polaris submarines. They were given Holy Loch off the River Clyde, very close to Glasgow. Thus Glasgow, Scotland's most populous city became the first target for a nuclear strike, whether pre-emptive or retaliatory. Macmillan was reassured by Eisenhower, that: 'In the event of an emergency, such as increased tension or the threat of war, the US will take every possible step to consult with Britain and other allies.' When at the end of 1962 the Americans cancelled Skybolt they had something for nothing. At the Nassau summit in the Bahamas of 17 December Macmillan insisted that President Kennedy should provide Britain with the Polaris missile at knock-down prices. Kennedy did so reluctantly—all his advisers were against giving Britain Polaris—but thereafter Britain's 'independent' nuclear force was to be inextricably linked to American technology.[16] Britain had just managed to stay in the nuclear club. At least Polaris came up to expectations and replaced Britain's V-bombers in 1969. What is extraordinary about the Skybolt-Polaris debate and the reluctance of the Americans to assist the British is that Britain could have argued: no missile and we will close down the deepwater base for US Polaris submarines. Instead, for turning the country into a major frontline base for the Americans, Britain was offered a minimum of assistance while there were periodic US pressures to suggest that Britain should abandon its nuclear programme altogether. Speaking as minister of defence in the House of Lords in 1961, Lord Carrington said of the British nuclear deterrent: 'It has been challenged at every level of consideration: on purely military grounds, that it is an unnecessary duplication of the American deterrent; on economic grounds that we cannot afford it; on political grounds that it is a barrier to disarmament; and on moral grounds, that it is iniquitous to use it.' Carrington went on: 'it was devastating and effective; that the US welcomed it as creating a greater dispersal of centres of decision'. Carrington did not address the question that British cities and bases should be put at risk but that decisions lay with the United States. He did, however, claim that Britain's deterrent increased British influence with both the United States and the Soviet Union.[17] Macmillan had put enormous effort into restoring the special relationship and obtaining, however reluctant, American assistance with Britain's nuclear programme but once he had obtained this assistance he appeared satisfied as though that was the end of the story. He never appears to have considered the downside of his achievement. He had alienated de Gaulle who in 1963 vetoed Britain's attempt to enter the EEC; Britain was never going to use the bomb on its own; the nation's prestige had not been increased but reduced as Britain was to be seen increasingly as an American satellite; and Britain itself was to be host thereafter to US nuclear bases that made the country a primary target in any direct confrontation between the United States and the Soviet Union.

When Polaris became obsolete, Britain, under Margaret Thatcher, continued with the Trident system. For Thatcher, Trident was an 'of course' decision. 'But, when the question of modernising and replacing Polaris again emerged in the late 1970s and when Mrs Thatcher announced the Trident programme in 1980 and NATO decided to deploy Cruise and Pershing missiles in the same year, a tidal wave of anti-American and anti-nuclear protest overwhelmed the Labour Party—resulting in the adoption of a totally unilateralist policy in 1981.'[18] From 1963 to 1991 Britain, with access to the US facilities in Nevada, conducted twenty-one underground tests. The nuclear debate thereafter was to come and go as part of the panorama of politics. The 1958 agreement was updated in 2004 and Britain and America jointly conducted sub-critical nuclear experiments in 2002 and 2006, to determine the effectiveness of existing stocks. These tests were allowed under the 1998 Comprehensive Nuclear Test Ban Treaty. Denis Healey argued for keeping Polaris. 'The real question was whether it was worth continuing with a programme whose real value lay in the ability to have a handle on the Americans, rather than anybody else, and I'm bound to say that one factor which strengthened my support for keeping the thing going was that MacNamara, and some other Americans, were so anxious we should get rid of it.'[19]

On 7 March 1983 there appeared in *The Times* a lead letter from Gene La Rocque, Director of the Center for Defense Information on NATO: 'The American nuclear weapons in Europe, and those that are to come, are totally under the control of the US Government. They will be used only if and when the US Government decides to do so. No prior understandings or arrangements about consultation will alter this fact. No member of NATO has a veto power over American nuclear weapons.' Members of NATO did, however, have a veto power about where those weapons should be based. 'This is why successive Administrations in Washington have never accepted a copy of the British version of the "agreement" between America and Britain on bases. Just before he died, Dean Acheson spoke admiringly of Attlee's attempt to achieve the promise of consultation, but added, "we had to unachieve that".' In 1986 the Americans used their bombers based in Britain to bomb Libya, provoking James Callaghan, normally a quiescent pro-American, to tell the House of Commons on 17 April that from his long experience as Father of the House and ex-prime minister, that it had never occurred to anyone when US bombers arrived in Britain in 1950 that these aircraft would be used for non-NATO purposes.[20] Gerry Northam, in his *Listener* article of 15 May 1986, put the position most succinctly: 'It may be impolitic to say so, but the fact of the 1952 "joint decision" agreement is that the United States President would make the decision, and the British Prime Minister would make it a joint "decision".'

During 1993–1994 the United States attempted to work closely with Yeltsin's Russia to create what they called a Global Protection System. This led to unease among other NATO countries. 'Intense, private British lobbying to change Washington's mind followed the signing of the Bush-Yeltsin agreement in June 1992. The deal had struck a raw Whitehall nerve. The credibility of the British independent nuclear deterrent rested on the so-called Moscow criterion: the requirement that Britain's warheads must be able to penetrate the Moscow defences.' Since the Cold War was officially over what was the need? 'The British government had fought against similar pressures when the SDI programme was launched in 1983. Despite the overtly warm relationship between Ronald Reagan and Margaret Thatcher, his Star Wars dream was anathema to her. The plan would mean abandoning the ABM Treaty, on which the viability of the British nuclear force depended.'[21]

The nuclear alliance at the heart of the special relationship was weakened when President Clinton extended a moratorium on tests in the Nevada desert in 1993 and pressed the then British prime minister, John Major, to agree to the Comprehensive Nuclear Test Ban Treaty. The British reaction was to describe the freeze as 'unfortunate and misguided', since it would invalidate the 'safety, reliability and effectiveness' of fail-safe mechanisms on upgraded warheads for the British

Trident II D5 missiles, and potentially the development of a new deterrent for the twenty-first century. Major, therefore, began to consider a return to Pacific testing while the Ministry of Defence turned to computer simulation. However, Britain was accused of using safety and reliability as a cover for testing a replacement warhead for the WE.177 free-fall bomb. The moratorium weakened the case for British reliance on Trident and led to the entente nucleaire with France in 1995 under a Joint Nuclear Commission.

The question of Britain's independent nuclear deterrent in the form of the renewal of Trident faced the new coalition government in 2010. Writing in *The Independent* in June 2010, Mary Dejevsky posed a number of pertinent questions about Trident and its renewal or phasing out. Does Britain need a nuclear deterrent? Should a country of Britain's size and limited wealth continue with a nuclear deterrent when the Cold War is over? Does it any longer make sense for Britain to pose as an independent nuclear power and does doing so increase British influence? Instead of making part of Britain's defence dependent upon the United States it makes more sense for Britain to help in the creation of an independent European defence system. Dejevsky quotes the US defence specialist Franklin Miller who argued that it was in the interests of Britain to renew Trident. He argued that all alternatives to the submarine-based Trident system were 'vulnerable' since they could easily be tracked, while Trident could not. Miller said a minimum defence system based on submarines should be three with an extra in reserve. He also argued that Britain saved billions by leasing the nuclear deterrent from the United States. Miller suggested that the United States would not trust its defence to France so why should Britain? Inherent in this point was the assumption that Britain also should not trust its defence to France but would trust its defence to a deal with the USA. He went no further, leaving open the question of choice. As a member of the EU Britain ought to be prepared for an EU defence system in which the leading countries—Britain, France and Germany—pool their defence capabilities rather than Britain retaining a system dependent upon the United States. If Britain is not to depend on France should it also not depend upon the USA?[22]

The illusory policy of a nuclear deterrent pursued by both Britain and France was for prestige and big power status rather than for use. It required expenditure that damaged the British (and French) economies. The object of maintaining big power pretensions has diminished steadily over the years and by 2010 made little sense. To quote Machiavelli, 'A wise prince must rely on what is in his power and not what is in the power of others.'

8

WILSON AND VIETNAM

During his first period as prime minister from 1964 to 1970, Harold Wilson spent most of his energies trying to sustain and keep viable the British economy while at the same time managing the Labour Party with its hardcore left-wing group constantly sniping at his middle-of-the-road policies. The pound was devalued from $2.80 to the pound to $2.40 in 1967. Throughout these years Wilson faced constant pressure from the United States to commit British troops to the war in Vietnam— a token force to show support. Wilson realised that Britain's two major overseas bases in Singapore and the Gulf had to be given up for economic reasons—a decision that should have been taken twenty years earlier. The decision to withdraw from Singapore came as a shock to the United States, which saw the British military presence in Asia as a contribution to its wider Cold War confrontation, then centred upon Vietnam. Wilson needed to reduce Britain's balance of payments deficit even as Johnson's over-extension of military power accelerated US economic problems. Despite disagreements the Johnson administration gave support in the IMF for loans to sterling that staved off devaluation until 1967. 'But it was on foreign support—especially American— that the government's ability to defend and maintain confidence in the currency rested. American goodwill, in turn, depended on Britain's continuing ability to serve US foreign policy as a reliable ally, giving moral or, as the White House increasingly hoped, practical help in Vietnam, performing a peace-keeping role East of Suez, and exerting an influence within the Commonwealth.' Inherent in US military needs and British economic weakness was a bargain: 'America's involvement in South East Asia, and Britain's increasingly urgent need for financial help, provided the basis for a working relationship with the new President. It was against such a background that Wilson visited Washington for the first time as Prime Minister in December 1964.'[1] The demand for British support in Vietnam increased as American commitment escalated and Britain's contribution to the alliance diminished. Even so, 'The British government became conscious as never before that the "special" relationship was actually a client one, at a time when the Americans had something specific to ask of their client.'[2] By the time Wilson became prime minister, the American 'disease' had taken firm hold both of leading members of the Labour Party and the mandarins of the Foreign Office. As Barbara Castle said of Gaitskell, 'The impossible convertibility goal had to be abandoned. Through all this [financial crisis] Gaitskell remained stubbornly loyal to America, not least in his foreign policy, which was increasingly dominated by cold war hysteria.'[3] Britain did hold one important military card and that was the presence of 30,000 troops in Malaysia to safeguard it against Indonesian 'confrontation' in Borneo. Even so, by 1965 US demands for a British commitment in Vietnam had become more insistent and in July, 'Johnson's special assistant McGeorge Bundy told the President: "We want to make very sure that the British get into their heads that it makes no sense to us to rescue the pound in a situation in which there is no British flag in Vietnam, and a threatened British thin-out both east of Suez and in Germany".'[4] At this stage in the Vietnam War the special relationship was turning into a struggle by the US to make its client give open military support, which the client was resisting to the best of its ability. Britain as a client state clearly had its uses but, as so often, was handicapped by the state of its economy.

The big question for Wilson was what to do in reaction to US pressures to send troops to Vietnam to participate in the war. The Foreign Office was clear: total and unhesitating commitment to the American cause, a viewpoint reflected in the statements of the Foreign Secretary Michael Stewart. Johnson wanted Wilson to give unambiguous verbal support to the US position in Vietnam and a token military force. Wilson was not prepared to do this and his statements were ambiguous.[5] There was an added problem in that Wilson and President Johnson did not respond to one another and when Wilson attempted to mediate in Vietnam—he was co-chairman with the USSR of the Geneva Conference—his attempts were not welcomed in Washington. Johnson regarded

Wilson as 'a creep' and was on record as saying, 'I won't tell you how to run Malaysia and you don't tell us how to run Vietnam.' It was not a happy relationship although politically Johnson did understand Wilson's problems with his left wing. The US Defense Secretary, Robert McNamara, insisted Britain should 'pay the blood price' by sending troops to Vietnam as 'the unwritten terms of the Special Relationship'. Wilson, however, refused to commit regular forces though he did permit special forces' instructors to be sent.

By the time Wilson became prime minister Britain had become so entangled in the Vietnam question that there was no easy escape. Thus, in March 1964, Douglas-Home had told the House of Commons that in recent talks with President Johnson, 'I reaffirmed my support for United States policy which—is intended to help the Republic of Vietnam to protect its people and to preserve its independence.' Douglas-Home gives the impression that he was not only concerned to maintain the special relationship but that he believed in the policy and that had Britain been stronger it might have become more fully involved. The myth was created that Wilson withstood all US efforts to persuade Britain to send troops to Vietnam but this ignores all the other assistance that Britain did supply. Wilson knew he could not carry the Labour Party with him in outright support for the United States. He did not hold back for ideological reasons (as the myth might suggest) but for Party political reasons and his personal survival.

Wilson allowed MI6 to assist the US in Vietnam and some of its personnel were attached to Australian and New Zealand SAS squads operating in Vietnam. An MI6 team made up of Malays and Borneo tribesmen (Dayaks) was sent to Vietnam to tour among the ethnic Montagnards in South Vietnam. Secret air flights from Hong Kong delivered arms, including napalm and 500 pound bombs and MI6 assisted the Malay government to transfer military supplies to Vietnam. British counter-intelligence experts were seconded to Saigon as part of the British Advisory Mission while some soldiers were seconded to Fort Bragg and then inducted into the US army. In addition, Britain trained US, Vietnamese and Thai troops at its jungle warfare school in Malaysia through to the late 1960s and for several years a leading British counter-insurgency expert, Sir Robert Thompson, who had been responsible for the Strategic Hamlet Programme in Malaya during the 1950s, advised the Nixon regime on Vietnam policy. As a consequence, 'America sought to defuse support for the communist insurgency by following Britain's strategy, employed in Malaysia and

Kenya, of resettling the population in model villages which were virtual open prisons.' Thus, Britain's main contribution was intelligence,
provided via MI6 stations in Hanoi and Hong Kong. Macmillan,
Home, Wilson and Heath each supported the US war in Vietnam diplomatically. Nor was there any questioning of the US right to wage this
war or criticism of the way it was done, for example by defoliation.[6]

The Labour Party was split on the issue of Europe—the 1960s wit-
nessed two British attempts to join the EEC, both vetoed by de
Gaulle—and unease about full commitment to Europe was matched by
willingness to make commitments to the United States. Only George
Brown, a brilliant if maverick member of the Labour hierarchy, saw
clearly what should be done when he argued, 'We've got to break with
America, devalue and go into Europe.'[7]

Wilson, like Churchill before him, favoured a mediation role for
Britain but his peace initiatives were to prove abortive. At the same
time he gave all the support he could to the US administration short of
open military aid while Britain continued to maintain contact and
trade with the two Vietnams. Both the Labour party and the Tories
supported the United States decision to bomb North Vietnam following the 1964 Gulf of Tonkin incidents. Privately, Wilson sought both
an end to the bombing and a negotiated end to the war and he
informed Johnson of his intention. However, he was unwilling to criticise US policy publicly, partly because of maintaining the special relationship and partly because he needed Washington's backing in
supporting the pound sterling. In the end, as Churchill had discovered,
mediation without power was unlikely to succeed and his initiatives in
1965 and 1966 came to nothing.

Part of the attraction of the special relationship for Britain, and especially for politicians of Douglas-Home's generation who were imperialists at heart, was that the US actions in Vietnam were probably what
they would have done had Britain been stronger. Many people at grass-
roots level in Britain were opposed to the Vietnam War but such opposition was not to be found among the political hierarchy of either the
Labour or Tory parties. Britain at this stage was still lamenting the
passing of its imperial world role. In March 1965, for example, Wilson
said: 'We fully support the action of the United States in resisting
aggression in Vietnam.'

The American ambassador to Britain from 1961 to 1969 was David
Bruce who supported the abortive attempt by Wilson in 1967 in col-

laboration with the Soviet Premier Aleksi Kosygin to bring an end to the war. Bruce was repeatedly obliged to defend the war in public although he personally became a sceptic. Popular anti-war feeling culminated in the huge demonstration in 1968 that came to an end in Grosvenor Square outside the American Embassy.

Denis Healey, once described as one of the best prime ministers the country never had, straddled the Labour Party from left to right. As a young man he was a member of the International Brigade that fought against Franco in Spain. He became a communist but in the aftermath of the Second World War he began a voyage from left to right. He worked closely with Ernest Bevin, he argued strenuously in print for NATO and the American alliance and was to forge personal ties with senior American politicians. Although he had started as a left-wing member of the Labour Party, Healey came down unequivocally on the side that opposed the power and potential aggrandisement of the Soviet Union. He became a Cold War warrior at a time when CND argued that nuclear weapons were wicked and that Britain should dispense with them.[8] It is a reflection on the ways in which the political establishment operated at this time that most of the Labour leadership—Gaitskell, Wilson himself, Crosland, Jenkins, Healey and most of the other university-educated members of the party—were pro-American. Healey sometimes appeared excessively pro-American and he seems to have had no doubts about American intentions towards Britain. President Kennedy, soft-talked and flattered by Macmillan, let Britain have Polaris to the annoyance of his own advisers, headed by Robert McNamara. 'Accordingly in the teeth of a major policy-making decision and effectively by caprice, the British independent deterrent, not British, not independent and only incrementally a deterrent, found indefinite continuance. But it kept America involved with the people she had nearly overlooked.'[9] It may be seen as a pity that Healey, with all his intellectual capacity, did not question the value of the special relationship to Britain or the extent to which it had come to dominate British foreign policy.

Nothing, however, could conceal the decline in British power. As the US secretary of defense, Clark Gifford said in 1968: 'The British do not have the resources, the backup, or the hardware to deal with any big world problem—they are no longer a powerful ally of ours, because they cannot afford the cost of an adequate defence effort.' Wilson at least came to terms with economic realities when he accepted that austerity meant military retrenchment and did what previous governments ought to have done and gave up maintaining a sizeable British force 'east of Suez'. This meant closing down the huge base in Singapore and reducing the size of the Navy. In addition, he announced the imminent intention of withdrawing from the Gulf. As Ben Pimlott suggested, Britain was 'the United States' hired help'. Edward Heath, shortly to become prime minister and take Britain into the ECM, was also beguiled by the American connection. He visited Vietnam and subsequently strongly supported the American intervention, believing it would be successful.

During the course of the Vietnam War Australia and New Zealand changed their allegiance—at least as far as security was concerned—from Britain to the United States by their readiness to send military forces to assist the Americans in Vietnam. In 1962 Australia sent the Australia Army Training Team Vietnam (AATTV), a thirty-man team of jungle warfare experts to assist the training of the Republic of Vietnam Army (RVN). In 1964 Australia increased its commitment to RVN in response to President Johnson's call for 'Free World Military Forces' to forge an alliance of 'Many Flags' in South Vietnam and the AATTV was increased to eighty personnel, who worked with US Special Forces. Under continuing pressure from Washington Australia increased its Vietnam commitment so that by October 1967 it had 8,000 combat troops in Vietnam. However, growing opposition to its involvement in the war in Australia led the government to withdraw its forces during 1970–1971 and by December 1971 they had all returned home, although a small Australian Army Assistance Group Vietnam remained in advisory roles until 1973. New Zealand sent both military and non-military aid to South Vietnam. Its rationale for such involvement was the decline of British power so that its security now depended upon the United States while it saw communism in Southeast Asia as threatening its interests. Shadowing Australia, New Zealand withdrew its small contingent of troops from Vietnam in 1970.

'Unlike all America's other European allies, Heath did not dissociate Britain from the United States' gratuitous bombing of Vietnam in 1972. "What you did," Nixon later told him, "didn't go unnoticed." All the same, Kissinger wrote in his memoirs, "we were witnessing a revolution in British foreign policy". It was hardly that; Douglas-Home (Heath's Foreign Secretary) merely told Kissinger that there was not much point in Britain unflinchingly supporting America when there was underlying disagreement.'[10] London gave full support to the policy of Vietnamisation but also supported the Nixon policy of continued bombing and mining of North Vietnamese ports. Further, Heath refused to condemn the US incursions into Cambodia. During the US terror bombing of Vietnam cities over Christmas 1972, *The Observer* reported that the British government had no intention of joining in the international condemnation of the United States. British official thinking supported the United States.[11] Heath was to take Britain into the ECM in 1973 when he had a golden opportunity to re-orient British policy away from the special relationship. Not only did he not take it but, as though to reassure the United States that Britain would remain a loyal satellite despite having joined the EEC, he went out of his way to support some of the least savoury US actions in Vietnam.

British Indian Ocean Territory

In 1962 the Pentagon sought bases in the Indian Ocean and looked to Britain for its colonial legacy to provide them. The best site was Diego Garcia where the United States wished to establish facilities for communications and military storage. The United States was to bear the costs and the facilities were to be jointly shared with Britain. By the spring of 1965 a plan of action had been agreed between the Foreign Office, the Colonial Office and the Ministry of Defence. At that time the Diego Garcia archipelago was part of the colony of Mauritius. In April 1965 the colonial secretary Tony Greenwood told the Mauritian leaders that before independence (scheduled for 1968) the whole group of islands, situated 1,200 miles north-east of Mauritius and known as the Chagos Islands, were to be detached from Mauritius and turned into a separate colony. Mauritius would be paid £3 million compensation. Later in the year the government created a new colony, The British Indian Ocean Territory (BIOT), which was to be ruled directly from the Colonial Office. A final agreement was signed and made public as an international treaty in December 1966. BIOT was to be leased to the United States with a minimum of fifty years with an option on another twenty. The British had wanted the lease to run for no more than thirty years but the United States insisted upon fifty. In effect, the United States was given a free hand to establish whatever base facilities it liked.[12] This treaty with the Americans was never debated in Parliament and the full story was concealed for years. Britain and America were to share the cost of removing the population, which was just over 2,000 strong and made their living from fishing, subsistence farming and the harvesting of copra. Their presence was inconvenient to the Americans who wanted uninhabited islands. The Americans insisted that Britain should be responsible for moving the islanders while the Wilson government was afraid that it would create a storm if the public learned of the forcible removal of the population. In effect the islanders were to be deported from the land where they lived and the removal was in direct contradiction of the UN Declaration of Human Rights—'no one should be subject to arbitrary exile' (article 9) and 'everybody has the right to return to his country' (article 13). The process of deportation was handled quietly by the government, which hoped to attract the minimum of attention. By 1973 all the people had been removed to Mauritius where they faced destitution; a decade later 80 per cent of the islanders wanted to return home. Britain had secretly spent £15 million setting up BIOT and removing its inhabitants. The Americans moved into Diego Garcia in 1971 and set about establishing a major naval base for the US Fleet in the Indian Ocean, which could handle nuclear-powered aircraft carriers. Later it was developed as an air base from which nuclear-armed B52s could operate. 'The fate of the remote island of Diego Garcia shows up the relative priorities that the Labour government gave to the demands of the American government and strategic considerations on the one hand and the rights of the native people affected by that policy on the other.'[13]

The BIOT story is a shameful one: handing over a British territory to the Americans—a special relationship 'deal' on the one hand, and the forcible deportation of the islanders, who were simply treated as an inconvenience, on the other. But the story did not end there. The islanders and their descendants in exile began to mount legal pressures upon Britain in the new century. In 2006, after years of stalling, Britain allowed 100 former residents of the Chagos archipelago to visit outlying parts of the sixty-five-island colony on a strictly 'humanitarian' trip. The exiles had been fighting through the courts for their right to return home. The exiled community of Chagossians, now concentrated in Mauritius and Britain, had become 5,000 strong. This return voyage, the first British gesture to the islanders after forty years, cost £400,000. Over the years compensation of £14.5 million had been paid, either to the islanders or to Mauritius. Although the British High Court had ruled in 2000 that the removal of the islanders had been unlawful Britain strongly opposed any permanent resettlement. Llana Rapaport, a spokesperson for Minority Rights Group International, said: 'Their removal and the persistent excuses and legal wrangling the UK Government have undertaken to deny the islanders their land rights is shocking. The Government have failed to explain why the Chagossians, themselves British subjects, still seem to be well below the Government's agenda of satisfying US foreign policy needs.'[14] Meanwhile, the United States argued that the return of the islanders would threaten US security. In May 2006 the Court of Appeal ruled that the British Government should not have prevented the islanders from returning to their homes. Moreover, the Court of Appeal refused to grant the government an immediate right of appeal. The Foreign Office then considered petitioning the House of Lords to review the case. It was clear at this time that the government would not give way to the demands of the Chagossians, despite the ruling of the highest court in the land.

In 2007 the islanders won another legal victory when the Court of Appeal ruled that the Chagos Islanders could rebuild a life that they lost in the 1960s. Islanders packed the court to hear the ruling and then called on the government to pay for about 5,000 of them to return and rebuild the life they lost forty years before. The story is one of legal confrontation between the High Court and the government. In 2000 the High Court had first ruled that the expulsion of the islanders was illegal but in 2004 an order passed by the British Government banned them from returning. The Court of Appeal ruled that the order, which was made under the Royal Prerogative without approval by Parliament, was unlawful and an abuse of power.[15]

In a new move designed to keep the islanders out of their former homeland, Britain decided to establish the biggest marine nature reserve in the world centred upon the Chagos Islands. The reserve is to contain fifty-five tiny coral islands sitting in a quarter of a million square miles of the cleanest seas on the planet that supports a pristine ecosystem teeming with wildlife. Although the plan was endorsed by environmental groups, it would also mean that no fishing would be allowed and fishing was the basic industry of the Chagossians before their forced removal. David Snoxell, a former British High Commissioner in Mauritius, and deputy commissioner of BIOT who was the co-ordinator of the Chagos Islands All-Party Parliamentary group, said of the proposals:

'I deplore the fact that the Chagossians have not been brought into this. It is as if they have been airbrushed out of the press release, and out of existence. The Government is clearly not going to take their interests into account, not until the decision at Strasbourg [the European Court of Human Rights to which an appeal had been made]. They are really pre-empting the Strasbourg decisions and attempting to influence the court.'[16]

The Foreign Office has been accused of misleading the public over the expulsion of the Chagossians. A secret US diplomatic cable released by WikiLeaks suggests that the Foreign Office had privately admitted that its latest plan to declare the Islands the world's largest marine protection zone would end any chance of the exiles being repatriated. National Archive documents reveal how the Foreign Office consistently lied about the eviction, maintaining a fiction that the Islanders had not been permanent residents. In May 2009, Colin Roberts, the Foreign Office director of overseas territories told the Americans: 'We do not regret the removal of the population since removal was necessary for Diego Garcia to fulfil its strategic purpose.' Roberts also stated that, according to the government's current thinking on a reserve, there would be 'no human footprints' or 'Man Fridays' (the Foreign Office's contemptuous reference to the Chagossians) on the BIOT uninhabited islands. A US State Department official commented: 'Establishing a marine reserve might, indeed, as the FCO's Roberts stated, be the most effective long-term way to prevent any of the Chagos Islands' former inhabitants or their descendants from resettling in the BIOT.'[17]

This is a most unsavoury story of US-UK collaboration, presumably in the name of the special relationship or Anglo-American alliance. The British hand over virtual control of a British territory to the Americans and at their bidding forcibly remove the inhabitants from the Island. By any standards Britain has abused the human rights of its own subjects in order to placate the Americans and over decades the Foreign Office covered up and lied about its actions.

9

HEATH TAKES BRITAIN INTO THE EEC

Edward Heath is the only British prime minister since 1945 who was wholly in favour of Britain in Europe and the only one who did not push the special relationship with the United States, preferring instead to speak of a 'natural relationship' based on shared culture and heritage. The special relationship was not part of his political vocabulary. He put consultation with Europe ahead of that with the United States. His premiership coincided with the presidency of Richard Nixon and it is ironic that these two cold, awkward men, who were uneasy in their personal relationships, should have held the highest office at the same time. Nixon wanted a special relationship with Britain but Heath did not reciprocate. Heath was persuaded that Britain's future was in Europe and that Britain should join Europe not reluctantly and calculatingly but with real conviction and he was determined not to make Macmillan's mistake of holding on to the special relationship. His commitment to Europe was profound.[1] In Heath's view the United States was a friendly country, entitled to the consideration that reflected its power and importance but that the special relationship was an obstacle to the British vocation in Europe. Of all British leaders Heath was also the least committed emotionally to the United States. It was not that he was anti-American; rather, he was immune to the sentimental elements of that attachment forged in two wars.[2]

Nixon had predicted, accurately, that Heath would win the British election of June 1970. 'At last, he said, there would be a kindred spirit in one major country, a group of leaders, who did not lean on us, whom we did not need constantly to buttress, and from whom we might learn a great deal.' The aura cast by the British political system clearly attracted Nixon. His first meeting with Heath took place at Chequers in October 1970. According to Henry Kissinger, Nixon's closest political adviser, 'The relationship with Heath was one of the most complex of Nixon's presidency. There was no foreign leader for whom Nixon had a higher regard, especially in combination with Sir Alec Douglas-Home, Heath's Foreign Secretary, whom Nixon positively revered.'[3] However, the relationship between them never flourished and the two men never managed to establish the personal rapport for which Nixon, at least, longed in the beginning. In any case, as Heath's commitment to Europe became clear some substantial rethinking took place in Washington. Agencies and Departments of the Treasury, Commerce and Agriculture were quick to air their fears of what British entry into the EEC would mean for American trade. A worst-case scenario of the consequences of enlargement as a result of British entry into the EEC was constructed that pointed to the emergence of an economic monster dominating world trade. Although in the years since 1945 the Americans had often derided or ignored the special relationship yet when under Heath a major realignment of British policy became apparent there was deep concern in Washington.

In December 1970 Heath made his first visit to the White House where an apparently cordial relationship was established. In response to Nixon's speech of welcome, Heath records that 'I declared that I did not favour the suggestion of a "special relationship" between our two countries. Such a relationship could be broken at a moment's notice by either partner. What was more, it could give offence to America's other allies, either in Europe or Latin America. I believed in a natural relationship, the result of our common history and institutions which nobody could take away from us.' This was fully accepted by President Nixon. He firmly believed in the creation of a strong European Community. 'When on 22 January 1971 Nixon sent his "warm personal regards", my advisers and I noticed with interest his statement that "I look forward to continuing our dialogue and to further strengthening the natural relationship between our countries and ourselves; and I hope you shall always feel yourself at home here in Washington".'[4] The trip in December 1970 was an undoubted success. The *New York Daily News* declared that the visit 'marked the first time since the

Eisenhower Administration that genuine personal friendliness has been enjoyed by the political leaders of the two nations.—This continued throughout my premiership.'[5] Heath's statement is at odds with Kissinger's view of their relationship.

By July 1971 Heath was in a position to announce that he would submit an agreement (with the EEC) to Parliament before the end of the year. This was the culmination of two decades of effort and American encouragement, and should have come as a gratification for the United States that had long pressured Britain to join Europe. Unfortunately, the British move coincided with a period when the frustrations of the Vietnam war were encouraging American xenophobia and an enlarged Common Market was seen as a threat to US economic pre-eminence. Over 20–21 December 1971 Heath and Nixon met in Bermuda. At this time Heath was more ready than President Pompidou of France to take Nixon at his word when he explained the US priority of Atlantic over East-West relations. Propounding his concept of European unity, Heath reassured Nixon that the European Community would be 'competitive' not 'confrontational'. This was an interesting but not entirely reassuring formulation. Heath's stand was very different from that of his predecessor Atlanticists. His idea of best procedure for Atlantic co-operation was for the Europeans to develop a common policy at a European summit and then to make an effort to coordinate policies with the United States. This was a positive reversal of the former special relationship approach, which was based on prior British-American consultations. As Kissinger pointed out: 'We—the United States—faced in Heath the curiosity of a more benign British version of de Gaulle.'[6] Heath's relations with Nixon were dominated by Britain's entry into the EEC in 1973 and though the communiqué they released at the end of the 1971 Bermuda meeting stated that British entry served the interests of the Atlantic Alliance there were clear US concerns that British membership would impair its role as (a US view) an honest broker. Despite these differences Heath was a strong supporter of US Cold War policies. When he became prime minister he argued vigorously that an American withdrawal from Vietnam under conditions that could be interpreted as a collapse of American will might unleash a new round of Soviet aggression in Europe.[7] This view, stated in 1970, might have given comfort to the United States but it was the impact such a retreat might have upon Europe that was Heath's first concern. Heath publicly supported the massive US bombing of Hanoi and Haiphong in April 1972. Heath's determined push towards Europe caused surprise and shock in Washington. Indeed, Heath was a new experience for American leaders: a British prime minister who based his policies towards the US not on sentimental attachments but on cool calculation of interests.[8] Once in Europe, Heath said, Britain would be constructive about US concerns though Britain would not act in Europe as a Trojan Horse for the United States. Heath's stand on Europe was seen as a radical change of British policy by Nixon.

Kissinger, who was National Security Adviser and Secretary of State to Nixon and President Gerald R.Ford (1969–1976), wielded huge influence as he was always deeply involved in making US foreign policy decisions. He presents a vivid picture of a startled American establishment coming to terms with a Britain led by Heath who was ready to put aside the special relationship in favour of a British role in Europe. Heath's policy upset all the US State Department calculations. Despite having pressed Britain for years to join Europe, when Heath demonstrated his determination to do so they did not know what to do and were suddenly fearful of a united Europe. It was ironical that Britain was slipping away from the special relationship that earlier US policy makers had derided or ignored. Moreover, Nixon's critics accused him of impeding the EEC's inclusion in the special relationship as Kennedy had originally favoured doing. American policy was to open European markets to US exports. Meanwhile, questions about European defence were raised when Heath came out in favour of a joint Anglo-French nuclear force. Unlike his predecessors or successors through to Blair, Heath did not want Britain to act as a bridge or go-between across the Atlantic. Heath, moreover, made clear that he was content to enjoy no higher status in Washington than any other European leader. Indeed, he came close to insisting on receiving no preferential treatment.

A major deterioration in European-US relations occurred during 1973 when differences over how to react to the Yom Kippur war between Israel and her Arab neighbours Egypt and Syria, and the OPEC oil crisis that followed, threatened Atlantic unity. These differences, moreover, took place when Downing Street was home to the least pro-American British prime minister since the Second World War. As Kissinger pointed out, Heath was the 'only British leader I encountered who not only failed to cultivate the "special relationship" but actively sought to downgrade it and to give Europe pride of place in British strategy'.[9] Heath described his response to the 1973 Middle East crisis as an effort to balance the Nixon administration's abandonment of an 'even-handed approach' to Arab-Israeli affairs.[10] When the Yom Kippur war broke out, Heath placed an arms embargo on all combatants and its major effect was to prevent Israel obtaining spare parts for its Centurion tanks. He refused to allow US intelligence gathering from British bases in Cyprus, leading to a temporary halt in US signals intelligence tap. Heath privately made clear that a request by Washington to use NATO bases in Britain for planes carrying supplies to Israel would not be welcome.[11] Heath's attempt to use the crisis of 1973 to move away from the US was poorly received by the Nixon administration, which publicly described the British as 'uncooperative'. Washington took particular offence at what it saw as a British breach of a promise to co-sponsor a UN Security Council resolution calling for an armistice.[12] Heath's position, however, was warmly welcomed by the West German chancellor Willy Brandt who, in November 1973, warned that the world's destiny cannot and should not be determined by the two superpowers alone. He said: 'Europe has become self-confident enough and independent enough to regard itself as an equal partner.'[13] The British-American relationship was further soured during the Yom Kippur war when Nixon failed to inform Heath that US forces had been placed on DEFCON 3 in a worldwide standoff with the USSR. Moreover, Kissinger misled the British Ambassador over the nuclear alert, which Heath only learned about through press reports. As Heath put it, 'I have found considerable alarm as to what use the Americans would have been able to make of their forces here without in any way consulting us or considering British interests.' The events of 1973 marked a low ebb in the special relationship. 'By 1973, there were many signs that America and Britain were drifting apart diplomatically. The special relationship seemed to be a thing of the past.'[14]

Heath proved to be the only British prime minister who warned the United States that it would follow its own, and possibly antipathetic, policies in relation to the United States. There was relief in Washington when Heath lost the 1974 election. By that date relations between Nixon and Heath were cool and less than special. A few months after Britain's entry into the EC Sir Christopher Soames, a former ambassador to Paris and an early EC commissioner said: 'A few months ago, a new entity was born—the enlarged Community with over 250 million people. We have no precedents on how such a Community should order its international relations. Our economic agglomeration gives us tremendous political potential—a heavy responsibility for the role we can play in the world.'[15] At the same time a British Foreign Office memorandum acknowledged during the first year of British EEC membership, 'there is an inclination—to regard us, the new boys in the Community, as having special capabilities in influencing Europe.' The return to power in 1974 of Harold Wilson, who was a staunch Atlanticist, and his need to hold a referendum on Europe to pacify his leftwing set the stage for a period of disillusionment in Britain that membership of the EC was not providing immediate economic or other advantages.

Wilson retired in 1976 to be succeeded by James Callaghan, who relates in his autobiography *Time and Chance* his reactions as a junior Member of Parliament to the American loan in 1946 and then to Churchill's 'Iron Curtain' speech. 'And I was mortified to discover that our economy was in such bad shape that we must borrow from the United States on terms which demonstrated our weakness. I was by no means anti-American at the end of the war. On the contrary—But because I underestimated both their strength and our losses, I saw no need for our policies to be slavishly yoked to theirs.'[16] He goes on: 'Nor was I at that time convinced by Churchill's famous speech at Fulton, Missouri in March 1946, when he first used the metaphor of an iron curtain descending across and dividing the continent of Europe from the Baltic to the Adriatic.' In the summer of 1950 Jean Monnet wrote: 'Britain has no confidence that France and the other countries of Europe have the ability or even the will effectively to resist a possible Russian invasion. Britain believes that in this conflict continental Europe will be occupied but that she herself with America will be able to resist and finally conquer.'[17] Callaghan (at this time) favoured Britain joining the Schuman Plan for Coal and Steel. The Labour Party was against. Monnet saw Coal and Steel as an expression of political will, a symbol of a federal Europe. Britain's membership was important to Monnet only if Britain accepted the federal idea. At this point in his autobiography, Callaghan is carefully establishing his credentials in relation to America and Europe. Later he upgrades the relationship with the United States and downgrades that with Europe. Writing of Attlee's government, he says: 'Over the European Recovery programme, the recognition of China, and the proposed use of the atomic bomb (by the US) in Korea, the Labour Government was able to demonstrate both independence and influence.'[18] Of developments in

Europe, as Monnet, Spaak and other founding fathers worked towards creating a united Europe, Callaghan says: 'The facts were self evident and they led to the apparent conclusion that, although it was vital to rebuild Europe, we would assist from the outside in joint partnership with the United States.'[19] This was a view of Britain and Europe that was widely held in both the Labour and the Conservative parties. There is a bland, emollient quality in Callaghan's writing that always conveys a sensible middle of the road approach to problems.

When Wilson won the 1974 election he had to deal with the demand from the left, led by Tony Benn, for a referendum on Europe. Callaghan went to the Foreign Office. Although in the end Wilson obtained a referendum vote for staying in the EEC, there were many members of the Labour Party who were either hostile towards the new European entanglement or dubious that it would be of much benefit to Britain. Had Heath won the election he might have been able to develop a more positive attitude towards Europe but the opportunity to do so did not occur. Instead, Callaghan downplayed the European policy by arguing for the Atlantic Alliance and the Commonwealth. A few days after becoming foreign secretary, Callaghan told MPs: 'I must emphasise that we repudiate the view that a United Europe will emerge only out of a process of a struggle against America.' Up to 1976 and then as prime minister from 1976 to 1979, Callaghan made plain his determination to maintain good relations with the USA.[20] Thus he said: 'Mr. Heath's deep and lasting commitment to Europe had weakened our relations with the United States, and as a strong believer in the Atlantic Alliance, I was determined that these must be strengthened.'[21] At the same time he advanced similar arguments on behalf of the Commonwealth. Thus, 'It also appeared to me that the Conservative Government's concentration on the negotiations to enter the European Community had given the impression of a diminished concern about the Commonwealth, and I was anxious to repair that.'[22]

Skilfully, by advancing the claims of the special relationship and the Commonwealth, Callaghan downgraded the importance of the EC without openly coming out against it. In February 1975 US Secretary of State Henry Kissinger visited Callaghan, whose record of their meeting provides an interesting commentary on the US attitude towards Britain in Europe. As Callaghan claims:

'A good relationship was established, [we] always treated on a basis of frankness. He responded with generosity and I took advantage of this to get his own views off the record. As I expected, he favoured Britain's continued membership, but said significantly that if the decision went the other way (the forthcoming referendum on Europe) we could be sure that the United States would do all it could to help Britain and to sustain the relationship between our two countries. It might mean that we would work together even more closely than before, taking into account Britain's economic problems, but in any event Britain need not fear that she would be cold-shouldered. This was genuinely meant and it was reassuring to know, but neither he nor I was under any illusion that a withdrawal could be painless or that a closer relationship with the United States would not involve Britain paying a price for such support.'[23]

Kissinger's message is clear enough: that the United States would welcome a British return to fuller engagement in the special relationship, and in this he reflects the US unease that Britain would first make Europe stronger and then make it less dependent upon the United States.

However, the Callaghan years 'were marked by an economic, rather than a political, crisis which—in clear parallels with the 1940s disputes—underlined how dependent Britain was on American support and goodwill'. Both the US Treasury and the Federal Reserve worked to ensure Britain did not adopt a siege mentality with import controls and other restrictions. Neither President Ford nor Kissinger wanted too much pressure applied to Britain since it might 'have destroyed Britain's ability to go on playing a major role in world affairs'.[24] The US assumptions here clearly suggest that by this time Washington had come to see Britain as a useful satellite. In 1976, after he had become prime minister, Callaghan used the occasion of the bicentenary of American independence as an occasion to celebrate the special relationship. There was a ceremony in Westminster Hall in May to mark the Declaration of Independence and a year of cultural exchanges and exhibitions that culminated in July 1976 with a visit of the Queen to the United States.

10

MARGARET THATCHER

Complimenting her predecessor in her autobiography *The Path to Power*, Margaret Thatcher says: 'Harold Macmillan's great and lasting achievement was to repair the relationship with the United States. This was the essential condition for Britain to restore her reputation and standing.'[1] This contradictory statement is like many others by leading politicians that Britain's standing depended upon the United States and not Britain itself. It amounts to a fundamentally defeatist view of the country that Thatcher herself wanted to be 'great'. Throughout her eleven years in Downing Street Thatcher was obsessed with America and the special relationship, which she put at the top of her international priorities even though she lectured US presidents and was not afraid to advance a tough contrary view. Her first visits to the United States were in 1975 and 1977 as leader of the opposition. 'Not for the last time, she was a tremendous hit with the Americans. It was the beginning of a relationship, which never broke down: which was, indeed, to be a definitive element of her foreign policy as prime minister. Having met, among others, Secretary of State Henry Kissinger, she said of the visit: "I feel I have been accepted as a leader in the international sphere, the field in which they said I would never be accepted".'[2] On a third visit to the United States in 1979 she met President Jimmy Carter. 'In December at the invitation of President Carter I made a short visit to the United States—the first of many as Prime Minister. In a short speech at my reception on the White House Lawn I went out of my way to reaffirm my support for American leadership of the West.'[3] In a lengthy interview on the ABC network in February 1981, Thatcher expressed regret for the 'complete misunderstanding about the European initiative on the Middle East'. She also reassured viewers that the US was the 'single most important nation and what it does is the single most important thing in the Middle East. And we all understand that in Europe and would like our American friends to know that we understand that.' (Press Conference for Washington Press Club, 26 February 1981.) Thus, early in her premiership Thatcher had appointed herself the European cheerleader for the United States. To the Conservative Party Conference later that year, she said: 'We cannot defend ourselves, either in this island or in Europe, without a close, effective and warm-hearted alliance with the United States. Our friendship with America rests not only on the memory of common dangers jointly faced and of common ancestors. It rests on a respect for the same rule of law and representative democracy. Our purpose must be not just to confirm but to strengthen a friendship which has twice saved us this century. Had it not been for the magnanimity of the United States, Europe would not be free today.'[4] Andrew Thomson, one of her biographers, goes on to say: 'She will be the first, of course, to explain and appreciate that all nations are unique and that she does not want the United Kingdom to become a miniature America. But the sheer rushing, gushing spirit of free enterprise in the United States will always reinforce her own vision for Britain.'

Thatcher never approached Europe with anything like the same spirit. 'Her ear was so attuned to the anti-Europeanism of the 1970s that it overlooked the anti-Americanism of the 1980s. For her, Americans are wartime allies and Cold War partners—attitudes formed, no doubt, before 1960.'[5] Sir Percy Cradock, Foreign Policy Adviser for the second half of Thatcher's premiership, said: 'Solidarity with the US as a cardinal principle of foreign policy acquired a special sanctity under Margaret Thatcher, but as a working rule it had been in place for many British Governments over many years.'[6] Thatcher believed that the Anglo-American relationship had done more for the defence and future of freedom than any other alliance in the world. Referring to NATO in 1990—her last year of power—Thatcher wrote: 'However fascinated I was by events in the Soviet Union and eastern Europe, I could not forget that the strength and security of the West ultimately depended upon the Anglo-American relationship,'[7] a view that relegated the rest of Europe to a Thatcherite obscurity. Elsewhere in her autobiography she claims that following the end of the Cold War a deep confusion existed about the future of Europe and Britain's place in it. She wrote that the special relationship had been allowed to cool to near freezing point. Contemplating future developments in the post-Cold War world—an Orwell-type division into three blocs or a return to a pre-1914 big power scramble—she says: 'Neither need come to pass if the Atlantic Alliance remains, in essence, America as the dominant power surrounded by allies which, in their own long-term interest, generally follow its lead.—And such collective security can only really be provided if there is a superpower of last resort.'[8] Analysis of this argument suggests an Orwellian outcome or a prolongation of Cold War tactics that would encourage Russia to reorganise its policies so as to oppose the spread of US hegemony. Constant emphasis upon Western security requires an answer to the question: security against which power or group of powers, and the implication is the continuation of rival bloc policies. Geoffrey Howe, after ten years of loyal service as chancellor and then foreign secretary and finally the non-role of deputy prime minister, at last fell out with Thatcher in spectacular fashion. Subsequently, in his memoir *Conflict of Loyalty*, he highlights points of difference between the United States and Britain and Thatcher's response to them. British policy was to uphold the International Court of Justice while the US either ignored or vetoed its jurisdiction as it did over the Contras laying mines in Nicaraguan waters. Thatcher insisted that rather than vote against the United States Britain should abstain. 'It was hardly a major issue. But I was nevertheless disconcerted by the strange sequence of events: first, Britain supports US action against Libyan terrorism, second, US supports Britain in action against Irish terrorism; third, Britain condones US-sponsored "terrorism" against Nicaragua. This was yet another occasion, on which Margaret insisted on carrying the "special relationship" perhaps one bridge too far.'[9] In all the differences between Thatcher and the Americans—there were several—she first argued that a good ally must disagree when necessary but always in the end came out as the agent—reluctant or otherwise—of the United States. Her strong words obscured her subservience. The change of government in the United States, which replaced Reagan with Bush senior and Baker as secretary of state, altered Washington's perspective on the special relationship. 'So neither Bush nor Baker was likely to accept the thesis, which Margaret Thatcher has re-enunciated, that "the ties of blood, language, culture and values which bound Britain and America were the only firm basis for US policy in the West".'

Thatcher managed to establish a remarkable rapport with President Ronald Reagan not least because they shared the same free-market approach to their respective economies. In 1981 Thatcher had her first meeting as prime minister with President Reagan at which she made plain her intended adherence to the Atlantic Alliance when she said: 'Your problems will be our problems and when you look for friends we shall be there.' These two 'ideological soul mates' reinvigorated what Thatcher described as the 'extraordinary alliance'. They shared a commitment to free trade, low taxes, limited government and strong defence. At the same time they rejected the concept of détente with the Soviet Union; they wanted to win the Cold War. The friendship between the two led to a revival of the special relationship, which had suffered a marked decline from the time that Heath took Britain into the EEC. There were to be four particular events that would test the special relationship: the Falklands War (1982); the US invasion of Grenada (1983); the US bombing of Libya (1986); and the ending of the Cold War, which raised acute fears in Britain that the United States would come to terms with the USSR without consulting its ally. 'The Thatcher-Reagan axis of the eighties will surely be remembered for developing a more robust capitalism and for achieving by strength and unity in the wider North Atlantic Alliance, disarmament treaties with the Soviet Union. Diplomats, businessmen and politicians have all played their part in securing these successes, but the pivot was the personal relationship of Ronald Reagan and Margaret Thatcher.'[10] In his biography, *One of Us*, Hugo Young claims that during the Reagan period Thatcher had established a significant hold on US opinion: first, her victory in the Falklands; second, an improving economy; third her rapport with the president. In December 1984 Thatcher visited Washington to tell Reagan that his Strategic Defence Initiative (Stars Wars) would not work. On another visit shortly afterwards in February 1985 she addressed a joint session of Congress: 'To maintain nuclear deterrence' she told Congress, 'it was necessary to ensure our research and capacity do not fall behind the work being done by the Soviet Union. That is why I firmly support President Reagan's decision to pursue research into defence against ballistic nuclear missiles—the Strategic Defence Initiative.'[11] She thus expunged her stand of the previous December. Also in the same speech to Congress, Thatcher said: 'No one of my generation can forget that America has been the principal architect of a peace in Europe that has lasted forty years. Given this shield of the United States, we have been granted the opportunities to build a concept of Europe beyond the dreams of our fathers.'[12] In none of her actions in relation to Europe did Thatcher do anything to advance this concept of Europe. The year 1985 was when the two countries celebrated 200 years of diplomatic relations and the occasion led to a two-way exchange of compliments with Thatcher claiming 'our relationship a truly remarkable one. It is special. It just is and that's that.' Reagan replied: 'The United States and the United Kingdom are bound together by inseparable ties of ancient history and present friendship.' The Reagan connection was of huge importance to Thatcher who went out of her way on a number of occasions to extol its merits: 'But Ronald Reagan's election was of immediate and funda-mental importance because it demonstrated that the United States, the greatest force for liberty that the world has known, was about to reas-sert a self-confident leadership in world affairs. I never had any doubt of the importance of this change and from the first I regarded it as my duty to do everything I could to reinforce and further President Reagan's bold strategy to win the Cold War which the West had been slowly but surely losing.'[13] The message in this statement was simple: everything depended upon the United States.

As far as Europe was concerned and especially a united Europe, Thatcher was always a 'little Englander'. In 1989 she tried but without success to delay German reunification, thereby antagonising both the United States and Germany, though not France under President Mitterrand. As Sir Percy Cradock observes, Thatcher 'did not like the Europeans; she did not speak their languages; and she had little time for their traditions'.[14] George Bush senior and his secretary of state James Baker and the State Department wanted to put the relationship with Germany rather than the special relationship with Britain at the centre of their European policy, which meant a downgrading of Thatcher's influence in Washington. If Thatcher was obsessive about the special relationship she was paranoid about Europe. When in December 1990, for example, the foreign secretary Douglas Hurd 'publicly advocated a distinctive European defence role through the Western European Union (WEU), which I had always distrusted, aware that others, particularly the French, would like to use it as an alterna-tive to NATO inevitably dominated by America'. Hurd's advocacy of a European defence role was entirely reasonable yet drew Thatcher's immediate opposition as did any suggestion about Europe acting outside the American orbit. Writing of regular meetings of EU heads of government, Thatcher says: 'By contrast, there was not enough contact and understanding between the European countries and our transatlantic allies in NATO—the United States and Canada. I hoped that my visit to Canada and the United States at the end of September [1983] would do something to put this right.'[15] There is a naivety about some of Thatcher's pronouncements in defence of the Atlantic Alliance that leads one to wonder whether she actually believed what she was saying. Thus, in *The Downing Street Years* she writes: 'Democracies are naturally peace-loving. There is so much which our people wish to do with their lives, so many uses for our resources other than military equipment. The use of force and the threat of force to advance our beliefs are no part of our philosophy.' Given the sheer size of the US military budget in relation to those of all other countries, the worldwide spread of its bases and the emphasis it puts upon spreading democracy such a statement hardly bears examination. Yet in 1999 she emphasised the divide in her own mind when she said: 'In my lifetime all our problems have come from mainland Europe and all the solutions have come from the English-speaking nations of the world.'[16]

When the Falklands War loomed Thatcher worried about the American stand and the fact that Reagan did not back her at once. However, the US defense secretary, Casper Weinberger, was an Anglophile and gave support with the supply of up-to-date weaponry while also providing communications intercepts. After a reproof for their tardiness, Thatcher reports: 'The Americans too, however irritating and unpredictable their public pronouncements on occasion, were providing invaluable help. I have already mentioned the Sidewinder missiles. They also provided us with 150,000 square yards of matting to create a makeshift airstrip. On 3 May Casper Weinberger even proposed sending down the carrier *USS Eisenhower* to act as a mobile runway for us in the South Atlantic—an offer we found more encouraging than practical.'[17] As Denis Healey claims, US assistance to Britain during the Falklands War was of—possibly—decisive importance. 'President Reagan, however, received his recompense in Mrs. Thatcher's unwavering support through every twist and turn of his policies over eight years.'[18]

In 1982 Thatcher obtained American agreement that the British Polaris fleet should be replaced with US-supplied Trident missiles.

When the United States switched to the more powerful D-5 Trident missile Thatcher was desperate to secure it to maintain the credibility of the UK nuclear deterrent and Reagan offered it to her at cost price. As with previous governments, Thatcher saw Trident as the best option for Britain's nuclear deterrent. But, of course, it was not an independent deterrent but depended upon the Americans. While accepting that Trident II was better than the alternatives the choice raised the more fundamental question of whether the UK could continue to maintain an independent strategic nuclear deterrent at all. However, 'In Britain, distrust of the United States surfaced on the question of whether there should be a 'dual key'—that is whether there should be a technical arrangement to ensure that the US could not fire these weapons without the consent of the British government.'[19]

During the second half of the 1980s Thatcher became increasingly anxious that the US Strategic Defence Initiative and Reagan's proposal at the Reykjavik Summit with Mikhail Gorbachev to eliminate all ballistic missiles would make the British deterrent irrelevant. Thatcher supported the principle of the Strategic Defence Initiative anti-missile defence project (though initially she had been opposed to it) despite deep misgivings in the Foreign Office and in contrast to French opposition, but she used her personal influence with Reagan to obtain a written commitment to the doctrine of nuclear deterrence. Tam Dalyell, a constant backbench critic of the prime minister, said of Thatcher's support for the proposed American project, 'This was British participation in the American Strategic Defence Initiative programme, popularly but misleadingly dubbed 'Star Wars'. Certainly the substantive decision about, and possibly even the Prime Minister's first public announcement of, British participation in SDI was made without proper consultation with the responsible Cabinet Minister, the Defence Secretary Michael Heseltine.'[20] Dalyell was taking the prime minister to task for bypassing parliamentary practices. In October 1986, when President Reagan and Mikhail Gorbachev met in Iceland for the Reykjavik Summit, which did not include Britain, the special relationship appeared to be wearing thin so that in November Thatcher flew to Washington to find out what the two super powers had agreed. This US-USSR meeting and the subsequent treaty between the two super powers signalled the possible emergence of two-power arrangements that would be made over the heads of other allies and so would mean the end of forty years of Atlantic Alliance. Even so, at crucial moments in the late 1980s, her influence was considerable in shifting perceptions in President Reagan's Washington about the credibility of Gorbachev when he repeatedly asserted his intention to end the Cold War.

Thatcher was a Cold War warrior but one whose 'warriorship' depended upon American support. In 1990, her last year as prime minister, Thatcher had to respond to Saddam Hussein's invasion of Kuwait. In terms of relative power it is interesting to speculate as to what Thatcher would have done had the United States refused to intervene. Her famous call to President Bush—'This is no time to go wobbly'—showed her at her most belligerent, the lieutenant urging on the leader and insisting that war was the only way to deal with a dictator who otherwise would end up in Saudi Arabia controlling far too much oil for the West's good. 'Suddenly a Britain with armed forces which had the skills, and a government which had the resolve, to fight alongside America, seemed to be the real European "partner in leadership".'[21] Even though Britain made a substantial contribution to the anti-Hussein coalition, President Bush was turning his back on the Reagan era and that included the special relationship with Britain. Wistfully, Thatcher records in her autobiography, 'By then I had learned that I had to defer to him in conversation and not to stint the praise. If that was what was necessary to secure Britain's interests and influence I had no hesitation in eating a little humble pie.'[22]

Michael Heseltine, who was Thatcher's minister of defence during the first half of the 1980s, did not believe in the special relationship though in defence terms he wanted and welcomed a strong US military presence in Europe. He said that since 1945: 'The wisest Europeans have understood that their continent's security depends on the continuing commitment of the United States, the power which twice within a generation has spent its citizens' lives and treasure in helping to end wars which were not of their making ... The Atlantic Alliance endures, and our peace still depends on America's commitment. That in turn will depend on where America in future believes her interests to lie.'[23] Heseltine makes plain that defence arrangements are of mutual importance to both sides and should be viewed unromantically.

'Europe [in which he includes Britain] is entitled to nothing from America. The long years of dependency after 1945, and the continuing and necessary reliance upon American protection within the mutuality of NATO, have sometimes engendered, especially I think among the British, an assumption that we are entitled to America's general support and goodwill ... The truth is that Europe can rely on American support, staunch though it has been, only so long as we continue to earn it.'

The British people, he argues, have no more right than other Europeans to presume on American support and friendship, which we are prone to do. He makes a clear, if debatable case, for an American military presence in Europe and as minister of defence justified the introduction of Trident missiles into Britain. Ignoring arguments about a special relationship that were so often advanced by Thatcher, he says: 'The basis of the Anglo-American relationship since 1940 has been the community of military interest between our two countries—but military necessity, and a common view of how world peace must be kept, has preserved and strengthened that bond.' More controversial was Heseltine's insistence upon the need for a US nuclear presence in Britain. Thus he says: 'No American government could continue to base substantial ground and air forces in Europe unbacked by a credible nuclear component.'[24] In contrast to Thatcher, Heseltine argues unsentimentally for a military tie-up with the United States and argued elsewhere that the only special relationship America had was with Israel.

The Falklands War

For seventeen years prior to 1982 Britain had appeared largely uninterested in its Falkland Islands dependency and had held sporadic if inconclusive talks with Argentina about their future. The Argentines had come to believe that the British wanted to offload responsibility for the islands and drew the logical conclusion from Britain's withdrawal of the *Endurance*—if Britain would not even pay the costs of keeping a survey ship in the region it was hardly likely to fight for the Falkland Islands. 'But information and analysis is not enough. You have to understand the temper of the country and of those in power—how they will react when the chips are down. Empathy may be more important than intellect.'[25] As Thatcher was to put it, the rock on which negotiations failed was the fact that the people of the Falklands wanted fervently to be British. Crucial to Britain was the fact that: 'In 1982 President Reagan was prepared to put the interests of Britain before his relations with South American neighbours. Without the cooperation of America it would have been impossible to have won in the South Atlantic.'[26] In any case, by 1982 Thatcher had already established with the Americans her strong Atlanticist bias and they recognised her as their staunchest supporter in Europe. The US secretary of state Alexander Haig tried to negotiate a settlement but when this was clearly not going to happen tells how the Argentine Junta would not believe that the British would fight. He sent Dick Walter (a State Department official and former Deputy Head of the CIA) to see Galtieri and tell him—in crystal clear terms—that if there was no negotiated settlement, the British would fight and win—and the United States would support Britain. Galtieri listened and replied: 'Why are you telling me this? The British won't fight.'[27] The British diplomat Sir Nicholas Henderson wrote: 'Some measure of the significance of American support for Britain over the Falklands can be gathered what it would have been like for Britain to have been detached from its most powerful ally as we were at Suez. From my discussions with service leaders since the event, I conclude that it is difficult to exaggerate the difference that American support made to the military outcome.'[28] For once, and very clearly, the special relationship worked in Britain's favour. When it came to the crunch the Americans gave Britain vital support both behind the scenes with information and in terms of equipment. This was given despite their longstanding interest in Latin America. 'Immediately the dispatch of Britain's task force was announced, Casper Weinberger, the US secretary of defense [an Anglophile] decided that maximum practical support should be provided. A British defeat would be a disaster for American policy—not just in terms of the humiliation of an ally but also as a demonstration that aggression might prosper. Accordingly a British defeat must be prevented and that required American assistance.'[29] One of the ironies of the war resulting from the special relationship was that Britain had to ask permission of the Americans for the use of Wideawake air base on Ascension Island. The decision was relatively easy because Britain actually owned the Island and under a leasing arrangement with the United States had reserved the right to use it in an emergency. The Americans provided aviation fuel, critical stores and spare parts, as well as weapons systems, including a variety of missiles—additional and more modern air-to-air Sidewinders, anti-aircraft Stingers and radar-seeking Shrikes. By the end of the war the aid bill, excluding the Sidewinders and the fuel, was $60 billion.

The British Embassy in Washington mounted a major public relations campaign to persuade American opinion to support Britain, which could be presented as not only the aggrieved party but also democratic and a close and long-standing friend and ally. A final word on the war comes from Ian Gilmour. 'The American tilt towards Britain was certainly influenced by the close rapport between President Reagan and Mrs. Thatcher.—A common ideology had brought Margaret Thatcher and Ronald Reagan together, and despite the occasional blip it proved a lasting bond. Mrs. Thatcher was Reagan's first visitor in the White House, and on his last morning there he wrote her a letter of appreciation.'[30]

Grenada, 1983

On 25 October 1983 President Reagan ordered US forces to invade Grenada. 'With the aid and encouragement of the government of Cuba,' a left-wing military group had murdered the prime minister Maurice Bishop and set up their own regime. Reagan argued that he had three objectives: to protect innocent lives including 1,000 Americans; to forestall further chaos; and to assist the restoration of law and order. The Americans went ahead without first consulting Britain. Thatcher was furious that she had not been consulted since Grenada was a member of the Commonwealth that acknowledged the queen as head of state. The day of the invasion there was an emergency debate in the House of Commons in which the foreign secretary, Sir Geoffrey Howe said that the limited amount of consultation possible with the Americans was to be regretted but that the outcome must not be allowed to compromise the alliance. On 30 October Howe was more forthright. He said the invasion was not justified on grounds either of threats to American lives or to the extent of Cuban presence on the island. Initially, Thatcher was more critical. Speaking on the BBC World Service (30 October) she said: 'If you are going to pronounce a new law that whenever communism reigns against the will of the people the United States shall enter, then we are going to have terrible wars in the world.' No matter what was subsequently argued by Thatcher, the fact is the United States went ahead without consulting Britain. As she reported in her autobiography:

'At the time I felt dismayed and let down by what had happened. At best, the British Government had been made to look impotent; at worst we looked deceitful. On the previous afternoon [to the US invasion] Geoffrey [Howe] had told the House of Commons that he had no knowledge of any American intention to intervene in Grenada. Now he and I would have to explain how it had happened that a member of the Commonwealth had been invaded by our closest ally, and more than that, whatever our private feelings, we would also have to defend the United States' reputation in the face of widespread condemnation.'[31]

Subsequently, while claiming that her advice against invasion had been good, Thatcher insisted to her cabinet that Britain's friendship with the United States must on no account be jeopardised.

The United States had already decided to intervene on 22 October so there was time to inform the Thatcher government. When the invasion took place Thatcher, Howe and Heseltine (Minister of Defence) were deeply disturbed but as Howe explains, 'Yet it was almost equally impossible for us to condemn the United States. For that would have done nothing for the future of Anglo-American relations already badly enough damaged—just for the sake of disagreement over a small island in the Caribbean.'[32] So Thatcher and Howe set about damage limitation. George Schultz, the US secretary of state, reacted harshly to Thatcher's complaints. 'We had turned ourselves into pretzels for Mrs. Thatcher over the Falklands crisis,' and he was puzzled that she had acted so negatively and 'without any particular concern for the "special relationship".' There is an interesting divergence of views here. The Americans simply assumed that Britain should support them while Thatcher was angry at the breach of allies' protocol since the British government as well as the queen, Grenada's head of state, had been kept in the dark. Britain's pride had been hurt. 'Not only was the invasion a plain breach of international law, it was a gross affront to British dignity, in particular that of Her Majesty the Queen, whose governor-general on the island had been compelled to accept invasion as a *fait accompli*.'[33] Thatcher's anger was at not being informed rather than at the invasion as such.

Libya, 1986

On 5 April 1986 the explosion of a terrorist bomb in a Berlin discotheque gave President Reagan the excuse he needed to bomb Libya. The United States had been building up a confrontation with Libya for the first half of the 1980s and this had culminated in a series of offshore naval exercises in the Bay of Sirte, which was claimed by Libya as part of its territorial waters. The discotheque in question was frequented by US soldiers and the bomb killed an American GI. On the grounds that the GI was defending Europe, President Reagan appealed to his European allies to support his initiative. Only Thatcher saw the issue in the same light. At the beginning of the year, 'on Tuesday 7 January the United States had unilaterally imposed sanctions on Libya with little or no consultation and expected the rest of us to follow—I [Thatcher] made it clear in public that I did not believe that economic sanctions against Libya would work. The US State Department was highly displeased!'[34] Whatever her reservations about Reagan's policy, Thatcher felt the need to repay the US for its logistical support during the Falklands War and in the end this sense of obligation led her to ignore policies and her own pronouncements that questioned the legitimacy of the American action. The United States mounted an exercise over 14–15 April to bomb Tunis with the aim of taking out Gaddafi. The US decision to use the F-111 fighter bombers based in Britain (Upper Heyford) was clearly dictated by diplomatic-political reasons to demonstrate that the United States had Britain's support and hopefully that of other European countries in face of the worldwide condemnation that the Americans expected would follow such a raid.[35] Despite the high likelihood of civilian casualties, Thatcher felt it was an initiative she had to support. It is instructive that the US request to use planes based in Britain only came through on the morning of the proposed raid as though the Americans were pre-empting the possibility of a 'No' from Thatcher. There was no military reason for using the F-111s but the Americans were counting on Thatcher seeing the issue as a test of the Western Alliance's resolve to combat terrorism and this is how she saw it. This, however, was not the reaction of other European countries. 'So ill-conceived did they imagine President Reagan's operation to be that France, Spain, Portugal and Italy would not even permit over-flying rights for the UK-based American aircraft. Alone in Europe, Mrs. Thatcher's Britain had entered into complicity with the Americans.' In a statement to the House of Commons Thatcher justified the raid as follows: 'The Government have evidence showing beyond dispute that the Libyan Government have been and are directly involved in promoting terrorist attacks against the United States and other Western countries, and that they had made plans for a wide range of further terrorist attacks.'[36] Earlier in the year Thatcher had told American correspondents: 'I uphold international law very firmly' but she put aside these sentiments 'when, after another terrorist outrage in Berlin, Reagan told the prime minister that he was going to attack Tripoli and would like permission to use British bases for the attack, she not only gave him the permission he sought, but decided that such an action was, after all, in accordance with international law and would also be effective.'—'The reason in fact why the United States wished to involve Britain was not military at all but political; the Americans did not want to be the only culprits.' According to Thatcher's own stated views about how allies should behave towards each other she was clearly failing in this instance. 'When a country is about to take a mistaken course of action, it is surely the duty of a good ally to try to dissuade it, not first to support it and then shower it with praise, as did Mrs. Thatcher—despite the views of the cabinet.'[37] As Tony Benn was to argue in his diaries, 'It was always assumed that the American base would not be used without the consent of the British Government, and when the bombing occurred, the Prime Minister informed the Commons that she had agreed to the action. Whether she was consulted or merely told has never been clear. But the fact that the US could use British bases in a conflict with a third country without seeking Parliament's approval gravely worried many people.'[38] According to Tam Dalyell, however, in the April 1987 issue of *Sanity*, Rear Admiral Eugene Carroll Jr., of the Center for Defense Information in Washington, was asked if, in his experience, it would have been practical to use the F-111s, and ask the British afterwards. '"That was the basis," said Carroll, "on which the plan was prepared." The implications are chilling.'[39]

At the Tokyo Group of Seven financial summit of May 1986 the US secretary of state, George Shultz, praised Britain's prime minister Margaret Thatcher for her support the previous April and described the action as a terrific statement 'for democracy, for freedom, for the fight against terrorism, for the cohesion of the West'. Thus was Thatcher publicly thanked for her support. However, the slavish acceptance of the American version of events by the British Foreign Office tells more about the decline of that institution than anything of its powers of independent judgement. Geoffrey Howe wrote scathingly of the American mindset. The action had to be justified on grounds of self-defence or not at all. 'This was always an unsteady concept for American minds: a society where there are 24,000 murders a year [and one handgun per head of the population] seems to think more instructively of a "suitable response"—in plain language, "retaliation". As distinct from self-defence, this is not a legitimate concept under any Western system of law.'[40] When not under pressure, Thatcher made sensible statements of principle. Thus, three months before the Libya air strike she said, 'I do not believe in retaliatory strikes that are against international law,' but three months later she supported such a strike fully. However, 'As the Foreign Secretary began to list some predictable Foreign Office doubts about this initiative, Mrs. Thatcher interrupted him—shrieking about the need to support the Americans and the need not to be fair-weather friends.'[41] Loyalty to America was clearly far more important to Thatcher than working with her parliamentary colleagues or pursuing just policies. 'One more proof of loyalty had been supplied, at a time when not one other European power was prepared to say, still less do, anything to align themselves with the American initiative. A resolution was introduced in Congress offering the British leader "highest praise and thanks" for her cooperation.'[42]

Norman Tebbit, generally regarded as a hardline Thatcherite, raised sharp questions about the United States. 'Understandably I worried about the path on which America seemed set—a worry which shaped my growing belief that Britain should not rely absolutely on even such a powerful ally but should also strengthen its European links.'[43] As he says, foreign policy and defence are to achieve security for a country. If they fail, everything else does. Speaking in 1969, he said: 'I do not believe that we can continue to rely, as we have increasingly done for twenty-five years, on America to do it [defend Britain] for us. We see today her lack of resolve to support her allies when the going is tough and vocal opposition at home is organised. We cannot let our security be jeopardised by riots of students on American campuses or a march of demonstrators on Washington.'[44] He argued over the Libya exercise that Thatcher was made to look vulnerable to the charge of being too eager to please the Americans at our potential expense. That was to put it mildly. Tebbit in common with Tony Benn, Ian Gilmour, Enoch Powell and some other assorted political figures, wanted to see a more independent Britain than the one fashioned by Macmillan and Thatcher who leant over backwards to extol the merits of the Atlantic Alliance and line up as loyal lieutenants of the leading super power. Unfortunately, countries get into habits they cannot find a way of throwing off when the habit has passed its usefulness. Thus from 1945 to 2000 Britain's old imperial instincts impelled it to intervene around the world for purposes other than its own safety and well-being.

Thatcher presents an interesting psychological case. She lauds the Americans and the special relationship at every conceivable opportunity. She claims the Americans saved Britain and Europe. She has stern quarrels and lectures Reagan and Bush to demonstrate her independence. She repays US assistance in the Falklands War by ignoring her stated principles when she acquiesces in the Libyan raid. And even when ignored or treated with contempt she insists upon the absolute value and necessity of the special relationship.

11

JOHN MAJOR

John Major was prime minister from the fall of Thatcher in 1990 to his defeat in the 1997 election by Blair. An underrated prime minister, Major demonstrated a toughness in his relations with the United States, and though he began as a supporter of the special relationship his relations with President Clinton were cool and sometimes angry. In the run-up to the 1991 Gulf War, after Saddam Hussein had invaded Kuwait (1 August 1990), Thatcher was in the United States and famously was reported as saying, 'This is no time to go wobbly, George.' After the resignation of Thatcher and the emergence of Major as leader of the Tory party and prime minister, he was to write in his autobiography: 'Just before Christmas, accompanied by Norma, I flew to Washington to meet President Bush. I had to secure the confidence of the Americans, who were still rocked by Margaret's departure.'[1] When Bush Snr. became president there was an initial coldness towards Thatcher and her special relationship with Ronald Reagan while James Baker in the State Department was not keen on the special relationship. Then, however, came the ousting of Thatcher and the annexation of Kuwait by Saddam Hussein and this led to a closing of the gap that had developed between Britain and the United States. By 1991 and the launching of the military operation to free Kuwait, the two countries were working closely together in the coalition that had been formed and Britain supplied the largest military contingent after the United States. President Bush called Major to confirm that military action would begin—as agreed—just before midnight GMT on the following day, 16 January 1991. He asked permission for US aircraft to use Diego Garcia airfield, a British territory in the Indian Ocean, and Major records that he 'readily agreed'. 'And above all, although it may be unfashionable to think in such terms, it was morally the right thing to do; it gave a signal that the world expected certain standards in international behaviour and would act to enforce them.'[2]

On the issue of Britain's relations with the EU and the United States, Major came down firmly in the middle. 'I had no time for the facile Euro-phobic argument that we should "choose" between our Atlantic alliance with the United States and our European partners in the Community. Our economic involvement with Europe was growing, but we retained substantial trade links with the United States, as well as a close military and security arrangement. We needed to nurture both alliances. Ray Seitz, the engaging and Anglophile diplomat who served as USA ambassador to Britain for much of my premiership, reinforced the view by telling me repeatedly that Britain's influence in America would grow as our role in Europe developed.'[3] Developing his theme, with clear bias towards the Atlantic Alliance, Major also said:

'We straddled the divide between the United States and Europe. We were the largest investor in the US, and the largest recipient of her investment. We were her closest ally in NATO. We shared a language. Our instincts and outlook were more often in tune with North America than with Western Europe.—The US did not want a fifty-first state. As successive American ambassadors made clear to us, the United States wanted Britain to be a strong voice in Europe, as geography, economics and common values suggested we should be.'[4] Just what kind of strong voice in Europe did the Americans envisage?

However, these sentiments were certainly to be ruffled by President Clinton. The Major government felt that the Clinton White House ran roughshod over British interests, taking a one-sided view, particularly over the granting of a visa to Gerry Adams of Sinn Fein to visit the USA in May 1994. This was in direct defiance of the wishes of Major and the advice of the State Department. Major wrote on 10 March 1994 that Gerry Adams would pocket American concessions but never deliver anything in return, which turned out to be the case.[5]

The passing of the Cold War deprived the special relationship of its former immediacy although military co-operation continued, as in the Gulf War of 1991. Moreover, on most international issues the Americans and British usually worked together unlike other important American allies such as France, Germany or Japan. With the collapse of the USSR that had been the Cold War's raison d'être greater weight would henceforth be given to other disputes. Clinton and Major did not get on and their personal relationship was described as especially awful. During the 1992 presidential election both the British Conservative and Labour parties sent advisers to assist the rival candidates, which amounted to inexcusable British interference in American home affairs. Moreover, Major allowed—or did not stop—Home Office press officers searching files for evidence that Clinton, when at Oxford in 1969 on a Rhodes Scholarship, had applied for British Citizenship to avoid the Vietnam draft. No evidence was found to justify this smear. Major had, it seems, allowed the special relationship to become a personal relationship with the losing candidate, George Bush. As *The Economist* suggested: 'The special relationship, declared dead scores of times since Suez, will soon face another burial.'

Over the war in Bosnia, Britain and France resisted the relaxation of the UN arms embargo and opposed US escalation of the conflict. They argued that arming the Muslims or bombing the Serbs would worsen the bloodshed and endanger the peacekeepers on the ground. Jointly they managed to prevent the US secretary of state, Warren Christopher, from lifting the embargo. At Copenhagen in June 1993, Clinton worked with the German chancellor Kohl to rally the European Community against the peacekeeping states—Britain and France—and an angry Major is reputed to have contemplated ending the special relationship. The following month at the UN the United States voted with non-aligned countries against Britain and France over lifting sanctions. US Secretary of State Christopher complained in October 1993 that US policy makers had been too Euro-centric. He said Western Europe was no longer the dominant area of the world. During February 1994 Major refused to answer Clinton's telephone calls for days over the president's decision to grant a visa to Gerry Adams, the Sinn Fein leader. Adams was listed as a terrorist in London. As it was, the US State Department, the CIA, the US Justice Department and the FBI all opposed the visa on the grounds that it made the US look soft on terrorism and could do irreparable damage to the special relationship. This line-up of US departments that argued the visa would do irreparable damage to the special relationship provides an interesting insight into US attitudes to the special relationship at this time. Adams had offered nothing new and the violence in Ireland escalated.

Following a nadir in US-British relations an improvement was achieved in 1995 leading Clinton to say: 'John Major carried a lot of water for me and for the alliance over Bosnia. I know he was under a lot of political pressure, but he never wavered. He was a truly decent guy who never let me down. We worked really well together, and I got to like him a lot.' This statement was Clinton making amends and in November 1995 he became only the second US president to address both Houses of Parliament. Even so, at the end of Major's premiership the special relationship had become so bad that the incoming US ambassador banned the hackneyed phrase from use in the embassy. Too often disagreements arose because the Americans did what they wished and then retrospectively expected the British to fall into line. On the big issue of Britain's relations with the EU and the United States Major sat in the middle.

12

TONY BLAIR

Blair and Clinton got off to a good start with each other. Clinton described their accord as a 'unique partnership'. He said, 'Over the last fifty years our unbreakable alliance has helped to bring unparalleled peace and prosperity and security. It's an alliance based on shared values and common aspirations.' This was Clinton at his most engaging. Blair believed in humanitarian intervention and 'bullied' Clinton into backing diplomacy with force in Kosovo in 1999. When the Republican George W.Bush won the election at the turn of the century, Clinton advised Blair to get close to his successor. Then came 9/11 and the terrorist attacks upon the World Trade Center and the Pentagon, and Blair at once flew to Washington to affirm British solidarity with the United States. In a speech to the US Congress, nine days after the attack, Bush declared: 'America has no truer friend than Great Britain.' Blair had pledged full support to the United States: 'This is not a battle between the United States and terrorism, but between the free and democratic world and terrorism. We therefore here in Britain stand shoulder to shoulder with our American friends in this hour of tragedy, and we, like them, will not rest until the evil is driven from our world.' Blair then went on a tour round the world for two months to rally support for military action: he covered 40,000 miles and had fifty-four meetings. The personal rapport between Blair and Bush served to highlight the special relationship or rather to highlight the Blair-Bush relationship despite major British opposition to the war in Iraq when that followed in 2003. Then, Blair's support for and involvement in the Iraq war tarnished his reputation and was deeply unpopular at home while also attracting strong opposition in the EU from France and Germany.

Even before 9/11 Blair put much effort into building up a relationship with Clinton while making clear his belief that British relations with America were a top political priority. Briefing American journalists at 10 Downing Street on 2 February 1998, Blair echoed Thatcher when he said, 'and to say to people in Europe, "You know, thank goodness there is America there because America plays a vital role and strong leadership role in the world which is to the benefit of all the world."'[1] According to a Downing Street spokesman Blair's object was to underline how 'we are proud to be America's closest ally' and how 'we in Britain are uniquely placed to bring the United States and Europe together in a way that is to our mutual advantage'.[2] Blair was allocating to Britain a middle or mediator role that had been tried from Churchill onwards and failed. He accepted—as other British leaders before him had done—that the special relationship was a permanency like the British monarchy. Blair loved manipulation but despite his flair and his acceptance in the White House and round-the-world missionary zeal as an American ambassador-at-large, he had to accept that Britain was still very much the junior partner in the special relationship.[3] Britain's foreign secretary Jack Straw was to pose the question in relation to Britain trying to get a UN resolution in favour of invading Iraq: 'Do you seek to encourage and influence America to put its faith in the multilateral system, or work in a way that they can make a choice and go unilaterally if they wish?' Later, Straw told British MPs, 'We will reap a whirlwind if we push the Americans into a unilateral position in which they are at the centre of a unipolar world.' That was the essence of the government's case. The Americans were determined to get rid of Saddam, and must not be left alone. Yet, both for domestic political and legal reasons, it is vital to do this under the cover of a further resolution.[4] Straw was preparing the ground for British intervention alongside the Americans whether they obtained a UN resolution in support or not. Blair, in exchange for his support over Iraq tried to persuade the Americans to choose the UN path and restart the Middle East peace process. The US did neither of these things. Blair never learned that it is always a mistake to pander to excessive power. A major Blair objective in his foreign policy was to avoid choosing between Europe and the USA. 'But an even closer relationship with

America at arm's length from Europe, as some Conservatives want, would undermine British independence and sovereignty just as much as becoming part of some European super state. A British Prime Minister has influence because he or she represents a country sympathetic to US values, which also has a leading role in Europe.'[5]

Blair argued that as the closest ally of the United States Britain should go with the Americans and not leave them on their own. It was part of an informal bargain: 'In return, America should "listen back" on issues such as the Middle East peace process, global poverty, global warming and the United Nations.'[6] This was a delusion and as Blair discovered the United States would go its own way on all these issues and not 'listen back'. Thus, Blair justified his close and constant support for the Bush administration because not to do so would encourage US unilateralism yet despite his support Bush always pursued a unilateralist course.

Britain's relations with the EU became an important factor in British-American relations. The disintegration of Yugoslavia and the Kosovo war in 1999 brought out both the military weakness and the indecisiveness of the EU, which could not deal with a relatively minor war situation on its doorstep without invoking American assistance and leadership. Blair was not a European idealist but as he told the Friedrich Ebert Stiftung at Bonn in May 1995, Britain should take steps towards building a stronger European foreign and defence policy in harmony with the Atlantic Alliance. Implicit here is the assumption of an Anglo-American alliance and a Europe that Britain looked at as an adviser from outside. Blair, in fact, saw himself as having a central role between the United States and Europe and that he should be the leader of Europe and act as a bridge between Europe and the United States. Blair's close support for the United States post-9/11 led Europeans to worry that Blair was too much the missionary, the number one ally, and not enough the messenger of European worries.[7] Throughout his premiership Blair tended to tell Europe to act as one while he (and Britain) would act separately in conjunction with the United States. Moreover, he believed that the British role in Europe was to keep it firmly linked to the United States—in other words to act as a Trojan Horse for the Americans.

Following 9/11 and the launching of the war in Afghanistan, Blair, having failed to obtain UN endorsement, nonetheless joined Bush in the March 2003 invasion of Iraq. By 2004 there were growing strains in the special relationship. Although it had been shaped by 11 September 2001, endorsed after action in Afghanistan and honed in Iraq, the 'special relationship' between Britain and the United States was tested in 2004 as the governments of Tony Blair and George W. Bush disagreed publicly on a major issue of foreign policy. In mid-March, Hamas leader Sheikh Ahmad Yassin was killed by an Israeli missile as he left a mosque in his wheelchair. One month later his successor, Abdel-Aziz al-Rantirsi was killed in a similar attack. Jack Straw, the British foreign secretary, condemned the killings as 'unlawful'. In contrast, White House spokesman Scott McClellan asserted that 'Israel has the right to defend itself.' That the two principal partners in the 'War on Terror' presented such starkly different conclusions on the legality of the Israeli action reflected their dissimilar perspectives on the Israeli-Palestinian situation, and on the relevant rules of international law.[8] This difference may seem irrelevant when related to the wider question of the value of the special relationship to Britain. The United States acts—and intends to go on acting—unilaterally in pursuit of its hegemonic interests. Britain, whether led by Blair or not, has a fundamentally multilateralist approach to world problems, and especially to those fraught with possible conflicts. It is closer to Europe in this respect. What Blair did repeatedly was raise multilateralist concerns to show where he stood intellectually and then ditch them and by doing so at the last moment in order to support the Americans, he destroyed any claims to a special relationship where Britain had 'influence' and as a consequence he earned the contemptuous appellation of Bush's 'poodle'.[9]

Despite President Bush's declaration in May 2004 that the war in Iraq was over, in fact both the Afghan and the Iraq wars were only just beginning. Differences between the United States and Britain over a growing range of issues surfaced during the year but always, when it came to the point Blair, like Thatcher, insisted that the special relationship—which meant the American view—should prevail. As one newspaper appraisal put it, 'Mr. Blair seeks to reconcile differences between the US and Europe, alert to the dangers of a divide between the two. In alliance, he is optimistic that Europe and the US will encourage the likes of Russia and China, the other great superpower, within a decade or two, to move in a similar democratic direction.'[10] There was little chance that either power would do anything of the sort and there was very little democracy about either Bush's decision to go to war or, still less, Blair's to do so in support. From this point onwards, Blair sought to justify his alliance with America on increasingly shaky grounds. 'On several levels Mr. Blair miscalculated. Europe and the UN could not be swayed. As he said in his speech at Labour's conference [that September]: "There was no third way over this. Believe me I tried."' In fact there was a third way and that of course was to cease supporting the United States. 'The most damning criticism of Mr. Blair's approach came from the former Washington Ambassador Sir Christopher Meyer, who revealed that he did not observe much private candour in discussions between the President and the Prime Minister.'[11] Blair's 'shoulder to shoulder' support for America was rejected by 64 per cent of the British people (in an NOP poll) who thought that having good relations with Britain's European Union partners was more important than with the United States. Despite this, Blair remained determined to act as a bridge between the United States and the EU.[12]

In February 2005 the British government announced proudly a London summit on the Middle East for March to be upstaged immediately by US Secretary of State Condoleezza Rice who announced a Washington summit for April/May. '"Prime Minister Tony Blair," Dr Rice declared in a sentence implicitly dismissing all London's hopes of being the peacemaker, "will convene an important conference to help the Palestinian people advance democratic reform and build their institutions. All of us support this effort." You can't get more patronising than that.'[13] Blair took such insults and persevered with a special relationship that to almost anyone else was only a satellite one. The brutal political fact was that Washington would do as it determined in the knowledge that Blair would follow suit, whatever alternative policies he might advance first.

It was not just on big issues that the United States acted unilaterally. It expected British compliance on quite small issues as, for example, the extradition of the NATWEST three (British bankers accused of fraud in the United States). The question of their innocence or guilt in relation to charges brought against them in the United States was not the issue. They were dealt with under fast-track arrangements set out in a UK-US treaty concluded in 2003, which did not require either side to make a prima facie case for extradition. The treaty had been enacted in the shadow of 9/11 and was designed primarily to deal with the transfer of terrorist suspects. The treaty should not have been used in relation to the three bankers. 'The real injustice, however, is that the men are being extradited under a reciprocal treaty that currently has no reciprocity. The US Senate, concerned about legal safeguards for US citizens facing extradition, has so far refused to vote on its ratification. So, while British citizens face fast-track removal to the United States, Americans face nothing of the kind the other way.'[14] In the House of Commons Blair insisted that the treaty had been concluded to bring the US into the international system, and he promised the men and their families 'all the support and assurances we can give'. He did not explain why Britain was honouring a treaty by which the other side was not bound. In simple terms, Britain was adhering to a treaty that was not ratified in the United States; it was a case of Britain doing what the Americans demanded without obtaining or even asking for a quid pro quo.

In mid-2006 Israel launched a heavy bombardment of Lebanon that caused outrage in much of the world but as the British newspaper, *The Independent* claimed, 'Britain today finds itself more isolated internationally than at any time since the invasion of Iraq. Our official position on the Israeli bombardment of Lebanon is at odds with the European Union, the United Nations and global opinion in general. By refusing to call for a ceasefire we find ourselves with only the United States and Israel itself for company.—The truth is that Britain no longer has what can be called an independent foreign policy. Our Prime Minister long ago threw his lot in with the Bush administration. And President Bush is adamant that Israel must be given a free hand in Lebanon. It is this—and this alone—that explains our government's refusal to call for a ceasefire.'[15] Meanwhile, the Israeli bombardment had killed more than 330 people, a third of them children. Neither the British cabinet nor the people shared Blair's approach to the Israeli bombardment and on 17 August 2006 the deputy prime minister John Prescott described British efforts on the Middle East 'road map' as 'crap'. When in November a US State Department analyst Kendal Myers said that the special relationship was a 'myth' with 'no sense of reciprocity' he was disowned by the State Department.

No matter how one-sided the special relationship between Blair and Bush, with no US commitments on climate change, poverty in Africa or the Middle East road map—subjects on which Blair especially pressed for change—he nevertheless defended a stance that he had made the cornerstone of Britain's foreign policy. 'An unrepentant Mr. Blair told MPs the relationship had given Britain more clout at the world's top table during his 10 years in power and insisted that it had resulted directly in progress on climate change, the Middle East and Africa. But his critics said little progress had been made on these issues and that Mr Blair had enjoyed little influence over President George Bush.'[16] Blair, indeed, was to expend much of his energies during his last year as prime minister defending the special relationship, of which he said, 'We shouldn't give that up in any set of circumstances.' He was at one with Thatcher on this issue. Both Blair and Bush appeared diminished figures in 2008 when they were about to step down from their leading political roles and by this time the special relationship that Blair had pushed so hard had been revealed as never before as one of a British client relationship that had belittled the prime minister and convinced the world that Britain had no independent foreign policy of its own.

Gordon Brown, who succeeded Blair as prime minister in June 2007, was always a proclaimed Atlanticist and frequent visitor to the United States. In 2006, he gave a prime-minister-in-waiting speech in which he warned that the fight against terrorism would be undermined unless Europe and the United States avoided a repeat of the divisions between them over the Iraq war. He told his Chatham House audience that there should be 'no future for anti-Americanism in Europe' because of the shared values of the two continents. 'If Europe and America cannot come together with a clear and common message, and then together work more closely with all continents, then this weakness will in itself be a tacit encouragement to terrorism,' he said and likened the fight against terrorism to the fight against communism after the Second World War.[17] Within a month of becoming prime minister, Brown sought to reassure the Bush administration that he would not depart from Blair's approach by distancing himself from the United States and spoke of forging stronger links between the two countries, an approach that was not acceptable to all his ministers.[18] Despite Brown's proclaimed acceptance of the special relationship, his period of office saw several minor yet contentious issues. A row erupted in June 2009 when the US failed to seek the approval of the British government before negotiating with Bermuda the resettlement to British territory of four ex-Guantanamo Bay inmates wanted by China. As a Foreign Office spokesman said: 'It is something we should have been consulted about.' The move prompted an urgent security assessment by the British government. Another row erupted over the US use of Diego Garcia for extraordinary rendition. One commentator described this as a 'wake-up call' and 'the latest example of American governments ignoring Britain when it comes to US interests in British territories abroad.' Then, in March 2010 the US secretary of state, Hillary Clinton, supported Argentina's call for negotiations over the Falkland Islands, which led to British protests and renewed scepticism about the value of the special relationship. President Barack Obama met Brown in March 2009 when he reaffirmed that, 'Great Britain is one of our closest and strongest allies and there is a link and bond there that will not break.—This notion that somehow there is any lessening of that special relationship is misguided.—The relationship is not only special and strong but will only get stronger as time goes on.' Brown appeared always to be seeking reassurance from the United States that the special relationship was as much accepted in Washington (which was not the case) as it was wished for in London.

Three wars: Afghanistan, Iraq and the War on Terror

Casualties from the war in Afghanistan have made front page news in Britain but the bravery of the soldiers has been offset against increasing doubts as to why British troops are there at all. In July 2010 British troops were withdrawn from Sangin where they fought against a classic guerrilla campaign with little success. As Patrick Cockburn reported: 'The area, where a tenth of the British troops in Afghanistan suffered one third of total casualties, is symbolic of Britain's involvement in Afghanistan, as a bit player whose contribution was always going to have little effect on the outcome of the whole campaign. There were never quite enough British troops to gain permanent control of Sangin, and the Taliban obviously sensed the vulnerability of British troops spread too thinly.—The only compelling reason for Britain to be fighting in Afghanistan is to retain its status as America's principal ally. Any suggestion that the British troops are keeping the streets of Britain safe has always been demonstrably untrue—and the idea that British forces could clear the way for good government for the people of Helmand has never made much sense.'[19] This judgement, coming from a veteran reporter, could apply equally to the legacy (or non-legacy) of British troops in Iraq. The troops are not to blame; they go where they are sent. Retaining its status as America's principal ally—ever since the Korean War—has become the principal reason for sending British troops anywhere. In his book *The Terrorist in Search of*

Humanity, Faisal Devji couples America and Britain together like international twins, although asymmetrical twins with Britain acting as a chorus to America. In this respect at least the special relationship appears to have survived. Devji claims that the actions of the Americans and British are prohibited by the same international laws and treaties, which they hypocritically claim to uphold and protect, and which they impose on others, even as they themselves violate them with impunity.[20] Whatever the reasons for going to war in Afghanistan (it did at least have the backing of the United Nations) the end result has been a disaster, and from the British point of view it has been a disaster wished upon the British people because a 'pliant British Prime Minister'[21] was determined to stand by the American president, regardless of where Britain's real interests lay.

The story of Iraq is somewhat different. One factor that is present amid all the violence and is often overlooked is oil, and oil in great quantities. In March 2003, just prior to the invasion of Iraq, Britain's two oil giants, BP and Shell, denounced reports that they had had talks in Downing Street about Iraq's oil. In fact, five months before the invasion, on 6 November 2002, the Trade Minister Baroness Symons told BP the government believed British energy firms should be given a share of Iraq's oil and gas reserves as a reward for Blair's military commitment to the plans for regime change in that country. BP was desperate to obtain its share of any oil carve-up. There were fears that the United States was entering into pre-event deals with US, French and Russian governments over oil but not with Britain. (Britain, as usual, could be taken for granted but the other countries needed to be mollified.) In public, however, BP insisted it had 'no strategic interest in Iraq' while privately to the Foreign Office it said Iraq was vital to its interests. Subsequently, after the invasion, twenty-year contracts were signed by various oil companies and these were described as the largest in oil company history. Oil was a vital British interest and the government colluded with the oil companies to give them access to Iraq's huge resources. A Foreign Office memorandum of 13 November 2002 argued that, 'Iraq is the big oil prospect. BP is desperate to get in there and anxious that political deals should not deny them the opportunity to compete. The long term potential is enormous.' In February 2003 Britain's prime minister Tony Blair dismissed the idea of an oil conspiracy as 'absurd'. On 12 March 2003 both BP and Shell claimed that they had not had talks with the government about oil in Iraq. Insur-

gency in Iraq after the war as well as other problems limited the country's oil output to 3m b/d. Meanwhile, all the big oil companies were
lining up to get their share of the eventual oil carve-up that was
expected to take place. They included BP, Shell, ExxonMobil, CNPC,
Lukoil, Statoil and Total. Oil had always been at the top of the Iraq
invasion agenda, something that was always denied. The oil companies
were determined to prise oil from Iraqi government control into the
hands of the oil majors. Days after President George W. Bush claimed
mission accomplished in May 2003, the British government was working to ensure that British companies got their share of the oil. Minutes
of a government meeting on 12 May reveal the extent of government
concern: 'The future shape of the Iraqi industry will affect oil markets,
and the functioning of OPEC, in both of which we have a vital interest.' London officials outlined a 'desirable' outcome for Iraq's crippled
oil industry as an 'oil sector open and attractive to foreign investment,
with appropriate arrangements for the exploitation of new fields'.
Plans to expand production from 2.5m b/d to 12m b/d are now under
consideration as a result of new contracts. The Iraq government under
duress has undermined Iraqi opposition to these huge sell-out contracts. This is a story of western hypocrisy and greed at its most dangerous. Even Iraqi oil experts who originally supported privatisation
now argue that it is not in Iraq's best interests.

By 2006 the military side of the special relationship was becoming
distinctly strained. The US Army published a criticism of its performance in Iraq by a senior British officer who accused American forces
of making a tricky situation worse with their cultural arrogance, over-
reliance on technology and inability to recognise the special challenges
of counter-insurgency warfare. This assault on US military competence
appeared in the *Military Review* under the name of Brigadier Nigel
Aylwin-Foster who served in Iraq from December 2003 to November
2004. The Brigadier wrote of the 'enigma' of the US Army with its
'unparalleled sense of patriotism, duty, passion and commitment ... and
in no way lacking in humanity and compassion'. Yet it was weighed
down by 'bureaucracy, a stifling hierarchical outlook, a pre-disposition
to offensive operations'. Unsparing in his criticism, the Brigadier went
on to say the US army showed 'a cultural sensitivity ... that arguably
amounted to institutional racism' and that it had failed to adapt to the
demands of counter-insurgency work, where military operations had a
vital political dimension. Unsurprisingly, this article provoked an angry

response. Colonel Kevin Benson, commander of the US Army's School of Advanced Military Studies, described Brigadier Aylwin-Foster as an 'insufferable British snob' in *The Washington Post*. According to the official Soldier's Creed, the US Army undertakes to 'engage and destroy' the enemy but not 'defeat' which would permit other political options to be tried.[22] The Brigadier's superior criticism is in a tradition that makes up for lack of military power on the ground.

In March 2006, the US secretary of state Condoleezza Rice visited Britain and went to Blackburn, the parliamentary constituency of Jack Straw, the British foreign secretary. She met with demonstrations both there and in Liverpool that underlined the damage the Iraq War had done to Anglo-American relations. 'The goodwill that flowed towards America after the 11 September terrorist attacks was dissipated within the year by maladroit US diplomacy. The invasion of Iraq and all that followed only deepened the rift.'[23] A comment upon Anglo-American relations in 2006 (they were not going well) appeared in an editorial and read as follows: 'But while Presidents and Prime Ministers come and go, the axis between London and Washington remains the most stable and strongest alliance in the world. Maintaining it has rightly been a foreign policy priority for every British government since the Second World War.' Meanwhile, Iraq had effectively broken up and civil war clearly threatened while Condoleezza Rice called for a 'strong leader' capable of uniting Iraqis. By this time all the signs indicated how the British-US alliance was fraying while Spain and other members of the coalition were withdrawing their troops under domestic pressures. Blair, however, insisted that Britain had a responsibility to stay and see the mission through. A retired US general, Jack Keane, said the British had lost control of Basra, which was descending into gang warfare. Statements by President Bush, Condoleezza Rice or Blair bore little relation to what was actually happening on the ground.

An analysis of Blair's attitude towards America was not to be humiliated. He was determined to show that he was not soft on 'defence' nor anti-American. Neil Kinnock, when leader of the Labour Party, had visited Washington to be snubbed by President Reagan who only saw him for a few minutes. 'Blair's guiding philosophy was never going to allow him to be placed in such a position, whoever was President.'[24] The Chilcot inquiry, which began in November 2009, would hear evidence of deep splits between British and American military chiefs, claims that Blair failed to prepare troops for the aftermath of the invasion and evidence that Blair's secrecy over his pact with former President George W. Bush helped fuel the post-war chaos. British military chiefs were furious at the lack of planning and failure to equip the troops adequately. These criticisms indicate that Blair was more concerned to be seen acting alongside the American president than preparing for a war that would inevitably put British troops at unnecessary risk. The British Chief of Staff in Iraq, Colonel J.K.Tanner, described his American counterparts as 'a group of Martians' for whom 'dialogue is alien'. 'Despite our so-called "special relationship", I reckon we were treated no differently to the Portuguese.'[25] According to Sir Christopher Meyer (giving evidence to the Chilcot inquiry) George Bush was so close to Tony Blair he felt the former prime minister was the 'only human being he could talk to' while the rest of the world's leaders were 'creatures from outer space.'

When Gordon Brown became prime minister his government secretly promised to limit the extent of the Iraq war inquiry to prevent damage to the United States. Such a pledge threatened to damage the credibility of the investigation. Brown had wanted the evidence to be heard in private but was forced to back down by public and political anger. Individually or in combination, the management of the Iraq war by the United States and Britain 'was planned for and undertaken in indefatigable, wilful ignorance of its history, ancient or modern, and the influence of history on the attitudes of the Iraqi people. Britain, which created, organised and administered the modern state of Iraq at the end of World War I; and thereby encountered determined ongoing Iraqi resistance.'—'Any western power intervening in Iraq would be well advised to inform itself about the influence of history on the attitudes of the Iraqi people. The evidence, however, shows that Britain and America preferred to invent their own versions of what Iraqis ought to think and feel, rather than consult expertise and opinion that was readily available.'[26] It is an irony of the special relationship that British military thinking and practices were often taken up by the Americans. Thus in Iraq, 'America responded to the insurgency and civil strife by following Britain's policy in Northern Ireland of building walls to separate communities on sectarian lines, thus concreting a problem it had created.'[27]

Why Blair went to war in Iraq to please Washington still requires elucidation. When he went to the United Nations prior to the invasion of Iraq the Americans saw this as a measure to help Blair politically, not as an option. Ultimately he was expected to fall into line and commit British forces, an expectation that made sense for Americans when they put it in the context of the special relationship. An apologist for Blair explains his decision: 'For Blair, the risks of a unilateral America outweighed the risks of going to war in the face of domestic and European hostility. And the Americans knew that. Bush always expected Blair to be with him at the crunch.'[28] Britain should never get into the position where it had to choose between the US and Europe but that is what happened in 2003 over Iraq. Blair made the wrong choice but no one, including Blair himself, has ever explained why. If not quite 'ready, aye ready' Blair in fact saw himself as always there alongside our ally, the United States.

The War on Terror that had been proclaimed by George W. Bush in the aftermath of 11 September 2001 paved the way for new US hardline approaches to international problems that were echoed by Blair. In the January 2007 issue of *Foreign Affairs*, the British prime minister Tony Blair wrote that the War on Terror 'is not a clash between civilisations; it is a clash about civilisation. It is the age-old battle between progress and reaction, between those who embrace the modern world and those who reject its existence—between optimism and hope, on the one hand, and pessimism and fear on the other.' These views were echoed by senior US policy makers.[29] It is unsurprising, in terms of both Blair's personal views and those of leading Americans, that the religious element enters the debate at this point. The US presidential candidate John McCain's 2008 defence of the invasion of Iraq was structured in terms of those who have Judeo-Christian values and those who don't: 'This just wasn't the elimination of a threat to Iraq— this was elimination of a threat to the West, part of this titanic struggle we are in between western Judeo-Christian values and principles and Islamic extremists.' One US official illuminated the debate when he said: 'Terrorists use violence because they don't have values; we use violence to spread democracy.' George Soros[30] made the point that by declaring a war on terrorism (at a highly emotive moment in US history) Washington in fact was creating a new concept that would permit US intervention almost anywhere. In terms of British participation in both Afghanistan and Iraq, Blair clearly aligned himself with this American view. Moreover, exaggerating the threats posed by terrorists only makes them worse. This was done by the Bush administration. While fear can be a useful tool in the hands of a government intent on

exploiting it to control its own people, it can also be used to unite people against a common enemy. Communism used to serve as the enemy:
now it has been replaced by terrorism.

13

BRITAIN AND EUROPE

Parallel with the saga of the special relationship, a relationship in which Britain was always destined to be the junior partner, ran the unbelievable story of Europe striving to end its violent past by creating a European Union, and in this case Britain could have taken the leading role but instead determined to sit on the sidelines. If ever a priceless political opportunity was thrown away this was it.

During a two-day debate (20–21 April 1944) on all aspects of the Commonwealth system, the Labour politician Emmanuel Shinwell appealed for co-operation with Western Europe: 'We ought to consider the possibility ... of effecting some kind of arrangement with the ... Scandinavian countries, the Netherlands, Denmark, Belgium, and certainly a free and independent France which can be dovetailed into an economic Commonwealth policy.'[1] In the period 1945–1950 Britain had every opportunity to take the lead in Europe but missed the chances or ignored the possibilities. 'But this was not to be. Duff Cooper, appointed in 1944 Ambassador in Paris, wrote to the Foreign Office urging a clear union with France but was frustrated, he complained, by the Treasury and the Board of Trade, anxious not to offend the Americans or Russians, or to diverge from Anglo-American plans for multilateral non-discriminatory free trade.'[2] On 19 September 1946, Winston Churchill gave a major speech in Zurich in which he called for a United States of Europe based upon co-operation between France and Germany. Britain, however, would not be a part of the organisation. This stand-off attitude towards Europe was to be sustained through to the twenty-first century: co-operation but not integration was to be the British line. In a number of post-war speeches such as that at Zurich, in which Churchill called upon France and Germany to forgive the past and 'build a kind of United States of Europe' Churchill gave the impression that Britain would be willing to play a major part in any moves towards continental union. 'Are we all, through our poverty and our quarrels, for ever to be a burden and a danger to the rest of the world? Do we imagine that we can be carried forward indefinitely upon the shoulders—broad though they be—of the United States of America.'[3] Calling in 1947 for the rejuvenation of a shattered Europe, Churchill talks as though Britain will be a part of the rejuvenation yet he also—he cannot leave it out—brings the United States into the equation. He exalts the relationship with France: 'But we have a proposal to make to France which will give all Frenchmen a cause for serious thought and valiant decision. If European unity is to be made an effective reality before it is too late, the whole-hearted efforts both of France and Britain will be needed from the outset. They must go forward hand in hand. They must in fact be founder partners in this movement.' Given such warm rhetoric in the 1940s it is little wonder Europe felt let down when it realised that Britain would remain outside. On 10 October 1947, speaking at Brighton, Churchill said: 'I am also an earnest advocate of a united Europe and of the important part which Britain must play in its achievement.' The United Europe Committee held a mass meeting in the Albert Hall on 14 May 1947, at which Churchill spoke (see above) so movingly about the future: 'We accept without question the world supremacy of the United Nations Organisation. In the Constitution agreed at San Francisco direct provision was made for regional organisations to be formed. United Europe will form one major regional entity. There is the United States with all its dependencies; there is the Soviet Union; there is the British Empire and Commonwealth; and there is Europe, with which Great Britain is profoundly blended.'

British awareness of its declining power affected the decisions it made or failed to make at this time. 'By 1947, British officials saw that the United States would soon be "plucking the torch" of world leadership from our chilling hands. Europe was now dependent on the United States for its own security and for global security.'[4] As the pattern of the post-war world took shape, the British probably took a view of power more akin to that of the Americans than did the Europeans. They had their Empire, they had developed a working mode of alliance with the Americans during the war and these helped persuade them that they were and perhaps should be apart from Europe. How, for example, was Britain to judge the Marshall Plan for the recovery of Europe? 'Was it, to borrow Churchill's description of Lend-lease, one of the most unsordid "acts" in the history of any nation, or was it a cynical and successful American instrument for prising Europe open for US business to penetrate while effectively driving the Soviet Union out of the reconstruction business and into its own grim and impoverished redoubt behind the Iron Curtain—the final stage on the two-year trail from Potsdam which doomed Europe to four decades of Cold War?'[5] Britain's role post-war was to work alongside the USA but in its own right and not as part of a European Federation or Union. Britain with its transatlantic and Commonwealth ties could and should be independent of Europe. As a consequence of such thinking it was to reject membership of the Schuman Plan in 1950. The Anglo-Saxons did not appreciate some of the imperatives that drove the Europeans together. 'Britain and, perhaps from time to time, the United States too, systematically underestimated the German desire for reunification. Britain and America were not threatened by the status quo. For them the division of Germany and the division of Berlin was a kind of solution. It was not especially satisfactory, but everyone got used to it. Leaders such as Macmillan and Kennedy were more interested in stability than change. De Gaulle, who had also lived through a period when his country was divided and occupied, was perhaps better able to understand Adenauer.'[6] The Americans became increasingly aware of Britain's ambivalence in relation to Europe. In 1949 George Kennan was called upon by the US under-secretary of state in the State Department to explain current UK thinking on Europe. In his response he said: 'The UK tended to exert a retarding influence on Western European plans for closer political and economic integration. The UK was most chary of entering into any arrangements which might tend to derogate from her sovereignty and she was continuously preoccupied with her Empire commitments. The net result was that UK participation tended to place a ceiling on Western European attainments towards unification.'[7] According to the US State department at this time, 'An attempt should be made to link the U.K. more closely to the U.S.A. and Canada and to get the U.K. to disengage itself as much as possible from

Continental European problems. It should assume more nearly the role of adviser to Western Europe and its problems, and less the role of active participant. It was hoped that the U.K.could be persuaded to disengage itself quickly from the Council of Europe.'[8] These American attitudes must have played their part in persuading Britain to stay aloof from many European initiatives, but she couldn't do so altogether! Such a policy of disengagement was bound to increase French suspicions of a partnership between the USA, UK and Canada from which they were excluded. At this point, perhaps, were sown the seeds of British distrust of Europe that in the case of France would lead to de Gaulle's vetoes of Britain's attempts to join the ECM in the 1960s. While the Americans wanted European integration, they accepted that Britain would remain outside. 'For their part the British were delighted to see the special relationship with the USA extended from defence to economics. They were equally relieved at American recognition of the impossibility for the UK, with its worldwide commitments, of integrating fully in some form of a European union.'[9] In 1950 the Europeans advanced the Schuman Plan as a first concrete step towards European unity and here a new and powerful advocate of Britain in Europe appears in the person of Dean Acheson. As he claims, 'Despite my earnest arguments in the next few days Britain made her great mistake of the post-war period by refusing to join in negotiating the Schuman Plan.'[10] Meanwhile, at American insistence, plans were going ahead to involve Germany in European defence—in other words German rearmament and as Acheson points out, 'We had obtained Attlee's grudging acquiescence in this compromise during the Washington visit.' Attlee, however, had to pay attention to his party's reservations about Europe. 'In a party pamphlet entitled *European Unity*, the trouble for doctrinaire socialists with the plan was shown to lie just where Schuman had suspected it would: in the binding effect of the High Authority's decisions. The issue was the sovereign right of a Labour Government to pursue democratic socialism. Important but secondary was the national policy of special ties with the Commonwealth and the United States.'[11]

Following the success of Marshall aid the Americans began to push the idea of a united Europe. Britain was the main obstacle. 'Knowing of the American support for the idea of an integrated Europe, Bevin wrote to Acheson just before the [1949] OEEC conference that while Britain would do everything possible to support the principle, in practice all concerned "must have regard to the position of the United Kingdom as a power with worldwide responsibilities, as a leading member of the British Commonwealth and sterling area".'[12] Speaking to a United Europe meeting in July 1957, at the Central Hall, Westminster, after he had retired as prime minister, Churchill said, 'It is a pleasure to me to take part again in a gathering to promote the cause of a united Europe, which has for so many years been near to my heart. I wish you all continued success in this great enterprise. Let us therefore go forward together with courage and patience.' He added, 'My message to Europe today is still the same as it was ten years ago—unite.' By this time it had become customary for Churchill to admonish Europe to unite but to do so from outside. Bob Boothby, a maverick political figure whose influence lay in the past, voiced common frustration when he wrote that the whole idea of an integrated European army was in fact blown up by Churchill's government of 1951. Anthony Eden was foreign secretary over the years 1951–1955 and was an imperialist who had little sympathy with the European experiment and did not want Britain to become entangled in it. Speaking in New York in 1952, he said: 'Britain's story and her interests lie far beyond the continent of Europe. Britain's family ties in every corner of the world were Britain's "life" and made it impossible for her to join a federation on the continent of Europe. This is something which we know, in our bones, we cannot do.'

Under Macmillan, Britain first withdrew (1957) from the Messina talks that would eventually lead to the Treaty of Rome and emergence of 'The Six', then in 1958 as it saw the ECM taking shape, it proposed a wider free trade area. In a cabinet note Macmillan argued, 'If the free trade area fails we should try to mobilise the Americans for the creation of a free trade area contemporaneously with the protectionist Common Market.'[13] Macmillan's next move was to create EFTA or 'Outer Seven', consisting of Britain and six small European countries—Denmark, Norway, Ireland, Portugal, Greece and Austria—as a rival bloc to the 'Six' but EFTA contained only one economic power in Britain whereas the Six included France, Germany and Italy. Thus, EFTA could not rival the Six and so Macmillan had to take the Six seriously, leading Britain to apply for membership of the ECM over 1961–1963 when de Gaulle used his veto to block British membership. By this time the Americans were becoming increasingly concerned about the direction of European politics and Britain's role in relation to the ECM. In

1962 the Cuban crisis focused attention upon American-European politics. 'The American response during the Kennedy-Khruschev encounter over Cuba was unwavering but this did not induce General de Gaulle to shift ground. Instead, he strove even harder for a self-dependent Europe as a substitute for Atlantic interdependence.'[14] Later, the same author argued, 'There would be less risk of any Third Force or anti-American aberrations if Britain belonged to a united Europe.' American concerns about a European defence force or where Britain should stand in relation to Europe would continue with varying degrees of intensity into the twenty-first century. 'What prompted Europeanisers among the British was the conviction that the British would run the show. And American hopes that the British would do so stemmed from distrust of precisely those European trends that Washington itself had long been fostering.'[15] Thus, in a celebrated speech on 4 July 1962, Kennedy announced that the United States would be ready to discuss ways and means of forming a concrete Atlantic partnership with a united Europe. From the American point of view the question was how Washington could control Europe. At that time the idea of an American withdrawal from Europe was not seen as in America's interest (and if for a moment we jump forward to 2010 and NATO, maintained and increased in size, this permitted the Americans to remain in Europe). It was all about the extension of US worldwide hegemony. Although at this time influential Americans advocated British membership of a European Federal Union, in fact had such British participation emerged this would almost certainly have detracted from American leadership of the West.

Britain and Europe or Britain and America were constantly advanced as political objectives about which Britain had to make a decision. When Macmillan made the decision to take Britain into Europe there were two consequences. The first: Britain would have to give up its attempts as under Attlee, Churchill and Macmillan himself to act as a mediator between the two superpowers. The second: the leadership had to overcome British fears about surrendering sovereignty to Europe. These fears about sovereignty have raised a question that has never been properly faced: why were there not equal fears upon the part of the British public at the amount of British power that had already been surrendered to the United States?

Charles de Gaulle came back to power in 1958, the same year in which the ECM of the Six began life as an independent entity. De

Gaulle spent much of his first year as president trying to persuade France's colonies in Africa to become members of the French Community, a move that in reality would prolong French control. In the new Europe de Gaulle was hostile to political integration and France became the most determined opponent of the European federal idea. Instead he promoted the concept of *l'Europe des Patries*, which was opposed to both European supra-nationalism and Atlanticism. He was nearer to the British position than ever appeared on the surface and opposed Community decision-making of the kind necessary to give the Community real power. He might have been persuaded to accept some form of Atlanticism had President Kennedy insisted upon treating France on a par with Britain by extending the special relationship to France but this, if it was ever a possibility, was thwarted by a jealous Britain. De Gaulle's attitude led Monnet to tell de Gaulle that if he continually put France to the forefront he was going to kill the European idea forever. In a private conversation between de Gaulle and the British ambassador Christopher Soames, de Gaulle argued that to create a truly independent Europe, capable of making decisions on matters of global importance, first of all it would be necessary for Europeans to free themselves from the encumbrance of NATO with its 'American domination and machinery'. A successful European political organisation would have to rely on a concert of the most significant European powers: France, England, Germany and Italy. In a brief to President Nixon concerning such a concert of Europe, 'It is also characteristic that de Gaulle would have recognised that such a concert would have to be based on Anglo-French agreement, although on the supposition that England would emancipate itself from any "special relationship" with the United States.'[16] There was no chance of such an outcome at that time and, as Adenauer remarked to de Gaulle, 'England is like a rich man, who has lost all his property but does not realise it.' Its policies were constantly intertwined—defence, the US relationship, Europe and NATO. As de Gaulle told Christopher Soames: Anglo-US talks were based on the thesis that eventually Europe would be independent of NATO and the ECM would change out of all recognition.[17] De Gaulle on the Macmillan attempt to enter the ECM, said: 'To France it seemed clear that if Britain were to enter she would back others in the Community to satisfy the Americans and endanger French agricultural interests.' The general's resolve (to bar UK entry) was strengthened by the Cuban crisis of 1962, which showed that when it came to the crunch the United States would 'always go it alone'. Throughout the negotiations Britain seemed to flaunt 'what it imagined to be its special relationship with the United States. While Nassau was not a decisive factor with de Gaulle, it must have been a welcome pretext. Macmillan did not seem to realise that for many in the Six, not just the French, his negotiations with Kennedy at Nassau provided fresh evidence that the British attached paramount importance to their link with the United States over those with Europe.'[18] De Gaulle was never convinced that the British would forsake their 'special' Atlantic relationship for a genuine European partnership. The British foreign secretary in 1969, Michael Stewart, made plain Britain supported a Europe that would remove the danger of French dominance. This attitude was well received by Italy, Germany and the Benelux countries. Then de Gaulle went from power. De Gaulle may have created a dominant position for France in the Six but this was as much resented as Britain's equally singular position of ambiguity.

Britain, increasingly, appeared to be at war with the European idea. Later, when it had joined the Six to make it Nine (with Denmark and Ireland joining at the same time) opponents of closer union used the stupidities of Brussels as an excuse for rejecting the EU concept. At certain levels British insistence upon its special relationship provided a convenient excuse for not making closer commitments to Europe. For centuries Britain had fought in all Europe's major wars yet at this point in its history when European union would prevent further wars Britain recoiled and began to deploy the argument (that was to continue into the twenty-first century) that closer ties with Europe would mean too many surrenders of sovereignty despite the readiness to surrender aspects of its sovereignty to the United States under the umbrella of the special relationship. The choice of full membership of Europe that always made the most sense would constantly be set aside in the years that followed because of old-fashioned nationalist sentiments and a false sense of grandeur based upon a vanished past. If right from the beginning Britain had accepted the European concept she could have been the dominant power in the early days of its formation and controlled the federal idea. The British mistake was always to sit on the sidelines rather than commit itself wholeheartedly to participation in the new Europe. Edward Heath did finally take Britain into the ECM but by then there had emerged a determined British antipathy and suspicion about Europe that could be traced back to Attlee's lukewarm approach to Europe. Writing in 2004, Timothy Garton Ash insists 'Britain—cannot go on doing the splits between an emerging federal super state, a United States of Europe run from Brussels, and the only remaining superpower, the United States of America.'[19] Although Ash clearly favours 'choosing' the United States, further on he argues: 'To choose Europe is to place a premium on social justice, solidarity, the environment, the welfare state and the quality of the public sphere. Many on the right agree: to choose America means, for them, to prefer the free market, an enterprise culture, the American business model, low taxes and the minimal state.'[20]

As the ECM of the Six enjoyed an economic boom, in the process suggesting a greater Europe to come, relations with the United States were not always easy. The United States was hostile to de Gaulle's determination to pursue an independent policy for France, suspicious of British imperialism, irritated by West Germany's policy of Ost-politik with the USSR and generally coming to see a United Europe as a rival rather than an acquiescent part of a Western alliance dominated by the US. These suspicions were to grow over the decades to the end of the century. As Yugoslavia disintegrated the Europeans claimed it was 'the hour of Europe' though humiliatingly it soon became apparent that the Europeans needed the United States to help bring about a peace, which they did with the Dayton Accord. Then the Kosovo war of 1999 demonstrated how difficult it would prove to be for the United States and its European allies to fight a war together. As Robert Kagan argues: 'Those who cannot act unilaterally themselves naturally want to have a mechanism for controlling those who can. From the European perspective, the United States may be a relatively benign hegemon, but insofar as its actions delay the arrival of a world order more conducive to the safety of weaker powers, it is objectively dangerous.'[21] For the fifty years after the end of the Second World War, Europe had fallen into a state of strategic dependence upon the United States while the American nuclear guarantee deprived the Europeans of the incentive to spend the kind of money that would have been necessary to restore them to military great-power status: this psychology of dependence was the legacy of the Cold War and the nuclear age. In the new century, however, more than a crack appeared in the Western Alliance as under President George W. Bush the Americans appeared to want—and to assume they could—remake the world in the American image. 'Not only is the assumption of the universality of American values disputed by many in Europe, Asia and Africa, but the strategy implies that America can impose its views without the willing cooperation of others, as opposed to their acquiescence.'[22] What these neo-conservative Americans overlook is the fact that once they have spread their hegemony worldwide there is only one subsequent development for them to face: worldwide revolt.

As far as the American-European alliance is concerned, one set of assumptions is almost always paralleled by another contradictory set. The Americans have seen Britain filling a useful role as a Trojan Horse in Europe. 'However, neither Washington nor London has seen Britain merely as part of a common or even joint EU approach. Rather, the Americans have regarded the UK as an ally arguing a common US-British line within Community institutions on everything from security and defence to trade. This is the 'Trojan Horse' view that has always aroused so much suspicion in Paris and was specifically rejected by Edward Heath.'[23] Such a British role was described in candid detail by Drew Middleton as early as 1963. His description of the role is both condescending and contemptuous of British values. 'Britain because she is trusted may well prove to be the best, perhaps the only agency, for the channelling of information on American policies and desires to a new Europe. President de Gaulle sees this clearly and, equally clearly, he doesn't like it. Yet once Britain, with her wealth, influence and diplomatic skill, gets into Europe, it will be almost impossible to stop—if Britain accepts the role. The United States will need a friend at court when moves have to be made that are better done quietly through a discreet friend than in open conference. What better friend than the British.'[24] Here is the Anglophile American assigning to Britain this demeaning role as though doing Britain a favour. How would enemies of Britain behave if a friend acts in this way? No wonder de Gaulle used his veto. As early as the 1960s, while pushing for European unity, American fears were surfacing that a strong Europe would go its own way independent of the United States, hence support for a British 'Trojan Horse' role.

Yet assessments of the American-British-European triangle rarely come up with a straight answer. Almost as soon as EFTA came into being it was clear that it could not act as a rival to the Six and when Macmillan, whose other policies had failed, applied to join the Six, membership of the ECM was never a shining collective goal in itself but a means of sustaining British power. As a concept, therefore, it was 'instrumental rather than inspirational'. The European failure to create a united defence force left the Six without any common organisation for defence other than NATO, where they are in a minority and where the US is emphatically the senior partner. Throughout the years 1959–1966 there were growing signs that the United States now regarded the Six as their most important ally in the Cold War, and that if forced to choose between Britain and the Six they would back the Six. In 1960 British policies were not going well. There was the collapse of the Paris summit between de Gaulle and Macmillan and when he visited the US in April 1960 he came under pressure to 'get into Europe'. American policy was now directed at creating a strong Europe, and this meant exerting pressures upon Britain to join. From the first the Americans had been enthusiastic advocates of the European movement. Arguing from the analogy of their own history, they believed that only union would make Europe strong again.[25] Again and again through the 1960s British policy was torn between the special relationship, its world role and Europe. A fillip to British difficulties came following her application to join the EEC in 1961 when the Belgian prime minister Théo Lefèvre said how the smaller EEC states wanted Britain to join to ensure equilibrium in Europe. However, the decade was to witness brutal divisions about Europe in the hierarchy of the Labour Party. At the 1962 Labour Party Conference, Hugh Gaitskell, who had become the leader of the party on Attlee's resignation, gave one of his greatest speeches against joining the EEC. He said that entry might mean the end of Britain as an independent state, 'the end of a thousand years of history'. Harold Wilson, in the chair, expressed delight, declaring Gaitskell's address an historic speech, which should be printed and sent to every member of the party.[26] George Brown, at the same conference, fought 'with all his might' for British membership of the Common Market, hoping to salvage the hopes of those who believed that Britain's destiny lay in Europe. Three years later, on 18 July 1965, Barbara Castle had a meeting with George Brown at which he said: '"We've got to break with America, devalue and go into Europe." "Devalue if you like," Castle retorted, "but I'll fight you on Europe." Brown replied, "But I believe in it passionately. We've got to go somewhere. We can't manage alone. That is what Pompidou said to us: "Devalue as we did and you're in".'[27] In an essay he wrote in 1968, Kissinger said: 'The United States could not expect to perpetuate the accident of Europe's post-war exhaustion into a permanent pattern of international relations. Europe's economic recovery inevitably led to a return to more traditional political pressures. 'A united Europe is likely to insist on a specifically European view of world affairs—which is another way of saying that it will challenge American hegemony in Atlantic policy. This may well be a price worth paying for European unity; but American policy has suffered from an unwillingness to recognise that there is a price to be paid.'[28] In June 1967 Harold Wilson and George Brown went round the capitals of the Six in the second bid to be admitted to the EEC. Wilson's final stop was in Paris where de Gaulle asked him: 'Was it possible for Britain at present—and was Britain willing?—to follow any policy that was really distinct from that of the United States whether in Asia, the Middle East or Europe? This was what France still did not know. The whole situation would be very different if France were genuinely convinced that Britain really was disengaging from the US in all major matters such as defence policy and in areas such as Asia, the Middle East, Africa and Europe.'[29]

Americans tried to balance the special relationship, as they saw it, with the price Britain had to pay in its relations with Europe. Thus, 'The British may have temporarily prided themselves on a special relationship with the Americans leading to special treatment. The price Britain paid was to exclude themselves from the economic dynamism which European integration entailed, locking them into a pattern of relative economic decline which steadily reduced their value to their American partner.'[30] Dean Acheson, backed up by the Pentagon, which saw Britain as strategically indispensable, was prepared to appease Britain's desire to have the financial privileges of European integration without surrendering a scrap of sovereignty or its global role. The US ambassador to Paris (and later to London) David Bruce complained that Britain's assumption of a special relationship with America, and of an exclusive position in Europe, could upset the whole Europe-wide purpose of the Marshall Plan. Many calculations about Britain's role during the years prior to 1970 were made when Britain was not in the ECM while at times it appeared as though she never would be. By 1971 it seemed reasonable to suppose that a regional Europe would be able to exercise both economic and political influence beyond its borders on geographically adjacent areas, beginning with the Mediterranean (a region that was tackled in this way enthusiastically some 35 years later by President Nicolas Sarkozy of France). Meanwhile, the fall of de Gaulle in France opened up real possibilities for Britain, which again applied to join in 1969. At the October 1972 Paris summit there was a particular attempt to improve co-operation in international affairs and the final communiqué expressed the Community's desire to establish its position in world affairs as a distinct entity. Henry Kissinger said 1973 was to be 'The Year of Europe' which it certainly was as far as Britain was concerned when Heath finally took the country into the ECM. Otherwise, it was to be the year of OPEC. By the end of 1973 the newly created and operational European Political Cooperation had shown itself to be entirely unsuited to deal with the problems it faced: the Yom Kippur War and the oil price, and the financial crisis that followed. Europe as an entity fell apart in the face of these explosive issues. The Netherlands had been openly pro-Israel in the 1973 Yom Kippur War and a Belgian diplomat said, revealingly: 'Eight European countries have observed strict neutrality. The ninth has followed public opinion. It is only normal that it should suffer the consequences.' Heath had finally got Britain into Europe to turn the Six into the Nine but only after years in which Britain had made wrong decisions or been thwarted by her European peers. Acheson had not been alone in his judgement that Britain made her great mistake of the post-war period by rejecting the Schuman Plan. Now, with Britain at last inside the EEC, the Americans had to think again. According to Ian Gilmour 'Heath was certainly not anti-American, but his commitment to Europe made him determined not to repeat Macmillan's mistake of appearing to be America's surrogate in Europe. Hence, according to Kissinger, the United States "faced in Heath the curiosity of a more benign British version of de Gaulle." Almost uniquely among recent British Prime Ministers—Conservative or Labour—Heath did not fawn on the White House; sensibly avoiding the phrase "the special relationship", he merely talked of the "natural relationship".'[31] Heath had taken the plunge and Britain at last had become a member of the EEC: joining was one thing, coming to terms with membership and accepting the changes that membership implied was something else. As one commentator put it, not very well: 'And although the long post-script to world power ended with Britain's belated entry into the European Community in the early 1970s it was plain that her political class found it exceptionally hard to adjust to membership.'[32] In his book *The World in 2020*, Hamish McRae poses questions about the future of the EU that reveal how precarious it may turn out to be. A crucial aspect of the growth, stability and influence (power) of the EU will depend upon the absorption of Eastern Europe—the former Soviet sphere—and how the EU deals with Russia. In this respect there is the malign influence of the USA. By pushing NATO to Russia's borders and the EU trying to include Ukraine, Cold War attitudes between the West and Russia have been prolonged. We shall return later to the malign influence of the USA. Europe, following the end of the Cold War, has searched uneasily for a degree of independence from the United States. At least Blair and Chirac obtained Europe-wide approval for creating a military force of 60,000 troops that could be deployed far from home and sustained for up to a year. It was not a full-blooded European defence force but rather a gesture telling the USA that sometimes the EU might act alone. Thatcher had little in common with her European peers and was not happy with Britain's membership of the EU but on one issue—the reunification of Germany—she found herself in agreement with France's President Mitterrand and both of them needed to be reassured by the Americans that all would be well. With the end of the Cold War a new world order began to emerge: that is, one of major states manoeuvring for influence in their regions. The world looks set to divide as follows: the United States, the European Union, Russia, China, India and Japan but there is no separate role for Britain. It can try to maintain the special relationship in which case it will lose any 'punch' it might have and become a satellite of the only superpower or it can 'join' the EU fully and commit itself to making the European experiment work instead of carping from the sidelines.

Mark Leonard, in his book *Why Europe will run the 21st Century*, makes some remarkable claims for the future though whether the EU will rise to them or not remains to be seen. 'After the horror of Bosnia, a new generation of European leaders was determined to back up law with force. This shift in mood paved the way for three new strands in European thinking on the use of force that sought to remedy the defects of European power so cruelly exposed in the early 1990s: humanitarian intervention, a European doctrine of pre-emption and state building.' By intervening in Kosovo, Europeans put military intervention back into a continuum of engagement that spanned diplomatic support, aid, governance assistance and sanctions. They have made an impressive shift in this direction, quietly doubling the numbers of troops posted overseas over the last decade (up to 2005). The average number of European troops deployed outside the EU and NATO areas was 70,000 during 2003 and up to 90,000 with UK troops in Iraq. EU troops were spread over twenty countries: in south-east Europe; in central Asia; the Gulf, and Africa. 'Europe's leaders now realise that the European Union cannot be prosperous if its neighbourhood is a hotbed of war and ethnic violence.' On the economy, Leonard suggests that Europe's strength in the world comes from the collective weight of the European economy rather than the size of its component economies. Germany, France and Britain can negotiate trade with the United States because they are in the European Union. Finally, the European Union is the only way that small countries can have a measure of control over global markets.[33]

The British dilemma over the EU showed little sign of being resolved in 2012 when a substantial segment of the Tory Party was demanding a referendum on whether or not Britain should remain in Europe at all. Part of the problem, as usual, was the United States. As long as Britain has the special relationship to turn to this provides an excuse for not making a real commitment to the EU. At the same time the EU was also facing the need to choose between economic union and political union. It can build out from economic union to political union, a course favoured by Germany. Or it can put political union on hold until the problems of the recession have been brought under control and, instead, build more open relations with the rest of the world. The greater the economic base the easier to move towards political union if that is the favoured path down which the EU would move. Any calculations about the EU's future must take account of Britain, the EU's maverick half member. If Britain were to throw its full weight into the EU, the situation could be transformed. Writing in the mid-1990s, Hamish McCrae argued: 'Britain has three substantial advantages over the rest of Europe: it is ageing less quickly than any other major European country; it has made the structural adjustment out of mid-technology manufacturing industry more quickly than the rest of Europe; and it has closer relationships with both North America and East Asia than its continental partners.'[34] Even when developments clearly favour Britain in Europe, was Eden correct when he said in 1952 that Britain could not join a federal Europe? 'This is something that we know, in our bones, we cannot do.'

American unilateralism became both a feature of US foreign policy and a threat during the presidency of George W. Bush and inevitably impinged upon Europe. Speaking at the Pentagon on Wednesday 22

January 2003, Donald Rumsfeld said: 'You're thinking of Europe as Germany and France. I don't. That's old Europe. If you look at the entire NATO Europe today, the centre of gravity is shifting to the east. Germany has been a problem, and France has been a problem. But you look at vast numbers of other countries in Europe. They're not with France and Germany on this, they're with the United States.'[35] Despite much diplomatic chaos and misunderstanding between the United States and the EU the Franco-German alliance was revitalised in antagonism to the Washington assumption that Europe should go with America and by mid-March 2003 Blair found himself out on a limb. Rumsfeld and the neo-cons preferred to work not through formal alliances such as the EU, and even NATO, which might restrict America's freedom of manoeuvre, but through 'coalitions of the willing'. This meant American dominated and led coalitions, as in both Afghanistan and Iraq. In these circumstances a divided Europe was not to be regretted, as in the past, but was seen as an advantage to Washington in recruiting supportive allies. Despite the special relationship, Washington saw Britain as a European power even if Britain refused to do so. By giving his wholehearted support to Bush's unilateralism Blair had isolated himself in Europe and not met any of the criteria for good membership of the EU as de Gaulle had indicated to Harold Wilson in 1967. One vital lesson that Europe learned from the Bush invasion of Iraq was summed up as follows: 'The wounds inflicted by the Iraqi disagreements run deep, and Europe cannot afford to rip itself apart every time a major international issue arises. One lesson from the Iraq war is that Europeans can have greater influence if they develop a common position before a crisis erupts, as they have done towards Iran.'[36] Yet, even as Europe sought to have its own policy, Blair interpreted the military and political indecisiveness of Europe as reinforcing the case for increased defence co-operation with the United States. There seemed little chance of Blair breaking his close tie-up with Bush's America. He took the line that Britain's value to America lay in its role in Europe and its ability to keep the EU outward-looking and firmly linked to the US on economic and defence matters. Here he is positively adopting the Trojan Horse role and sees nothing wrong in acting as an agent for US interests in Europe even though the result of adopting such a position undermined the possibility of taking a leading role in Europe. Blair constantly claimed he wanted Britain to be at the heart of Europe yet all his actions, apart from rhetoric, suggested that he really wished to be in the US camp. In the last column he wrote before his death in 2003, Hugo Young despairingly reflected on the way Tony Blair's attachment to the 'special relationship' with the United States had led his country into the Iraq war. 'What does this mean?' he asked and answered: 'That we have ceased to be a sovereign nation.'[37]

A YouGov survey, conducted in December 2010 on behalf of the Fabian Society and the Foundation for European Progressive Studies, found first, that almost 45 per cent of those polled thought that Britain's membership of the EU was a bad thing and anti-Brussels feelings were predictably hostile, but it nonetheless saw the role of the EU in a much more favourable light when some of the things it did do were considered. About 71 per cent said EU countries should co-operate more closely on fighting terrorism and international crime; 55 per cent thought member states should work more closely on climate change; and (despite the government and the City) 53 per cent said they should do more to regulate the banks jointly. Further, on core economic issues (the area in which successive governments have tried to prevent national sovereignty being transferred to Brussels) more people took the view that EU member states should work together than not. The subjects that attracted more positive than negative support make interesting reading. Despite generalised antagonism towards the EU, a majority of respondents saw the EU carrying out useful functions and suggested it should do more along the same lines. As Charles Grant, Director of the Centre for European Reform said of the EU that while its institutions such as the European Commission or the Council of Ministers were 'inherently unlovable', 'the British people do appear to realise that one middle-sized European country can actually achieve more in many areas of policy if it acts with its neighbours than if it tries to go it alone.'[38]

Some thoughts about the European Union

The erosion of the nation state 'is most marked in the European Union, which is at the time of writing, trying to dictate to one of its members [Austria] how its own elected government should be composed'. The concept of 'soft power' and its use has developed alongside many attempts by the EU to solve political problems. Will the recession have the long-term effect of teaching the EU to have a more cohesive overall economic structure? Europe has the opportunity to recreate an integrated economy, such as it had before the First World War and again between the wars. Is Europe going back to its roots? Any consideration of the direction Europe is taking at once invokes a discussion of its differences with the United States. Thus, the EU's strategic doctrine is very different from America's. Military force is about building peace, not projecting power. Force may be necessary to defend Europe's values, but it will never be the heart of European foreign policy. 'However, we must recognise that the persistence of different views is a strength rather than a weakness, and that the EU's structure is robust enough to accommodate disagreements of monumental proportions.—The genius of Europe is that it carries on trying. And from every setback it has everyone emerges stronger.'[39] 'With Russia prostrate, the attraction of Europe, along with the promise of the American security guarantee, pulled just about every nation to the east into the western orbit.—The gravitational pull of Europe shaped politics in Ukraine and Georgia, as well as in Turkey.'[40] When the EU expanded to the east and took in former Soviet satellite countries it automatically became embroiled in a geopolitical power confrontation with Russia. This post-Cold War expansion of the EU could be the template for other unions though first, and the answer lies in the future, we have to see whether the huge expansion of the EU will work. Is this EU expansion a foretaste of how the world will be organised during the twenty-first century or is it merely a return to imperial expansions of the past? Samuel P. Huntington predicted that the coalescing of the European Union would be 'the single most important move' in a worldwide reaction against American hegemony and would produce a 'truly multipolar twenty first century. What Europe in its own sometimes messy way has been doing ever since the end of the Cold War and collapse of the Soviet Union is pursue a form of Realpolitik based upon "soft power" that is the antithesis of American perceptions of power and its uses and the gap between the two is widening all the time. The logic of European integration is that Europe should, sooner or later, develop a common foreign policy and a common security policy and, probably, a common defence.' Such a development so that for example, EU forces had the capability of being deployed in other parts of the world as are US forces, would represent a real challenge to the current spread of US hegemony worldwide.[41] Multilateralism—for which the European Union stands and which is in some way inherent in its construction— is more than a refuge for the weak. It embodies at a global level the ideas of democracy and community that all civilised states stand for on the domestic level. But multilateralism, if it is to be effective, needs to be backed by strength, including armed strength. If the European Union cares about the multilateral system, it must do more to support it. The extent to which, already, the members of the EU have mixed their affairs with one another means, even if the Union as such collapses, there can be no return to the Europe of individual states that preceded it. The key to Europe ridding itself of the US incubus lies in its relations with Russia. In the aftermath of the Cold War the EU allowed itself to be used by the United States to put huge pressure upon Russia with the expansion of NATO that ensured a continuation of Cold War attitudes and suspicions. Only the EU can reverse this situation. Britain as was the case after the war when Churchill persistently called for European unity, is again in a position where it can alter the entire US-EU power balance by throwing in its lot with the EU. Britain trades 3.5 times more with the twelve-country Europe (eurozone) than with the United States. Meanwhile, Europe's economic weight across the continent is leading it to ease progressively the political and military power of the United States by, for example, tightly surrounding with its real physical mass the American bases on the periphery of Europe. 'Europe is thus becoming an autonomous power almost in spite of itself. What is worse, from an American perspective, is that Europe stands to annex new spaces on its margins by virtue of their mere contiguity and existence as priority trading partners.'[42] As the 2003 invasion of Iraq forced the US and Europe to define their positions and policies, Pascal Lamy, the European trade commissioner, said: 'Stop pretending that the United States and Europe share a common view of the world, recognise that we have different world views and interests, and then manage our relations.' Or, as Timothy Garton Ash said, 'America has too much power for anyone's good, including its own.' How do you induce the 27 EU members—or even the Big Three—to speak with one voice in international affairs?

14

CAMERON AND OBAMA

BONDING

Writing in the *Financial Times* during October 2009, Phillip Stephens examined the possible impact upon the special relationship should David Cameron emerge as Britain's prime minister in May 2010. Foreign policy's David Rothkopf summarised how the relationship may look: 'US-UK history and culture are such that the relationship will always be different from that we have with other countries. But it seems quite possible that with an unsentimental post-modern president in the White House (Obama) who seems destined to have a chilly partnership with the odds-on favourite to be the next Prime Minister of the UK, the special relationship will be considerably less special in the future than it has been at any time in recent history.'[1] Inevitably speculation by the press and the Foreign Office was to be expected. The binding force that held the special relationship together from the late 1940s to the fall of the Berlin Wall was the Cold War and part of the speculation was whether no Cold War meant the end to the special relationship. Those who worry about the special relationship should understand that its demise would not bring an end to co-operation over security and other matters of mutual concern. Sarcastically, Stephens looks at Blair's determination to stay close to the Americans and be their Top Pal. The big question at this time was whether Cameron as prime minister would behave any differently towards Washington than did his Labour predecessors Blair and Brown.

On his first visit to Washington as British prime minister in July 2010, Cameron was concerned to tell President Barack Obama that he 'deeply regrets the pain' caused by the release of the Lockerbie bomber Abdelbaset al-Megrahi and that it was a 'wrong' decision by the Scottish court. Writing from Washington, David Usborne said: 'Everything has been set to ensure David Cameron gets the biggest bang for his buck during his 48 hours in America: He has a major network interview [ABC News], three hours in the White House, meetings on Capitol Hill with Nancy Pelosi et al, and a brief foray by train to New York City. But in truth, Mr Cameron's going to Washington is never going to bring Main Street America to a stand still.'² Perhaps it could be argued at this stage that British politicians believed (wrongly) that the special relationship made Britain appear to be more important than it was.

In his article in *The Wall Street Journal* Cameron said that relations between Britain and the US were absurdly over-scrutinised, picked over by analysts with a zeal once reserved for decoding the mysteries of the Kremlin. The two countries were bound to have their differences. They were natural and battle-tested allies but—and here he inserts a measure of necessary subservience—Britain was obviously the junior partner. At least Cameron was supported in his more realistic approach to the special relationship by the recommendations of the House of Commons Foreign Affairs Committee, which had concluded the previous March that the phrase 'special relationship' was 'potentially misleading' and 'its use should be avoided'. And as Cameron said, 'I care about the depth of our partnership, not the length of our phone calls.' He argued that the partnership was 'entirely natural'. 'Yes, it always needs care and attention, but it is resilient because it is rooted in strong foundations.' He said he was 'unapologetically pro-America' and 'loved' America and 'what it's done for the world'. There was more gushing praise but the most interesting point he made related to developing economies. He said the US is a global power and is strengthening its ties with the world's rising powers, pointing to his forthcoming visits to Turkey and India as evidence that Britain is doing the same thing. In a world of fast-growing, emerging economies, there was a responsibility to engage more widely and bring new countries to the top table. 'To do so is pro-American and pro-British, because it's the only way we will maintain our influence in a changing world.' Examining the prime minister's *Wall Street Journal* foray, and leaving aside his carefully scripted admiration for the United States, Cameron attempts, dangerously in diplomatic terms, to suggest that Britain is far more influential than it is when he describes Britain's unique relations across the world: 'throughout the Gulf States and with India and Pakistan, not to mention the strong ties with China and our links through the Commonwealth with Africa and Australia'. Is Cameron positioning himself as loyal lieutenant of the United States for the confrontation to come between the two superpowers when China is ready to mount a real challenge to the United States?

Over the years issues of defence and Britain's contribution in troops have been the necessary glue for what has always been an asymmetrical alliance. This became clear in October 2010 when budgetary cuts included a major downsizing of the British military establishment. US Secretary of State Hillary Clinton, attending a NATO conference in Brussels, expressed American fears that the Coalition Government's determination to slash defence spending could threaten NATO's capabilities. Explaining her fears Clinton said a commitment to the common defence was essential. 'NATO has been the most successful alliance for defensive purposes in the history of the world … but it has to be maintained. Each country has to be able to make its appropriate contributions.' (This was an argument that periodically surfaced between the United States and its European allies throughout the years of the Cold War.) Defense Secretary Robert Gates, accompanying Clinton said: 'My worry is that the more our allies cut their capabilities, the more people will look to the United States to cover gaps.' Cameron then sought to reassure the Americans and told General David Petraeus that Britain would stay the course in Afghanistan. The British foreign secretary, William Hague, stressed that Britain would continue to provide a 'flexible, highly deployable force that will remain within the context of NATO, a military power of the first rank.' Meanwhile, major cuts in the British military continued.

Leaked US Embassy cables revealed that Conservative party politicians had promised they would run a 'pro-American regime' and buy more arms from the United States if they won the election. The despatches also revealed how US diplomats in London are amused by Britain's 'paranoid' fears about the special relationship. One (diplomat) said the anxious British attitude 'would often be humorous if it were not so corrosive' and that it was tempting to take advantage of this neurosis to 'make London more willing to respond favourably when pressed for assistance'. The UK was said to offer 'unparalleled' help in promoting America's aims. Promises of support by the incoming Conservatives were apparently spontaneous. Thus Liam Fox, who became defence secretary promised to buy American military equipment while William Hague, in what could be described as a sell-out, offered the ambassador a 'pro-American' government and told him that the entire Conservative leadership were, like him, 'staunchly Atlanticist'.[3] Fox, indeed, asserted that some within the Conservative party were less enthusiastic about the special relationship and took the line that we were partners with, not supplicants to, the United States. But Fox said he rebuffed these assertions and he 'welcomed the ambassador's reassurance that senior US leaders value the UK as an equal partner'. Hague appeared to fall over himself in pledging loyalty, not to Britain, but to the United States. British personnel at the Washington Embassy worried about whether Obama in his inaugural speech would send a signal of approval of the special relationship and were shocked when Obama had the bust of Churchill that had been displayed in the Oval Office sent back to the British Embassy. The US deputy chief of mission in London, Richard Le Baron, said: 'This period of excessive UK speculation about the relationship is more paranoid than usual.' He said, the sting in the tail, 'The UK's commitment of resources—financial, military, diplomatic—in support of US global priorities remains unparalleled; a UK public confident that the USG values those contributions and our relationship, matters to US national security.'[4]

The BP oil spill in the Gulf of Mexico threatened to cause a rift in the special relationship. The *Christian Science Monitor* noted that a 'rhetorical prickliness' had come out of the Obama administration criticism of BP almost as though it was a welcome opportunity to criticise Britain and downplay the special relationship. The repeated use of the term 'British Petroleum', despite the fact that BP does not use it, suggested this. Cameron said he did not want the president's toughness on BP to become a US-UK issue and he noted that the company had a balance of US and UK shareholders. President Obama seemed to soften his attitude when Cameron made his first visit to the United States as prime minister in July 2010 when he said, 'We can never say it enough. The United States and the United Kingdom enjoy a truly special relationship'.—'We celebrate a common heritage. We cherish common values—and above all, our alliance thrives because it advances our common interests.' Cameron responded in kind. Compared with the promises and statements of loyalty made by such obsequious Tories as Liam Fox and William Hague, Cameron appears to be almost cold in his statements about the special relationship yet he managed to mar his statement when he concluded 'we are obviously the junior partner' which was a pity.

As Britain downsized its armed forces, Cameron and Sarkozy of France worked in an unlikely alliance to bring an end to Colonel Gaddafi's rule in Libya. The British prime minister demonstrated his Blairite tendencies when he decided that Britain should act in Libya, even despite Washington's reluctance to become involved: instead, he ought to have been re-appraising his country's role in the world. Ever since the disaster of Suez in 1956 British interventions have been alongside the Americans—Iran, Iraq, Afghanistan—and this perhaps more than anything else has provided the raison d'être for the special relationship. It has also revealed the hollow fact that Britain has no foreign policy of its own except being useful from time to time for the Americans and helping them to spread their hegemon worldwide. During the debate about intervention in Libya, Robert Gates, the US defense secretary, showed his contempt for the British when he pointedly said that creating no fly zones would require American support and the use of more than one aircraft carrier: 'It is a big operation by a big country.' As it happened, just, the British and French managed largely without the Americans.

Traditionally, the Conservatives had always claimed to be the patriotic party concerned with safeguarding the British way of life. The resignation of Liam Fox in October 2011 revealed an American connection with right-wing Tories that was ideologically opposed to accepted party policies. Thus, several senior members of the cabinet were involved in an Anglo-American organisation whose objectives were at odds with the party's environmental commitments and pledge to defend free health care. Fox had had his own charity, Atlantic Bridge, whose purported aim had been to strengthen the 'special relationship' that was wound up in 2010 after an adverse report on its activities by the Charity Commission. According to *The Observer* many of those who sat on the Anglo-American charity's board and its executive council, or were employed on its staff, were lobbyists or lawyers with connections to the defence industry and energy interests. Fox's organisation formed a partnership with an organisation called the American Legislative Exchange Council. This powerful lobbying group received funding from pharmaceutical, weapons and oil interests as well as backing from the Koch Charitable Foundation, whose founder, Charles G. Koch, is a generous donor to the Tea Party movement in the United States. As a connection it was clearly welcomed by the hardcore reactionary members of the Conservative party. As the Liberal Democrat peer Lord Oakeshot said: 'Dr Fox is a spider at the centre of a tangled neocon web. A dubious pattern is emerging of donations through front companies.' While Fox as an individual has the right to hold extreme views and develop links with similar-minded Americans, as a cabinet minister his first loyalty must be to British interests and this was clearly not the case, hence his resignation. Moreover, such ties laid Fox open to massive pressures about military defence procurements.[5]

The war on terror, unsurprisingly, is promoting the practice of secret justice which goes against every principle of the British legal system stretching back to Magna Carta. 'Secret justice looks set to be a regular feature of British courts and tribunals when the intelligence services want to protect their sources of information. Civil courts, immigration panels and even coroner's inquests would go into secret session if the Government rules that hearing evidence in public could be a threat to national security.'[6] These proposed changes were introduced in Parliament in October 2011, following lobbying by the CIA. Binyam Mohamed, a British resident, who was held in Guantanamo Bay for five years, launched a claim for damages from the UK government, which he accused of complicity in torture. The Court of Appeal released a summary of CIA intelligence, which supported Mr Mohamed's claim that British intelligence officers knew about the torture of suspected terrorists. The CIA was furious and halted the flow of information from its headquarters in Langley, Virginia. Faced with angry CIA colleagues in Langley, the British government paid out to sixteen terrorist suspects at a cost of £20 million to prevent further damage to relations with the United States. There are two issues here. The first, will British courts continue to see that justice is done to people who have been mistreated both legally and physically? The second, is Britain to allow the CIA to dictate how the British justice system works—and that, fundamentally, is far more serious.

At the very time that the government was seeking to change the law at the behest of the Americans, the Conservative Eurosceptics were demanding the repatriation of powers from Europe. Furthermore, it was not just the extreme Eurosceptics who sought repatriation. Thus, as in 2011 every department had to draw up cuts, in July 2012 every department was instructed to look at every aspect of European legislation to see where it overlaps with British law.

The changing pattern

In the 1950s, although a reliable NATO ally, 'Britain was becoming much less important to America in the Middle East at the same time that Britain's differences with America were becoming more significant.' The Anglo-American intervention in Iran (to oust Mossadeg) concluded with the Americans as the dominant outside power in the country, as well as with the United States taking a share of the once exclusively British oil concession: post-Suez US primacy in the Middle East became obvious. By 1958—the US intervention in Lebanon and the British in Jordan—it was clear that Britain was a 'very junior partner'.[7] But it still had its—potential—uses. Thus Dean Rusk, Secretary of State to President Johnson, wanted a token British force in Vietnam, 'All we needed was one regiment. The Black Watch would have done.' In 1969, to Louis Heron of *The Times*, he said: 'Well, don't expect us to save you again. They can invade Sussex, and we wouldn't do a damn thing about it.' Once Macmillan and Kennedy were gone, and after the fleeting premiership of Douglas-Home, the special relationship in general was diminished. Wilson got on badly with Johnson and Heath kept Nixon at bay as he went all out for Europe. It only really recovered under Thatcher and Reagan. 'British self-esteem had ever since Suez, except under Edward Heath, been connected to its sense of how valuable it was to the United States.'[8] The reality, which was to become clearer over the years, was that a genuine alliance of unequal powers was not possible. Denis Healey, who in many respects was a clear-headed political operator, seemed like so many of Britain's political elite to be besotted with the American connection. He was to argue: 'Britain's fundamental interest in unity with the United States will remain supreme.' Such an attitude helped bind a once independent Britain to the United States as a 'lieutenant'.[9] An examination of biographies and autobiographies of leading British political figures from 1945 onwards reveals a similarity of views across the political spectrum about the American connection as though they had all attended the same master class on the special relationship.

In the aftermath of Britain's prime minister Tony Blair being described as President George W. Bush's 'poodle', the press at last began to present the Anglo-American alliance in humorous and sometimes derisive terms. Thus, in February 2009, in *The Independent* Leonard Doyle (the US editor) opens his article as follows: 'It was a poignant moment for British diplomats, as they listened to Hillary Clinton sing the praises of her "friend" David Miliband. The two top diplomats gushed over each other, with Mr Miliband declaring he was "delighted" to be meeting with Mrs Clinton exactly three months after Mr Obama was elected, two weeks after his inauguration and one full day after Mrs Clinton was formally sworn in. Whew. Their talks were "detailed, substantive and friendly", Mr Miliband recounted.'[10] Later, Doyle refers to a pre-election confidential assessment by Britain's Ambassador Sir Nigel Sheinwald revealing deep anxieties: Mr Obama was a fence sitter given to 'assiduously balancing pros and cons and he does "betray a highly educated and upper middle-class mindset".' Clearly, getting to know what makes Obama tick was to be a top Foreign Office priority. Americans may laugh at British paranoia in connection with the special relationship but full marks to British diplomats who constantly manage to persuade top Americans to endorse the alliance. Following Miliband's 'substantive' talks with her, Clinton told reporters that the bilateral relationship had 'proven very productive whoever is in the White House, whichever party. This relationship really stands the test of time.' In his turn, Miliband praised the Obama administration's commitment to 'share the burdens and responsibilities' of global leadership—Miliband had made an early dash to Washington in order to beat the French or Germans or anyone else in greeting the new US administration.

In November 2009 the new US Ambassador to Britain, Louis Susman, made his first formal speech to the Pilgrim Society and, as was to be expected spoke of the closeness of the two countries. In particular he referred to the queries that had been raised about the special relationship. He said: 'Over the last few months there has been comment in some circles that the special relationship between our countries has diminished. Anyone who accepts that analysis is wrong and is ignoring the lessons of history. In war and peace, in prosperity and in times of economic hardship, America has no better friend and no more dependable ally than the United Kingdom.' Thus the ambassador set the tone for the Cameron-Obama relationship.

Cameron and Obama: bonding

According to a major story in the *Telegraph* that appeared just after Obama's inauguration, he would play down Britain's importance and cast it as merely 'one of the crowd' of countries with which America has a special relationship. Instead, he intended to move away from tight links with Britain forged under George W. Bush and develop closer links with a far wider range of countries. Foreign Office officials admitted that they felt threatened by Obama's plans 'to flirt with others' and saw that British influence in Washington could wane as Obama looked elsewhere to forge friendships and alliances on the world scene. British diplomats remained hopeful that their close personal links with US officials and Britain's shared interest in rebuilding the global economy and getting to grips with such problems as Afghanistan and Iran would eventually reassert the importance of the special relationship. According to a British official, 'The public line has always been that we are happy for America to flirt with other countries, and it makes sense for Obama to snuggle up to France and Germany. But in truth we are a little bit threatened by that.' This contradictory statement tells us a good deal about British attitudes. On the one hand it is proprietorial—we don't mind if he snuggles up to France and Germany, much as though we own him. On the other hand we feel threatened as our two major European rivals appear likely to move into a relationship more like ours. It was clear from the beginning of his presidency that Obama had no interest in meeting Gordon Brown, already by then a lame prime minister—he could wait until the G20 economic summit in April. A British official said: 'There is a surprising level of disagreement behind closed doors, but there is an understanding that it is kept private. People don't routinely leak it all like the French do.' However, British diplomats in Washington do expect to have Obama's ear as he tries to ease the worldwide economic downturn and thaw relations with Iran and they hope to steer him towards a new international climate change deal by the end of the year. The role of British Ambassador Sir Nigel Sheinwald and his team in establishing links with Obama's team was praised: 'They have a breadth and sophistication of contacts that has left the French and Germans lagging. British officials admit they are sensitive to changes of mood in the special relationship because unlike most other countries, the huge amounts of intelligence and military technology that the UK gets from the US means that staying close to

America is a fundamental goal of foreign policy in itself.' According to one hopeful diplomat, 'With Obama, there's the chance that we can have a relationship more like Thatcher with Reagan. She was not frightened to tell him what she thought. We will be scared to test the love too much, but we will flex a bit more muscle.'[11]

Obama's 'laid back' attitude to the special relationship provided an opportunity, had it been taken, for Britain to break the connection and adopt a more robust and independent policy towards the United States. Instead, the British diplomatic machine went into high gear to ensure that the special relationship should be adopted by the Obama administration. The possibility of changing the government's attitude towards the United States was provided by the Commons Foreign Affairs Committee, which argued in March 2010 that the government needed to be 'less deferential' towards the United States and more willing to say no. While the Committee agreed that the link between the two countries was 'profound and valuable' and the Foreign Office said the two nations shared a 'unique' bond, the Committee nonetheless said that the phrase 'the special relationship' did not reflect the 'modern' Anglo-American relationship. Recognising that British influence had 'diminished' as its economic and military power had waned, the Committee argued that the phrase 'the special relationship' was potentially misleading and 'we recommend that its use should be avoided'. Furthermore, 'The overuse of the phrase by some politicians and many in the media serves simultaneously to de-value its meaning and to raise unrealistic expectations about the benefits the relationship can deliver to the UK.' Tilting at the Blair-Bush relationship, the Committee said: 'The perception that the British government was a subservient 'poodle' to the US administration leading up to the period of the invasion of Iraq and its aftermath is widespread both among the British public and overseas. This perception, whatever its relation to reality, is deeply damaging to the reputation and interests of the UK.' The Committee pointed out that President Obama had taken the same 'pragmatic' attitude towards relations with Britain.

Responding to the Committee's report, a Foreign Office spokeswoman said: 'It doesn't really matter whether someone calls it "the special relationship" or not. What matters is that the UK's relationship with the US is unique, and uniquely important to protecting our national security and promoting our national interest.' Was this the Foreign Office giving notice that thereafter it would refer to the 'unique' relationship?

In May 2011 President Obama and his wife Michelle came to London on a state visit. Obama's popularity in the United States had just been boosted by the successful operation of the Navy Seals to take out and execute Osama bin Laden. The media, true to form, set about discovering how close or otherwise were relations between Obama and Cameron—they were nowhere near the Thatcher-Reagan or Blair-Bush intimacy: rather, Obama's refusal to meet Gordon Brown at the 2009 UN General Assembly had led a senior State Department official to say: 'There's nothing special about Britain.' As the British daily, *The Evening Standard*, pointed out hopefully: 'It is a tradition among American presidents, especially Democratic ones, that they start out feeling the special relationship is an anachronism, then slowly come to appreciate it, particularly when America needs a comrade in arms.'[12] Whatever the expectations, Obama's stay in London was a world away from that of President Bush in 2008. His stay was infinitely more relaxed, spontaneous and simply friendlier and in deference to British sensitivities, he did speak of the special relationship. During his visit Obama stopped short of endorsing the coalition government's big spending cuts but suggested that nations would need the flexibility to change course if their strategy was not working—a clear reference to Chancellor George Osborne's refusal to contemplate a Plan B. He did, however, say that success in pulling the world out of recession was in large part due to the concerted action between the US, UK and other countries. The president insisted that he and Mr Cameron wanted to arrive at the 'same point'—sustainable growth without leaving a mountain of debt to future generations. The discussions were straight-forward and the US did not do what Tory officials had hoped he would before the visit got underway, and that was endorse the policy of cuts then being followed by the British government. A bonus for Cameron was that he was under less pressure than his predecessors to prove that Britain was a willing military ally to the US. *The Independent* summed up the visit: 'This is largely a ceremonial sequence. The real test comes with events. Although they agree about the dangers of imposing democracy from outside, their actions in Libya come close to doing so. And there is a shared reliance on an economic recovery and a sense that only one of them can be right. Playing table tennis and serving hamburgers in a sunny Downing Street is the easy bit. It is too early to judge whether Mr Obama and Mr Cameron will forge a more subtly effective partnership than Mr Bush and Mr Blair did.'

In March 2012, it was Cameron's turn to visit the United States. On the eve of the visit the US ambassador, Louis Susman, speaking in Washington, said Obama 'relies on David Cameron more than any other world leader—and makes his first call in a crisis to Downing Street'. He went on to hail the 'essential relationship' and could hardly have done better had his script been written for him in Whitehall. He went on to describe the relationship between Michelle Obama and Samantha Cameron as 'very, very warm'. Such endorsements of what appears now to be the 'essential relationship' would certainly be welcome in Whitehall but what do they mean in terms of political reality? Afghanistan, Iraq, Libya, Iran, global security and world global economy should all be on the agenda. The visit came at a difficult time as far as Afghanistan was concerned. In an editorial plea, *The Evening Standard* came close to the knuckle when it argued that the United States had to allow Britain some influence in decision-making. 'The British-American relationship is ever in flux and we do not always see eye to eye: the US, for instance, is more favourable to EU integration than Britain is. Yet on most issues, the US can expect the UK to act as a friend, not least in the UN Security Council. But the US must be willing to allow Britain some influence in its decision making where the effect of those decisions affect us all, notably, at present, on Iran.'[13] Just what allowance, if any at all, will Washington extend to London? The essential relationship will be without point unless Britain has room to manoeuvre in its own way rather than acting as a backup for decisions already fashioned and then taken by Washington. Stage management in London for Obama and the next year stage management in Washington for Cameron have certainly helped to project an image of harmony between the two leaders and their countries but what does it mean? 'A truth rarely acknowledged in the recent history of British-US relations is that the care either side lavishes on preparations for a leader's visit tends to be in inverse proportion to the warmth of the relationship. That it is the appearance, rather than the substance, of the Prime Minister's trip to Washington which has been front and central in recent days speaks volumes about the personal distance that remains between Barack Obama and David Cameron.'[14] In America, Cameron said: 'I think the special relationship survives. It's increasingly strong, based on common interests and common values.'

Escaping from the toils of the special relationship will not be easy even for a young politician like Cameron who has always tried to play down the concept and the attendant ballyhoo. Obama was touched by his reception in London in 2011 and clearly wanted to reciprocate but the stage-managed bonhomie is no substitute for the real thing: that consists of hard-headed answers about complex questions—Afghanistan, Syria, Iran and the troublesome extradition treaty between the two countries, and though the two leaders paid lip service to their joint interests in fact their interests will often be apart. From the British point of view the perception of its relations with America is as important as the reality of the joint decisions which the two countries reach, if this is ever true. After the shame-making performance of Blair no British prime minister, ever again, wants to place himself in the position of an American poodle.

15

PROBLEMS

Ending an empire is never easy and may end in blood and tears but finding a new role is endlessly hampered by visions of the past. If the empire has straddled the world the memory of what that meant— showing the flag, peacekeeping, sending gunboats, dictating solutions and, moreover, being expected to do these things because you always had done them and had the power to do them—makes the transition to another role extremely difficult to carry out or bear. When in a lecture at West Point Dean Acheson said Britain had lost an empire and not yet found a role he was perfectly correct, but that did not make what he said acceptable. Indeed, it met with antagonism in Britain because it was true and came too close to the core problem facing Britain at that time and so became the subject of an angry tirade from Macmillan. The British were having a hard enough time finding or trying to find an alternative role and, above all, did not want helpful suggestions from those who would most benefit from the disintegration of the British Empire—the Americans. This brings us to what were British interests, a mixture of pros and cons, at this time. There was across the spectrum of British politics, despite Churchill's rhetoric on the subject, a reluctance to be too close to Europe and a way out of this dilemma without giving overt offence was to argue that Britain's commitment to the special relationship with the United States (as well as its worldwide Commonwealth) made it impossible for Britain to become involved in the federalising activities of Europe. This was not true and later Britain had to find other reasons for her persistent reluctance to recognise that the country was as much a part of Europe as was France. Thus, the special relationship became the excuse for British aloofness with regard to Europe: it saw itself as a sympathetic ally on the sidelines but barred from closer association by its ties to the United States. Moreover, yearning for a continued place in the political sun—Britain had played a leading role in the creation of the United Nations and the Breton Woods financial institutions of the World Bank and IMF—British leaders saw a close alliance with American leaders as a way of maintaining its place at the 'top table', a phrase much used by Douglas-Home. Britain may have been skilful in handing over power to its former colonies but it was still determined to manipulate them as long as it could—it was the period when neo-colonialism became a policy, as Ghana's Kwame Nkrumah quickly recognised.

A crucial question that has rarely been faced is simply: when did the special relationship really coincide with British interests? As a great trading nation Britain had surrendered many of its markets, especially in Latin America, to the United States while Britain itself concentrated on the war. In the post-war world it should have put all its efforts into rejuvenating the economy and recapturing lost markets. It worked very hard at earning dollars but did not match the French or the Germans at rebuilding its industrial base from scratch. Churchill, meanwhile, tried to create a middle role for Britain—mediating between the two new superpowers—but neither the Americans nor the Russians saw any need for this. They could bypass Britain and talk direct to one another. Adopting a form of isolation was also a possibility—splendid isolation had worked under Lord Salisbury at the end of the nineteenth century when Britain was the world's leading power—but was hardly the answer in the late 1940s. In any case Churchill had pre-empted alternative British roles when in 1946 at Fulton, Missouri, he had delivered his 'Iron Curtain' speech that actually put Britain ahead of the United States in formulating a Cold War policy of confrontation with the USSR. Ever since the publication of Adam Smith's *Wealth of Nations* Britain had been the home of modern capitalism and Churchill, the avowed enemy of communism, had led the way in creating a capitalist-communist conflict. The huge baggage of Empire, despite independence for British India in 1947, still needed to be dealt with and by the 1960s the area of concentration was Africa. Decolonisation, the rise of the Commonwealth and issues of racism came together even as Britain was making tentative moves—second thoughts—about joining the ECM. There still appeared to be several possible choices for new policy commitments but none was easy. What Britain needed to do was break the existing pattern and to do this meant coming to terms with the loss of her big power status—and that Britain could not bring itself to do. British political leaders at this time could have done well to remember Palmerston's famous aphorism: Britain has no permanent enemies, nor eternal allies, only its interests are everlasting. Meanwhile, as the United States replaced Britain as the world's leading hegemonic power, the special relationship appeared to fill the role of grooming Britain to become Washington's lieutenant in spreading the US hegemon.

In his book *The Lost Victory* Corelli Barnett went against—even in 1995—the grain of establishment arguments about how Britain should have handled the peace. Inherent in his arguments is distrust of a civil service—Oxbridge—that wanted the comfortable old role that pre-dated the disaster for Britain of the Second World War. He argues that between 1945–51 Britain threw away the opportunity to modernise itself as an industrial country at a time when her rivals—Germany, France, Japan—were still crippled from the war although they were rapidly restructuring their industrial bases. Most important, Barnett claims the root cause of her failure to modernise was the illusion that Britain was and could remain a great world power, one of the Big Three, along with the USA and the USSR. In other words, the problems that Britain faced over these years were temporary difficulties to be overcome rather than a fundamental change of status. At the same time, the Labour government was responding to the promises of a New Jerusalem and the yearning of the British people (post-1945) for the government to eliminate the terrible poverty that existed in 1939 and had been accepted as a necessity during the war but should be no longer. There was a public sense in Britain at this time that after the sacrifices of the war the country now deserved a respite although how that was to be paid for was another matter. The problem in 1945 that would stymie all other programmes was how the cost of introducing the welfare state and maintaining Britain's role as a great power could be paid for from an economy that was bankrupt and a country that was industrially backward. Attlee and his cabinet decided to use both the Keynes Loan and Marshall aid to pay for the New Jerusalem instead of investing it in industry and infrastructure. Rebuilding the economy ought to have been the first consideration after the war. Both Germany and France used Marshall aid to modernise their economies while Britain used it to introduce the welfare state and support its world role as a Great Power.

Attlee and Bevin clearly recognised the fact that British supreme power was passing and they fought hard at every turn to maintain it or at least prolong it. What they failed to do was identify an alternative policy, instead falling back upon the special relationship as though it was an American interest to shore up British power. It was not. Nor did they see that the power shift was permanent and negative as long as they sought US assistance to prop up British power. In June 1952 Churchill's ministers warned of the grave state of the economy. Eden,[1] in his role as foreign secretary, produced a paper on 'British Overseas Obligations' in which he argued that to maintain all existing policies was placing a burden on the country's economy 'which it is beyond the resources of the country to meet'. He then ran through the various geographic areas, such as the Middle East, and argued they could not be cut without Britain sinking to the level of a second-class power. In the longer term, relief would be contingent on setting up international defence organisations. He advised, therefore, that 'Our aim should be to persuade the United States to assume the real burdens in such organisations while retaining for ourselves as much political control—and hence prestige and world influence—as we can.' It was a sleight of hand policy—using US real power to maintain Britain's position. Such a policy would reduce Britain to second power status anyway and the thinking behind the suggestion was itself second class. A few years later, Adenauer's remark that Britain was 'like a rich man, who has lost all his money but does not realise it' aptly captured the essence of the British approach to its waning power.

In his autobiography Denis Healey frequently speaks of his close friends in the United States and makes clear both his admiration for the United States and his willingness to work with it.[2] Later he surrenders to the American political allure: 'I had long since abandoned the idea that Britain might be able to organise a Third Force between the United States and the Soviet Union; this dream was still attractive to the Labour Left. Though it was difficult to live with the Americans, I was convinced it was impossible to live without them. For post-war America, isolationism was no longer an option; if she could not cooperate with allies, she would go it alone.'[3] Here is the birth of the reasoning that lasted through to Tony Blair as prime minister: that if the United States could not co-operate with allies (or rather, that if they would not co-operate with the United States) she would go it alone. This leads to the British justification that it should go with the Americans, right or wrong, to help keep them on the right path. Such thinking would become a weak justification for supporting wrong policies such as Blair supporting Bush's Iraq policy. Timothy Garton Ash in his book *Free World* makes assumptions about Anglo-American and Anglo-EU relations as though they are immutable. He also, by titling his book *Free World* assumes or implies that everyone he does not embrace is not free, which is nonsense. More important still, by writing of the Free World he is creating or adding to a divide that implies his 'non-free' must be enemies.[4] Another Cold War warrior defending the stands of the United States is Chris Patten who tells us that America has been prepared to support the values that have shaped its own liberalism and prosperity with generosity, might and determination. Sometimes this may have been done maladroitly: what is important is that it has always been done. Now the United States has to continue, unthanked, to stand up for these values in Asia—Patten then balances the United States and the EU, but his real target is China. 'Washington will only have spasmodic support from European countries, whose pretensions to a common and honourable global policy are, alas, regularly turned inside out by China's facility at playing off the uninformed greed of one against the unprincipled avarice of another.'[5] According to Patten, the United States is the knight in shining armour, the Europeans are unprincipled and clearly not to be trusted and China is the villain. 'America' he tells us 'is still the only big kid on the block, prepared to accept a global leadership role despite the fact that those who most benefit from it will rarely if ever concede that they have cause for any gratitude.'[6] Patten's eulogising of the Americans ignores the harsher rules of international relations: that there is no gratitude in politics because actions by powers are always self-interested. Patten was writing in the immediate aftermath of Britain, which he represented, handing over Hong Kong to the Beijing government. Prophetically he says that for the indefinite future it will be American military power that provides the guarantee of security for most Asian countries. He was speaking before the American interventions in Afghanistan and Iraq or the policy announced by President Obama in 2012 that the United States would concentrate its military in the Pacific region.

By 1964, following the Cuban crisis and the revamping of the special relationship by Macmillan and Kennedy, it was time to take stock. The advantages of the special relationship were straightforward. It linked Britain to the greatest power in the world and offered the best available protection against possible aggression by the world's other superpower, the USSR. It permitted Britain to decline further in world-power terms in the least painful fashion, standing alongside the United States and taking decisions that would affect the world. In fact, the United States would take the decisions and Britain would endorse them. The United States even encouraged Britain to hold onto imperial outposts in case these could be useful to the United States: the story of BIOT which was turned into a US base emphasised this possibility. The Americans needed it to support their global strategy, Britain no longer did so. The relationship also covered the attractions of sentiment and emotion: the same language, similar institutions, a comparable way of life, adherence to the same basic values. The continuance of the special relationship suited the old Dominions for reasons of security (the ANZUS pact covered Australia and New Zealand) and, in the case of Canada in particular, because of her geographic and political middle position between the two great English-speaking countries. Finally, of possible policies that Britain could pursue, the special relationship was the easiest to embrace. It had developed out of the wartime alliance, it allowed the US to replace Britain as the world's leading power with minimal anguish, and it was dictated by Cold War necessities.

Its disadvantages were different. It tied Britain to American anti-communist policies with all their rigidities: the hardline, massive-arms-build-up, defend 'free world' approach emphasised the creation of a massive western bloc while ignoring the fact that many of the uncommitted countries saw such a grouping as just as threatening as the communist bloc. Inherent in the western free world Atlantic Alliance approach of the rich white nations was the possibility that it would ignore and grow apart from the poor non-white countries of Africa and Asia. Next, it aided US expansion at Britain's expense. It can be argued that this would happen any way but outside the ties of the special relationship Britain could have held some of her independent decisions longer. The increasingly subordinate role that the special relationship offered to Britain went against the national inclination and in the long run threatened to devitalise the country whose politicians and civil servants came to treat making the special relationship work as a policy in itself. The fact that the United States was involved in a major power struggle with Russia led her to exert pressures upon Britain to make it adopt policies that enhanced the American position but not that of Britain or anyone else. Finally, remembering Palmerston's aphorism, the United States would only keep Britain as its special ally as long as it suited her to do so.

Approaching the subject from the British point of view it looks somewhat different. Towards the end of the war the United States became the dominant partner in the alliance and Britain increasingly had to defer to American wishes. This was no more than a recognition of the hard facts of political power. After the peace, in a world where the old order could not be restored, Britain's policy makers realised that the best chance of preserving an international order in which British interests had most chance to flourish lay in the continuance of the American alliance. Once the nature of the communist threat had become apparent it was easy to present the special relationship as the 'necessary alliance'. As the years passed the East-West struggle was redefined as a power struggle rather than an ideological one since there was no possibility that either side would abandon its ideology for that of the other. In any case, this power struggle was complicated by the rise of China and the resurgence of Europe. In these circumstances, allies and satellites became little more than pawns of the two superpowers. The disparity in power between even the strongest ally, such as Britain and the two giants was so great that at most British influence over the United States could only be marginal. In addition, the United States had been constantly increasing its world influence at the expense of Britain. Thus, the question arose: how much longer could Britain afford a policy that placed first an alliance in which her influence was steadily reduced and then replaced by that of her ally while her status as senior lieutenant was gradually whittled away? British dependence upon the United States was seen as inevitable in the immediate postwar world. The fact that during these years Britain was painfully attempting to readjust to a vastly reduced status and was searching for a new national purpose made acceptance of the alliance all the easier. Parallel with a search for a new purpose, there persisted the delusion that much of the old world, so favourable to Britain, could be salvaged. Just as the alliance represented the best chance of prolonging a position in world affairs that had already been lost so all Britain's energy went not into finding a new purpose but rather into finding new ways to maintain her former pre-eminence. Macmillan first used the word 'interdependence' to describe the alliance. Like Churchill he wanted to act as a mediator between the two superpowers but once Kennedy had become president he gave up the attempt. Macmillan's famous analogy of the Greeks and the Romans tells us a great deal about the official state of mind at that time: The clever Greeks whose empire had withered act as mentors to the new giant American Rome. The comparison was dangerous for though it may have been intellectually appealing it was nationally devitalising, reflecting too much the desire to avoid searching for any policy that would require Britain to act alone. The flaw in the Greek-Roman comparison was that in the end Greece became a Roman province and a not very important one at that. In the 1960s British politicians, journalists, lecturers or others were constantly explaining Britain and the Commonwealth to the Americans whose lecture circuits were cluttered with British speakers. *The American Scholar* (Autumn 1961, vol. 30, No. 4) contained an article titled 'An Englishman's Reflections on the Change of Administration', by David Butler, whose opening sentence reads, 'The President of the United States is the President of Britain.' It would be hard to take sycophancy much further. It was time for Britain to rethink its attitude towards an alliance that otherwise would reduce the country to an American cipher.

The special relationship has been central to British foreign policy ever since 1945. If, in a much-changed world, it is to be continued the justifications for doing so will be very different to what they were in the immediate aftermath of the Second World War. If, on the other hand, the special relationship is finally seen to have run its course, what do we put in its place? Why did successive British political leaders always opt for the special relationship and work to enhance it or revive it depending upon its status when they came to power? Why were alternative policies never discussed even when the Americans had acted in a cavalier fashion over British intentions and pretensions? How is it that so many British politicians accepted the special relationship as a 'given' policy without examining alternatives? Perhaps, most intriguing of all, what policies would Britain have pursued had there been no special relationship? The European experiment ought to have occupied a far greater amount of British attention than ever was the case: how much were British attitudes towards Europe affected by the American view (and pressures) as to what Britain ought to have done about Europe? When Acheson said Britain had lost an empire but not yet found a role was he also hinting as a friend of Britain that it was time it went its own way? When Eden's one time foreign secretary Selwyn Lloyd visited the US secretary of state John Foster Dulles on his deathbed Dulles said to him in reference to Suez, 'why ever didn't you go through with it?' Who of British political leaders saw that clinging to the special relationship always meant the whittling away of Britain's capacity for independent action? How many British policy decisions have only been made after first checking upon the American view or position? What, without reference to the special relationship, are British priorities: trade, peace, the Commonwealth; good relations with the Arab world, Europe, Russia and Iran; prevention of a return to a bipolar world; learning to punch at our weight and not trying to punch above it? The biggest question of all is why Britain—backed by an enviable history—cannot break the connection? Who ever of British politicians asks, 'What do we get out of the special relationship?' and how often have governments not followed their instincts in foreign affairs through fear of offending the Americans? To what extent have the Americans encouraged the British to believe in the special relationship in order to use them as a fifth column in an expanding Europe? Despite Macmillan's concept of the British Greeks to the American Romans, yet it was in the end the British who were patronised by the Americans, 'We can always rely on Harold, Jim, Margaret or Tony.'[7] What has been the mesmeric attraction to British leaders that has prevented them from breaking the White House umbilical cord and why have British leaders acceded to the special relationship as though it was an absolute fixture, like the monarchy? Why, when he came to power, did David Cameron push the 'independence of Britain in relation to the United States' and then say, 'of course we are the junior partner'. Do the British like being the junior partner and is it necessary to be partners at all? Why cannot Britain just have good or bad relations, depending upon circumstances, as do France and Germany? When American presidents—Kennedy or Obama—have indicated they want to have better relations with France and Germany (on a par with those with Britain) the Foreign Office has become frantic to prevent what it sees as a catastrophe. Would British leaders not have preferred a British policy as distinct from an American special relationship policy? Every time the United States let Britain down, for example over sharing nuclear know-how, the British ought to have used the occasion to break the US stranglehold on its decisions. Instead, Britain then worked extra hard to appease the Americans with the lure of British reliability as an ally. Is the special relationship in fact a product of British racism—a deep-seated sense that we must maintain a white western alliance? Are the British content to be a base country for the deployment of US power and if so why? We always come back to the same question: what has impelled the British hierarchy to stick so unswervingly to the special relationship despite all American rebuffs? Has it not passed its 'sell-by' date? 'In spite of everything that has been said against it, of all the announcements of its demise, the 'special relationship' between Britain and the United States remains. There are, indeed, misunderstandings; there are those in each country concerned to exacerbate these. But at a profounder level, the word 'foreigner' is never used in Britain of an American.[8] The special relationship has turned Britain into a subservient adjunct of the US imperium.

16

DIFFERENT PERSPECTIVES

The special relationship had become a contentious issue in Washington when Richard Nixon was president although he himself was positive about it. US advocates of European unity, however, saw it as an obstacle and wanted to terminate it. Henry Kissinger, whose influence was paramount at this time, was a defender of the special relationship. Writing in his memoirs in the following decade, he said: 'For the special relationship with Britain was peculiarly impervious to abstract theories. It did not depend on formal arrangements; it derived in part from the memory of Britain's heroic wartime effort; it reflected the common language and culture of two sister peoples. It owed not a little to the superb self-discipline by which Britain had succeeded in maintaining political influence after its physical power had waned.' This description could well have been written by the Foreign Office. Kissinger went on to say that: 'The special relationship was, in effect, a pattern of consultation so matter-of-factly intimate that it became psychologically impossible to ignore British views.' Kissinger's laudatory description of the special relationship is all the more surprising, coming from a man who generally was sparing of praise.

'Above all, they [the British] used effectively an abundance of wisdom and trustworthiness of conduct so exceptional that successive American leaders saw it in their self-interest to obtain British advice before taking major decisions. It was an extraordinary relationship because it rested on no legal claim; it was formalised by no document; it was carried forward by succeeding British governments as if no alternative were conceivable. Britain's influence was great precisely because it never insisted on it; the "special relationship" demonstrated the value of intangibles.'[1]

Prior to the president's trip to Europe in February 1969, Kissinger briefed Nixon: 'My own personal view on this issue is that we do not suffer in the world from such an excess of friends that we should discourage those who feel that they have a special friendship for us. I would think that the answer to the special relationship would be to raise other countries to the same status, rather than to discourage Britain into a less warm relationship with the United States.' On Harold Wilson, he said: 'His emotional ties, like those of most Britons, were across the oceans and not across the Channel in that region which in Britain is significantly called "Europe".'[2] Not all the incumbents of the White House across the years would accept so extravagant a defence of the special relationship.

It should always be remembered and taken into account that it was Britain—before America—that was the cradle of modern capitalism. This point was rammed home by George Soros who claimed that since the election of Ronald Reagan in the United States and Margaret Thatcher in the United Kingdom, market fundamentalism has become the dominant creed in the Western world.[3] Market fundamentalism is destined to play a major role as the world divides again into East and West as seems increasingly likely and here the British role will be of supreme importance. Writing in *The Financial Times* on 3 December 2000, Mark Curtis, tongue in cheek, says: 'The world should be grateful that the most powerful nation in all history wields its military and economic might so benignly.' On the special relationship Curtis argues that its essence is British support for US aggression. This dates back to the end of the Second World War when British planners recognised their role of 'junior' partner in an orbit of power predominantly under American aegis. The junior partner role was adopted by British elites as a way of preserving some 'great power' status and of organising the global economy according to western interests. As Curtis goes on to argue, to begin with the special relationship was often competitive until the US had effectively replaced the British, especially in the Middle East. Later, the Americans came to realise how valuable the British residual imperial presence round the globe was for an extension of Anglo-Saxon influence—that is, US control round the world. The two powers, Britain subordinate, nonetheless wanted the same result: the liberalisation of the world economy to benefit US/UK business. Thatcher was angry at the way the United States ignored Britain or took it for granted as in Grenada in 1983 or the bombing of Libya in 1986 yet in the end she always insisted that Britain should accept the US action and support it because ultimately the special relationship had to be maintained. This policy of supporting the United States even when disagreeing with their actions did not emerge with Thatcher but much earlier under Eden. There is especial irony in the fact that in his memoirs Eden said of US pressures upon Guatemala: 'Anglo-American solidarity was of overriding importance to us and the West as a whole. I believed that even if one did not entirely see eye to eye with the United States government in their treatment of the Guatemalan situation, we had an obligation as their principal ally to go as far as we could to help them.'[4] (Two years later Eden forgot his own advice when he embarked upon his Suez adventure with scant reference to Washington.) The US war in Nicaragua in the 1980s led the World Court to judge that US actions in Nicaragua were illegal but this made no difference to British support. Throughout the US war Britain preferred to maintain what Thatcher called the fundamental alliance between Britain and the United States. Indeed, Thatcher's defending the credibility of the special relationship gave birth to a particular kind of dishonesty. The US bombing of Libya in 1986 was described by Thatcher as an act taken in self-defence. Britain, again, was the only major state to support the American invasion of Panama in 1989. Thatcher's determination to defend any American action did not give rise to any protest by civil servants or the Foreign Office. Subservience reached new depths under Tony Blair almost as though a mechanism to support was triggered every time the United States resorted to some form of violence. Thus, after the US bombing of a pharmaceutical factory on the outskirts of Khartoum, Blair said, 'I strongly support the American action against international terrorists.' The factory manufactured matches. Under Blair, 'The current phase of British soldiers standing shoulder to shoulder with the US military comes when it is crystal clear that our primary ally is in fact the world's greatest outlaw state. Post 9/11 US policy became openly imperial under the cloak of the war on terror. Meanwhile, British leaders continue to steadfastly praise the US for remaining committed to the values it is openly demolishing, indeed continuing to offer unstinting support.'[5] Under Blair Britain was so closely the leading apologist for US foreign policy that the relationship between the two came to resemble that between the former Soviet Union and its satellite republics of Belarus and Ukraine. Continuing his diatribe, Curtis argues that in its major foreign policy, Britain is largely a US client state while its military has become an effective US proxy force. Thus, British forces are not really needed for military purposes. 'Rather, Britain provides a token military commitment, its more useful function being to uphold the pretence of an international coalition, where only the US and its faithful "junior partner" are seriously interested in military action.' As Curtis says, 'Most client states feel bound by their masters; Britain is different in choosing to support US actions or in being willingly subservient. Many of the worst US policies are supported by British elites because the latter agree with the US quite independently, not simply out of loyalty to a special relationship. Those elites acted with complete disregard for moral standards when they ruled the globe so it is hardly surprising that their successors give the same latitude to the US.'[6] Here Curtis has touched upon one of the most important reasons why the special relationship has survived: because a significant proportion of the British governing elite would have behaved in exactly the same way had they been in power.

Sir Nicholas Henderson composed a valedictory despatch for the foreign secretary when he gave up his post as ambassador in Paris in 1979. This was normal practice. He concentrated upon how Britain's standing in the world was due to its economic decline. 'Sir—Since Ernest Bevin made his plea a generation ago for more coal to give weight to his foreign policy, our economic decline has been such as to sap the foundations of our diplomacy. Conversely, I believe that, during the same period, much of our foreign policy has been such as to contribute to that decline. It is to the interaction of these delicts, spanning my time in the Foreign Service, that this valedictory despatch is devoted.' He goes on to compare British economic performance with those of Germany and France.[7] Britain's economic failings contribute a constant background theme to its foreign policy. 'In stark terms, Britain in 1945 no longer had the economic sinews to sustain a world and imperial role abroad while constructing a welfare state at home. This was not a prospect either of the main political parties addressed in 1945. Few in politics or in Whitehall did and when they tried they were shunned.'[8] Hennessy examines the missed opportunities of the years 1959–64 and claims that neither Macmillan nor Home paid sufficient attention to the economy. Macmillan ought to have more than anyone else in the post-war period to that date because at the time of Suez he had turned the tables on Eden on the grounds that UK economic weakness made it impossible to follow through alone without American aid. In other words, Britain's economic difficulties made it impossible for the government to carry out many of its external policies—Britain's economic difficulties undermined the credibility of the government's foreign and defence policies. What seems remarkable in retrospect is that many able public figures drew attention to the failure of successive governments to relate foreign performance to economic performance yet achieved little impact upon the government to which they addressed their fears. Post-1945, both front benches accepted a threefold commitment to full employment, to a welfare state and to the co-existence of large public and private sectors in the economy. 'The notion of a public purpose which is more than the sum of private purposes is apt to seem dangerous or meaningless or both ... The result is an intellectual and moral vacuum at the heart of the political economy. Since the war, at the latest, Britain has had a substantial public sector and a large capacity for public intervention. But because the notion of public purpose is alien to it, her political class has had no philosophy of public intervention or of what might be called the public realm.'[9] As David Marquand says at the end of the 1980s, Britain's 'economic performance has been, on almost any reckoning, the worst in the developed world' and the crux of his argument, 'Britain's inability to adjust to the economic upheavals of the 1970s and 1980s lies in her failure to become a developmental state.' And as Alistair Horne, Macmillan's biographer, points out, 'What nobody, however—neither Macmillan in the 1930s, nor the Labour Utopians in 1945—appreciated just how much the welfare state and nationalisation were going to cost.'[10]

Clive Ponting, a disturbing figure in the background, spent time looking behind the scenes of the British establishment. He points out how close were relations with the Americans in the financial field. 'The Americans were normally consulted before any raising of the Bank Rate. Walter Heller, Chairman of the Council [US] of Economic Advisers, told President Johnson: "in spite of the British secrecy, Jim Callaghan told me last November 7—for your eyes only—what was going to be in their budget a few days later".' Thus the Americans were told details of Callaghan's first budget four days before it was made public and three days before he told the Cabinet. Moreover, Callaghan told the Cabinet that informing them in advance about the budget would be 'subverting the constitution'.[11] In 1968 the US secretary for defense, Mark Clifford, said: 'The British do not have the resources, the backup, or the hardware to deal with any big world problem—they are no longer a powerful ally of ours because they cannot afford the cost of an adequate defence effort.' Part of the British problem was that its successive governments took the economy for granted, maintaining it on worn out machinery and old techniques while Germany, Japan and France rebuilt from scratch and politicians only really paid attention to the economy when a crisis arose. Why was the need for a strong economic base so often overlooked or taken for granted when it wasn't there? Bevin's plea to the coalminers to give him an extra million tons of coal a year and he could have a strong foreign policy said it all. The parlous state of the British economy was at the heart of the country's weakness. Bevin, as a highly popular former trade unionist, made his famous appeal to the coalminers to give him an extra million tons of coal a year to transform the economic outlook. 'You cannot carry out—as I want to do—a completely independent British policy dovetailed in with other people, until we can get out of this economic morass we are in—I should hate to think that we are going to become a sort of financial colony of someone else.'

'Too poor to hang on, but too proud to let go, Britain had clung by its fingertips to the traditional status and commitments of a great imperial power, with its troops and ships stationed around the world. The terrible winter of 1946–47 proved too much, and the commitments had to go.'[12] But they didn't—only Greece and Turkey. In his book *The Stagnant Society* Michael Shanks points out that Butler suggested at one stage during his chancellorship that if all went well Britain might just manage to double her standard of living in twenty-five years. Even if we do manage this—which is by no means certain—it will be a rather modest achievement compared to what many other countries are doing.

As the power disparity between Britain and the United States became more obvious so anti-Americanism became a feature of the British political left. Peter Shore summed it up as follows: 'Defence and foreign policy their hostility to German rearmament and their suspicions of US policy, particularly of the then US Secretary of State, John Foster Dulles, together with an over-optimistic assessment of Soviet intentions and capacities, led them to an increasingly neutralist stance in contrast to the careful, bipartisan, but by no means wholly uncritical pro-Americanism of the party leadership.'[13] This attitude was matched by that of Eden as foreign secretary (1951–55) who in private was distinctly ambivalent about the Americans. As he noted to Lord Salisbury, 'They like to give orders, and if they are not at once obeyed they become huffy. This was their conception of an alliance—of Dulles' anyway.' Resentment at US power was never far beneath the surface during the 1950s and it raised the question of what compulsion was needed to break the US attachment despite all it did to Britain's pride and world and European position. Maintaining the special relationship was the easiest policy for Britain to follow and it could be used to give an illusion of British power that was unreal. It pandered to the inherent British suspicion of Europe and the British determination to remain at the top end of the world power structure. But it also reduced Britain to the status of a US satellite although for a time this could be disguised. Essentially the special relationship emasculated Britain, making it more and more dependent upon decisions taken in Washington. Moreover, it created a habit of Britain checking with Washington as to what policies were acceptable. The sense that only by an alliance with America could Britain play a full part in international affairs turned into a scrabbling determination at all costs to be a faithful ally of the United States so as to persuade it to maintain the charade of a special relationship.

Much more productive from a British point of view, by the new century Britain's major defence and aerospace company BAE Systems had obtained an important foothold in the US defence market. Despite the US fixation upon secrecy in its arms business, this had not prevented BAE expanding its business at speed in the USA to become the seventh largest defence company operating there so that by 2006 the US accounted for 40 per cent of BAE's sales and more than half its 86,000 workforce. In business terms BAE has established a ground floor position for itself in the United States and this gives it a voice in the complex and lucrative US defence business. Possibly the most enduring aspect of British-American co-operation is in the business of collecting and sharing intelligence. This originated during the Second World War in the shared business of code-breaking. This led in 1943 to the BRUSA agreement signed at Bletchley Park. In 1948 there was the anti-communist UK-USA Security Agreement which brought together the SIGINT organisation of the USA, UK, Canada, Australia and New Zealand. The custom has grown so that the head of the CIA station,

London, attends the weekly meetings of the British JIC. The result of such past agreements is the UKUSA Community, comprising the USA's National Security Agency, the UK's Government Communications Headquarters, Australia's Defence Signals Directorate and Canada's Communications Security Establishment collaborating on ECHELON, a global intelligence gathering system (UK-USA members do not spy on each other). This is one area where the Commonwealth 'spread' has clearly been of value to the American global reach. Following the 2006 transatlantic aircraft plot, the CIA began to assist the Security Service (MI5) by using its own agent networks in the British-Pakistani community. Security sources estimate 40 per cent of CIA activity to prevent a terrorist attack in the US involves operations inside the UK. One intelligence official commented on the threat against the United States from British Islamists: 'The fear is that something like this would not just kill people but cause a historic rift between the US and the UK.'

In his book *Colossus* the historian Niall Ferguson repeatedly draws attention to the parallels between the British Empire and the current spread of US hegemony, to such an extent as to suggest that the former imperialism of the British and the current spread of its imperium by the Americans together form an important bond, almost a raison d'être for the special relationship. It is important to the Americans to justify their empire by making comparisons with others. Ferguson does this job for them, a befitting occupation for a British historian. 'As Senator J. William Fulbright observed in 1968, "The British called it the 'white man's burden'. The French called it their 'civilising mission'. Nineteenth-century Americans called it 'manifest destiny'. It is now being called the 'responsibilities of power'." But the resemblances between what the British were attempting to do in 1904 and what the United States is trying to do in 2004 are nevertheless instructive. Like the United States today, Great Britain was very ready to use its naval and military superiority to fight numerous small wars against what we might now call failed states and rogue regimes.—Just as Americans propound the benefits of globalisation—even if not practising what they preach—British statesmen a century ago regarded the spread of free trade and the liberalisation of commodity, labour and capital markets as desirable for the general good.' Today, the Americans take it for granted that they can count on the Brits. None of this, however, answers the question: what is in it for the British? Why, Ferguson asks, did the British prime minister risk his political life for a plan of action against Iraq that was designed in Washington with American needs primarily in mind? In the end the war cost the British a great deal and ensured that they became the third target of Islamist zealots after the United States and Israel. Almost all British prime ministers have succumbed to American pressures when Washington has needed their support. Ferguson paints a dramatic picture of Harold Wilson resisting all pressures from the Americans to send even a token military force to Vietnam. 'Be British,' pleaded one American official when the foreign secretary George Brown went to Washington in January 1968. 'How can you betray us?' Dean Rusk would have settled for 'just one battalion of the Black Watch'. 'When the Russians invade Sussex,' he grumbled when this too was denied, 'don't expect us to come and help you.'[15]

Between Korea (1950) and Suez (1956), Britain's military strengths changed dramatically. In the late 1940s and early 1950s Britain tried to maintain a leadership in Western Europe while simultaneously clinging to the shreds of Empire overseas. In 1950, when forces had to be found to send to the Korean War, Britain had: in Germany—two infantry divisions, an airborne brigade plus seven armoured regiments, an artillery regiment and two infantry battalions; in Austria—one infantry brigade; in Trieste—two infantry battalions and an anti-tank battalion; in the Middle East—one infantry division, three artillery and two armoured regiments; in Malaya—one Gurkha division, one infantry and one Commando brigade; and in Hong Kong—one infantry division, one artillery and one armoured regiment. The RAF maintained 120 squadrons around the globe. The Royal Navy deployed a fleet in the Atlantic, another in the Mediterranean and another in the Indian Ocean. It could still send an aircraft carrier, two cruisers and four escorts to the Korean crisis from the China Station.[16] Prior to the Korean War, Britain's reoccupation of Hong Kong and its hopes of trade with China led her swiftly to recognise Mao's communist government, even though the United States refused to do so. Britain still had a formidable list of resource concerns in the Empire. Tin and rubber in Malaya led to a seven-year guerrilla war and the deployment of more than 30,000 British troops on the peninsula while a range of mineral wealth in South Africa and copper in Northern Rhodesia would dictate British policy in southern Africa for decades to come. Back in 1942 that unrepentant imperialist Leo Amery recorded in his diary a cabinet discussion about what to do with regard to Burma after the war: involve the Americans and the Chinese in an imperial problem.

'This appalling defeatism about our mission in the world horrifies me. The place seems full of people who really think that the solution of everything is to hand it over to the Americans, or the Chinese, or the Russians, or some mixed committee of all of them. I only wish sometimes I were in a free position to say what I think about the Atlantic Charter and all the other tripe which is being talked now, exactly like the tripe talked to please President Wilson—Just before the Cabinet I saw a further telegram from Chiang Kai-shek to Roosevelt urging him to interfere in India; I sped it on its way to Winston with a strong telegram urging Winston to tell Roosevelt to tell the Generalissimo to mind his own business.'[17] Jumping forward half a century, after the Iraq War an article in *The Guardian* stated: 'Britain has now lost its sovereignty to the United States and has become a client state.' Sir Malcolm Rifkind, a typically cautious Tory said in 2003: 'British interests are best served by a close relationship with the United States, but Blair has yet to learn that unqualified endorsement of US policy is a bridge too far.'[18] A little bit of free thinking, then back to the safety of the special relationship.

The Cold War provided the background raison d'être for a close military liaison between the United States and Britain—as it did for the other West European countries—but not necessarily for a wider special relationship. Yet, though in power terms Britain was sliding into a secondary role it had long been the world's leading defender of capitalism and many British Tories were by nature hardline opponents of communism, which made them natural supporters of the American anti-communist paranoia that was a feature of the 1950s (the McCarthy era). Such British attitudes emerged in relation to Britain's only South American colony, British Guiana. In close co-operation with a paranoid America, Britain was to behave in an absurd fashion towards this minor colony after Chedi Jagan, a mild Indian socialist won the 1953 elections. 'For a period of 11 years, two of the oldest democracies in the world, Great Britain and the United States, went to great lengths to prevent a democratically elected leader from occupying his office.'[19] Jagan was the grandson of an Indian indentured labourer who had trained as a dentist in the United States. He had formed the People's Progressive Party, which had won the first pre-independence elections in 1953. Indians formed 46 per cent of the population. Jagan's programme was not revolutionary. It included encouragement of foreign investment in the mining sector and was set to encourage liberal reforms that were generally acceptable anywhere. Only four and a half months after Jagan took office Churchill's government turned him out. This arbitrary act followed a relentless media campaign to dub him a communist orchestrated by the two powers. Britain sent naval and military forces, suspended the constitution and removed the entire government. In London the colonial secretary explained: 'Her Majesty's Government are not prepared to tolerate the setting up of Communist states in the British Commonwealth.' The whole paranoid story is told in detail in *Killing Hope*.[20] Paranoia, hypocrisy, lies, the manufacture of false information, distortion of facts and endless scare tactics became part of the Cold War armoury of the United States—and to a lesser degree—Britain in the early years of the Cold War. In 1990, at a conference in New York (Jagan was present) Arthur Schlesinger publicly apologised for his past role in collaboration with the British in manipulating the constitution to keep Jagan out of power. When in 1994 it was time to declassify the British Guiana documents under the 30-year rule, the State department and the CIA refused to do so because 'it was not worth the embarrassment'. These documents include a direct order from the president to unseat Jagan. This story raises the question of how far the Cold War was used as an excuse to prolong the special relationship. A major problem throughout the Cold War was defence—conventional weapons and nuclear weapons—and the result was a huge drag on the economy, one of the reasons for successive British financial crises. As the Cold War became settled, what choices faced Britain? To act as a US satellite appeared to be the easiest and was chosen as a British policy. Every prime minister from Attlee to Wilson (Attlee, Churchill, Eden, Macmillan, Home, Wilson) appeared transfixed by Cold War threats and this became the dominant theme of foreign policy that affected all other aspects of it. The Cold War allowed the United States to entrench itself in British tactical and strategic thinking: the two countries were allies against the Soviet Union. Churchill, in any case, had sparked the Cold War with his 'Iron Curtain' speech and saw it as a way of keeping the United States committed to Europe with a permanent military presence there. Aware of Britain's weakness, Churchill wanted to ensure that the United States did not retire into isolation again. His dramatic intervention in British Guiana was as much an exercise to please the Americans and demonstrate that Britain was equally as tough on communism as they were, as it was motivated by real fear of what Jagan in power would actually do.

17

THE GROWING AMERICAN IMPERIUM

Professor Philip Zelikow, who was Director for European Security Affairs in the National Security Council in Washington as the Cold War ended, described Britain's special qualifications for a special relationship with the US. 'In part because the British share our values and share our broad goals as to how the world ought to evolve. There are not so many powers that share our fundamental objectives so completely that we can afford to dispense with a crucial power that does.' While the professor was thinking of how to safeguard capitalism, the British diplomat Sir Anthony Parsons pondered about the British-American link: 'In all my dealings with the Americans over many years, particularly in the United Nations, I've always noticed that they very much like to have company in what they are doing.' (Britain was their number one choice.)[1] All US policies, it should be remembered, are aimed at maintaining the US position as the most powerful nation in the world. This is what is to be expected of the leading power but is it a British interest to assist the spread of US world hegemony? According to one analyst, the success or failure of United States foreign economic peace aims depended almost entirely on its ability to win or extract the co-operation of Britain. The growth of the US imperium has been paralleled by the collapse or whittling away of the British Empire. Even prior to 9/11 the US neo-conservatives had fashioned their manifesto, 'Rebuilding America's Defenses'. The document emphasised the extraordinary opportunity the US now had with the collapse of the USSR and called for nothing less than American dominance in every conceivable sphere of life—economic, political, military and cultural—but bemoaned the probability that the plan could not be operational without a 'catalysing event like a new Pearl Harbor'. Then came 9/11.[2] The author (a touch of hubris) goes on to make the point: Of course the so-called civilising mission was always ultimately a lie. The real venture was to take land and resources from others and transfer these to the conquerors, or to open or maintain sources of gain that would deprive the other of self-determination. Over the years as they decried it the Americans were both admirers of the British Empire and envious of it. Their chance to begin replacing the British Empire with the US imperium came in 1940, when a desperate Britain had to begin surrendering its worldwide power in order to buy American support for its war with Germany. As Maynard Keynes said at the end of the war: 'America must not be allowed to pick out the eyes of the British Empire.' But that is what it began to do. Lend Lease, extolled by Churchill, bound the United States and Britain in a de facto alliance and in August 1941, meeting secretly with Churchill aboard a navy vessel in the North Atlantic, Roosevelt gave his blessing to an armed alliance.[3] Although the United States acted as though it was an ally, working with Britain in reordering the world system in the aftermath of the war, in reality it sought to oust Britain from various economically vital areas and replace it with its own presence. This applied in particular to oil. According to a State Department position paper,[4] 'Our petroleum policy is predicated on a mutual recognition of a very extensive joint interest and upon control—of the great bulk of the petroleum resources of the world—US-UK agreement upon the broad, forward-looking pattern of the development and utilization of petroleum resources under the control of the two countries is of the highest strategic and commercial importance.' As Attwood points out: 'The inclusion of the British government in this proposed condominium was quite disingenuous, since American policy all along had been to displace Britain at the top of the system, to remake it on American terms: to ply Rome to Britain's Athens.' In the aftermath of the Second World War Britain discovered how it may have won military victories but was rapidly losing the empire it had sought to preserve.

Although the Americans often derided or scorned the British insistence upon a special relationship, belittling Britain in the process, they still invoked the special relationship when it was useful in support of their policies and the United States was prepared to help Britain when to do so meant drawing it into their political orbit. By 1950 the United States was well set on its path towards world hegemony. The Americans admired the structure and longevity of the British Empire and wished to take over parts that were 'available'. Thus, the Americans flattered Britain with the special relationship but were not prepared to treat it as an ally and equal. The special relationship could be resurrected in Washington when it suited the United States although sometimes this did not work, as for example when President Johnson failed to persuade Wilson to commit troops to Vietnam. On the other hand, as long as President George W. Bush needed Blair to stand with him there was an incentive to accept the myth of a special relationship though doing so did not mean accepting British policy suggestions. It was in the field of defence that Britain was most important to the United States, both as an offshore base and as a worldwide information listening post. Tony Blair, who seemed mesmerised by the mere possibility of linking British defence activities to those of the United States, faced opposition in Britain when it emerged in February 2007 that he had been in secret negotiations with Bush to put anti-ballistic weapons on British soil. He did this moreover just when large demonstrations were planned against the renewal of Britain's Trident nuclear weapons. Negotiations had been to station ten interceptor missiles at US bases in Britain as a fallback option since at the time the United States was having problems persuading Poland and the Czech Republic to allow a missile defensive shield on their territory. The possibility of such missiles being based in Britain had been denied by Downing Street until a Downing Street spokesman said: 'The Prime Minister thinks it is a good idea that we are part of the consideration by the US. We believe that it is an important step towards providing missile defence coverage for Europe, of which we are a part.'[5] Defence coverage of Europe appears to be an afterthought and there is no explanation as to the threat that requires the defensive missiles in the first place. The Labour MP Harry Cohen accused President Bush of using Britain to kick-start a new Cold War to try to achieve US military dominance. He said: 'We will be asking "Whose finger on the trigger?" We know the answer and it won't be ours.' In August 2007 among ministerial announcements before the end of the parliamentary term, the defence secretary, Des Browne, announced that he had given his approval for the RAF Menwith Hill monitoring station in North Yorkshire to be used as part of the US missile defence system. This announcement and the way it was slipped in among other business is typical of the clandestine way British governments make Britain an important part of the US worldwide military system. Unsurprisingly, Russia reacted angrily to the US defensive shield, whether based in Britain or Eastern Europe, and ridiculed the argument that it was designed to deal with rogue states. It is a statement of relations between the United States, Russia and Britain. According to one estimate, as of 2009 there were 909 US bases in forty-six countries and territories and of these fifty-seven were in Britain. The bulk of the US basing system was established during the Second World War, beginning with a deal with Britain for the long-term lease of base facilities in six British colonies in the Caribbean in 1941 in exchange for fifty fairly decrepit US destroyers. Although the United States reduced the worldwide spread of its military after the war this was soon reversed as the Cold War developed. There followed the codification of US military access rights around the world outlined in a comprehensive set of legal documents. These established security alliances with states in Europe (NATO), the Middle East and South Asia (CENTO) and Southeast Asia (SEATO). Also bilateral documents with Japan, Taiwan, South Korea, Australia and New Zealand. The United States has based nuclear weapons in Britain since September 1954. The Lakenheath base is home to the 48th Tactical Fighter Wing of US Air Force in Europe with an estimated 110 B61 nuclear weapons based there. The 1958 Mutual Defence Agreement provides the basis for the extensive nuclear collaboration between the United States and Britain. Since the Second World War and the Berlin Blockade the US has maintained substantial forces in Britain. In July 1948, the first American deployment began with the stationing of B29 bombers. RAF Fylingdales radar facility is part of the US Ballistic Missile Early Warning System.[6]

Threats to the continuance of this apparently fixed military arrangement are likely to increase as the popularity—or at least the public acceptance of the special relationship—is questioned by the British people. The advent to power in the United States of President Obama in 2009, his apparent desire to downgrade the special relationship and the apparent concurrence of the British prime minister, David Cameron, in such a change was brought to a halt when Obama made a state visit to Britain and the Foreign Office worked overtime to resurrect the special relationship, while carefully downplaying the use of the term, did at least suggest a new approach to the alliance on both sides of the Atlantic. Whatever the eventual outcome from this new questioning of the special relationship, the British involvement in the Iraq war at the insistence of Prime Minister Blair did enormous damage to Britain's international standing. By 2012 the concurrence of several parallel developments threatened the long-lasting cosy acceptance of the special relationship. First came the Obama indifference to it as a staple of US foreign policy. Second came a public reappraisal of its value in Britain, assisted by the ambivalent attitude towards it of David Cameron. Third came the question of China and the US attitude towards that country. If there is to be a power confrontation between the United States and China—and the indications multiply that this will happen—where does that leave Britain and the special relationship? On the one hand, the United States will be looking to renew its crumbling alliances with Europe to strengthen its hand in facing China. On the other hand, Obama's announced shift of policy to concentrate US military power in the Pacific-Asia region means removing the confrontation away from Europe so that Britain, should it elect to do so, could adopt a neutral stand to a Pacific confrontation that is removed from its immediate involvement. At this point in time this is no more than a thought but one that could solidify into a policy. America's long-standing European allies of the Cold War era became increasingly dissatisfied with the US policies in the Middle East—Afghanistan, Iraq, Iran and Israel—under the Bush presidency and despite the problems Europe faces in regard to the recession and the Eurozone there are many indications that Europe would like to shed its close policy connections with the United States, a policy shift that would isolate a US-China confrontation in the Pacific. Even before 9/11 and the wars in Afghanistan and Iraq there were distinct signs of a shift in the political outlook in Europe. 'Europeans who had for long been loyal children of a respected paternal power began to suspect this supreme authority of a possibly dangerous lack of responsibility. And though far from complete, there began to emerge the unthinkable—a common international sensibility uniting the French, German, and British people.' German loyalty to the United States was clearly becoming suspect. 'The new hesitancy on the part of America's British ally is no less surprising. The alignment of Great Britain alongside the United States was a fact of nature for American strategic analysts—a congenial condition solidly affirmed in a shared language, temperament and civilisation.'[7]

As the same author adds: 'Only one threat to global stability hangs over the world today—the United States itself, which was once a protector and is now a predator.' Writing in the *New York Times* (9 April 2002), Timothy Garton Ash said, 'America has too much power for anyone's good, including its own.' An increasing number of American writers who specialised in foreign policy were beginning to question American aims and the preponderance of its power, real or imagined. These critics of the American imperium were indicating their concern at America's overweening arrogance (hubris) and sense that its destiny was world control. If comparisons are to be made between the American imperium and the British Empire this is the obvious place to make them. Just as Kipling raised doubts about British self-assurance at the time of Queen Victoria's Diamond Jubilee in 1897, when Britain was at the height of its imperial reach, and the sun never setting on her empire, so Obama has at least raised a query as to the US ability to settle all the world's problems. Once the Cold War had come to an end so too did some of its restrictions with the result that the United States made fewer concessions to international public opinion, paid less deference to allies and believed it had more freedom to act as it saw fit—unilateralism instead of multilateralism. Global public opinion polls suggested a strong international desire for a diminished American role, a move towards greater multipolarity and equality in the international system, in other words a rejection of US unilateralism. Nevertheless a decade after the end of the Cold War the United States remained and clearly intended to remain the dominant strategic force in both East Asia and Europe.[8] The arrival of Barack Obama in the White House appeared at first to herald a change of policy. He deliberately restrained US participation in the Libyan war, leaving France and Britain to act as the West's key players. Then he gave a speech in which he said that the United States could not be expected to solve all the world's problems. However, power politics have a momentum of their own and by 2012 Obama was announcing a shift in emphasis: the United States would concentrate its military resources in the Asia-Pacific region to face China although this was not spelt out in so many words.

British subservience to American views on how the world should be managed run like a thread through her international policies. In his book *Breach of Promise* Clive Ponting,[9] a former civil servant, provides a chapter 'The American Connection' in which he gives a detailed and scathing account of Britain's subservience to America under Harold

Wilson (1964–1970). Areas of Anglo-American collaboration from 1945 onwards were two: intelligence and nuclear weapons. All governments up to Wilson saw these links as of fundamental importance and central to a special relationship. (No one ever appears to have questioned why Britain could not have had those two areas of collaboration without the need for a special relationship) The most important contribution to the relationship forthcoming from Britain was the system, based on the Cheltenham headquarters (GCHQ) of key intelligence stations around the world—such as Cyprus and Hong Kong—that provided information not available to the Americans. 'This information was regarded as of the utmost importance within Whitehall and Britain was prepared to pay a high price to ensure that this information continued to flow from the Americans ... The UK was therefore highly dependent on the United States in two key areas—intelligence and nuclear matters. This dependence, combined with the US dominance of the multilateral framework, set strict limits to the ability of any British government to institute independent policies and reduced the British role to one of junior partner to the Americans. To help disguise this dependence the myth of the "special relationship" was assiduously cultivated.' The US Ambassador in London for most of the 1960s, David Bruce, told the State Department in 1967 that, 'The so-called Anglo-American special relationship is now little more than sentimental terminology.'[10]

Wilson was little short of sycophantic in his pursuit of the special relationship. 'Wilson was in constant touch with the President through the special telecommunications link between No 10 and the White House and he was to make much of his relationship with President Johnson ... Indeed, the overwhelming impression of the first few months of the new government is that it actively sought to increase British dependence on the United States and develop its relationship with the American administration into the central pillar of its policy in the strategic, foreign, defence and economic fields ... In the defence field not only did the Labour government accept all the existing US bases in the UK but it did everything possible to help develop worldwide US capabilities.'[11] Wilson made his first visit to Washington as prime minister in early December 1964. He wanted to establish a close relationship with the US president. Johnson wanted British support in Vietnam. Wilson agreed to provide support backstage but would not commit any troops to the conflict. When the United States made demands upon Britain it was always in relation to matters of defence. In this case what the Americans wanted was a UK presence in Vietnam and they were only prepared to help with the (British) economy, then in crisis, if such help was tied to other political/defence measures such as keeping troops in Singapore. Wilson was not prepared to put British troops in Vietnam but was prepared to provide a number of other support measures. He knew he could not carry the party with him on sending troops to Vietnam. The extent to which policies were geared to fit in with American requirements is astonishing in retrospect and yet no one appears to have challenged the government—'this is not a British policy, it is an American one'. John Stevens, the Treasury representative in Washington, explained: 'Johnson had made it clear to Wilson that the pound was not to be devalued and no drastic action east of Suez was to be undertaken until after the American elections in November. In return the pound would be supported to any extent necessary.'[12] George Brown said Wilson was 'bound personally and irrevocably to President Johnson and had ceased to be a free agent'. Wilson tried to sustain the special relationship but after 1967 it was no longer possible to do so. 'The period from 1964 to 1967 was Britain's last-gasp effort to continue as a world power in both the military and economic spheres. This desire was egged on by a United States eager for help in defending the over-exposed dollar, and its military and diplomatic posture in the Far East. The period after 1967 is one of the British beating retreat—not just from East of Suez but in economic terms too.'[13] At least at this time Wilson and Johnson needed each other; the special relationship was not all one way.

18

BRITISH OPTIONS AND MISSED OPPORTUNITIES

Prerequisites for an independent British policy after the Second World War first required a rejection of the American loan and second a continuation of Bevin's policy of Britain going ahead with its own nuclear weapons programme without seeking US assistance. And then in 1950, the Korean War set the pattern for Britain's role as the faithful lieutenant to the United States. Britain could have kept out of that war and left it to the Americans. Meanwhile in Iran, Mossadeg was taking the first steps that would lead to a major confrontation with Britain and lay the ground for the US to begin whittling away at British power in the Middle East. Then came the Suez Crisis of 1956 and very nearly a total breech between Britain and America. That breech presented the perfect opportunity for Britain to kill off the special relationship and experiment with going it alone. The opportunity was passed by. Instead, Macmillan who had succeeded Eden as prime minister, bent over backwards to resuscitate the special relationship and ensure decades of a deferential satellite role for Britain. Although Wilson refused to commit British troops to Vietnam to propitiate the Americans and got praise for his action, in fact he provided all kinds of help behind the scenes and only held back on deploying troops because he knew the Labour Party would not stand for it. Otherwise, Wilson was mesmerised by the power of the US presidency and claimed a relationship with President Johnson, which was not reciprocated. Only Heath was prepared to break the pattern by taking Britain into Europe yet, having done so, he too supported US activities in Vietnam. Then, over a quarter of a century, first Thatcher and then Blair worked with extraordinary determination to entrench the special relationship as the keystone of Britain's foreign policy and they did so when the opportunities for a new direction were better than they had ever been. At the beginning of the new century the terrorist assault upon the United States—9/11—provided a unique opportunity for Blair to advise his American ally, playing the Greek role but instead, to his eternal shame, he opted for the 'poodle' role.

What became clear over the years was that almost no prime minister or other influential figure gave any serious thought to an alternative to the special relationship that they appeared to accept as a guiding principle. And throughout these years the question of Europe remained in the background to confound other British policies; it offered opportunities that the British always sidestepped. The fifth Marquess of Salisbury, who was a dominant elder statesman in the Tory party after the war, told a cabinet meeting in March 1952, not long after they had returned to power, 'We are not a continental nation but an island power with a Colonial Empire and unique relations with the independent nations of the Commonwealth. Though we might maintain a close association with the continental nations of Europe, we could never merge our interests wholly with theirs. We must be with, but not in, any combination of European powers.'[1] He laid this down like a mantra, which has been automatically adopted by most British politicians ever since. But how did Salisbury view, as an alternative to Europe, a more binding British relationship with the United States? As long as they lasted, the Soviet threat and the Cold War became the principal overt reasons why Britain insisted upon adhering to the special relationship. Despite changing conditions and the end of the Cold War British leaders still behaved as though the special relationship was engraved in stone. In logical terms the end of the Cold War ought to have spelt the end of NATO and also of the special relationship. The fact that it did not do so depended upon the American resolve to use the changing situation to spread its hegemony and the British resolve, like scavenging jackals, to go with them. A major power, such as Britain, should pursue its own policies as far as that is ever possible in the world in which we live but by adhering to the special relationship, indeed, raising it to the level of the top priority in international relations, Britain deprived itself of almost any capacity to act alone since it had to consult with its ally first and then fall into line with whatever Washington had decided to do. Britain needed to break the mould that the special relationship had created, but no leading figure was prepared to take the lead and do so. Another action that demanded attention was an exercise in simple accounting: what could Britain afford to do? Wilson came closest to such an exercise. The 1966 Defence White Paper still assumed a worldwide role for Britain, which Wilson favoured, but two years later when he made the crucial decision to close down the huge Singapore base he was finally acknowledging that such a role was no longer possible. Just as Singapore had represented British imperial power in Asia until its fall to the Japanese in 1942, so in 1968 the closure of the British base signalled the final reality of the end of empire. By the time the Wilson, Heath and Callaghan generation came to power the elite and the establishment had been brainwashed into accepting the special relationship as a necessary part, indeed the necessary part of Britain's foreign policy and they did not see any shame in their subservience to the United States.

It is possible to find many faults with the special relationship but what are the alternatives? We can pinpoint particular occasions when breaking the mould would have been relatively easy—Suez is a prime example, but what then? None of the first four post-war prime ministers examined closely what the reality of a break might have meant. Churchill, it is true, toyed with the idea of Britain becoming a mediator between the two superpowers but abandoned the concept as unrealistic in power terms. He then gave his celebrated speech in which he placed Britain at the centre of three intersecting circles representing, respectively, the Commonwealth and Empire, the Atlantic Alliance and Europe but having done so had no suggestions as to how the three circles should be managed. Macmillan, when he came to power, spent all his energies trying to mend the relationship that Eden had all but destroyed. But each of them, on examination, appeared to have accepted a world in which the Americans were paramount and everyone else had to follow them. President Truman had tried to ignore or over-ride the special relationship over the years 1945–47 and by 1950, five years after the end of the war, Britain should have emulated Truman and branched out on its own. Instead, repeatedly, Britain refused to cut its cloth according to the reality of its strength, hence its recurring financial crises. Thus, while Britain maintained its worldwide bases, France and Germany rebuilt their economies. The same question keeps recurring: why did Attlee and Churchill who both had experienced at first hand the ruthless, hard bargains imposed upon Britain in 1940–41 choose nevertheless to go along with America after the war in a relationship that gradually reduced Britain to satellite status—superior satellite maybe—but satellite all the same?

Three very different characters argued for an independent British role in international affairs to that which adherence to the special relationship ordained it should follow. They are Sir Stephen King-Hall, Enoch Powell and Anthony Nutting who each argued that Britain should break the mould into which its post-war American alliance policy had consigned it. First, Sir Stephen King-Hall: He had a high reputation as a writer and broadcaster, he had founded the King-Hall News-Letter in 1936, he was an acknowledged expert on defence questions and was an independent MP. In 1962, the year of the Cuban Crisis when the Cold War reached its zenith of post-war intensity, he published a book and argued on the dust jacket that 'only by this bold policy can Britain once more become powerful in world affairs and avoid the otherwise inevitable result of becoming more and more an American camp-follower in world power politics'. The front cover of his book reads as follows: '*Power Politics in the Nuclear Age* by Commander Sir Stephen King-Hall in which he expounds a controversial policy for Britain'. In his introduction he writes: 'The recommendation is that Great Britain should, preferably with like-minded nations, but if necessary alone, renounce the use of nuclear energy for military purposes and do so for two reasons. First, because it would make a substantial contribution to the world problem of the nuclear arms race; and secondly, because the adoption of this policy would restore Great Britain to that pre-eminence as a *great* Power which she enjoyed during the 19th century.' As he argues, in a general sense all politics are power politics because the business of politics is concerned with the possession and use of power in different forms. Politics have been defined as the organisation of power. King-Hall pinpoints the core reason for Britain's post-war weakness when he says, 'Our Victorian ancestors were conscious of the fact that it was beyond a nation's capacity to create power based on resources it did not possess.' The special relationship deluded Britain into believing it could create an American power resource that was at Britain's disposal. In fact, British weakness was starkly revealed at the beginning of the Second World War. Driven out of France, the Low Countries and Norway, subsequently she could not liberate Western Europe without American aid while it was inadequate to defend its positions in South East Asia. He asks what was to be the hope for the future. 'Some felt that salvation lay in the fact that the USA had stepped up to the throne. Here at any rate was a Pharoah who did know Joseph and shared most of the British Joseph's spiritual values—even if Pharoah in Washington was at times most unreasonable about colonialism and brash in its foreign policy. This school of thought believed that henceforth we must shelter in the shadow of the American monarch, hoping to stand at his right hand as a trusted counsellor, but not holding the sceptre.'[2] Central to King-Hall's argument is the fact that nuclear weapons are logically unusable. If this be true then the offensive element of the nuclear weapon is operating in the field of psychology and that is where the defence should be sought; and this book shows the true defence against nuclear violence is not to have counter nuclear violence. One of the reasons originally put forward to justify the British independent deterrent was that, since by itself it would be effective, this would enable Britain to hold her own in an argument with the Americans. However, this did not take account of the cost. As one of the senior American technical advisers on defence remarked to the author: 'The defence market is getting too costly for you people to operate.' King-Hall considers the likely consequences should Britain adopt his proposed policy. They would include: the British withdrawal from NATO; a re-appraisal of the Anglo-American alliance; a substantial reduction of conventional armed forces; and the establishment of a prototype international inspection team. Such a policy would require the Americans to remove their bases and missiles from Britain. Further, Britain would have to make clear to the Americans that in no circumstances whatsoever did we wish to be protected by, or in any way associated with, their nuclear capacity.[3]

Enoch Powell was a curious yet brilliant maverick figure in British politics. He hated the Americans—this comes out repeatedly—but not just because of their policies. He believed they were whittling away at British power whenever they could while simultaneously spreading their own worldwide hegemony. 'Powell had not stopped believing that the principal aim of America's foreign policy in the twentieth century had been solely to diminish the power of others, including her nominal allies, to establish herself as the leading world power. Above all, he blamed her for the loss of India.'[4] As his biographer points out, 'Powell was aggrieved that Britain had—while he was a member of Macmillan's government—chosen to adopt a nuclear strategy that depended on America's selling Polaris missiles to her. He felt the strategy was wrong, and the reliance on America wrong too. Powell scornfully derided the notion of a "special relationship" and said it had often been more imaginary than real, a product as much as anything of our own wishful thinking. In Vietnam every American action had received British endorsement, with Britain acting like an "obedient commentator". He quoted Christopher Mayhew's resignation statement [Mayhew had been Navy secretary] over Healy's policy. Mayhew had described Britain "not as a power in our own right, but as an extension of the United States power, not as allies but as auxiliaries of the United States".[5] As in Vietnam so also did Britain support the United States in its arguments with Iran after the 1979 hostage crisis.

Powell became increasingly worried by the developing closeness of Thatcher and Reagan. On 3 March 1981, the House of Commons debated a nuclear deterrent. Powell argued that Britain did not have a nuclear 'independent' deterrent. 'Through NATO Britain was bound in to the nuclear deterrence policy of the United States, and bound thereby to America's "strategy", to its view of the world and to its concept of the politics of the world as a whole.' In a speech in Somerset on 16 September 1983, Powell accused Sir Geoffrey Howe, the new foreign secretary, of 'slavishly' following American policies, notably in the Middle East. The country needed a radical review of foreign policy to avoid the further 'Finlandisation' of Britain in respect of America— where sovereignty was only notional. Powell's constant theme was of Britain's obsessive belief that Britain is necessitated to 'join with American forces' upon demand whatever they are doing and wherever they are doing it.[6] Speaking of Britain's involvement in the 1991 Gulf War, Powell derided the idea that it was to uphold the 'authority of the United Nations'. The exercise (in the Gulf) was to allow the United States to project its new-found power in the defence of something called 'the world' against a moral anti-body known as 'communism'. According to another biographer, Powell had become convinced by the time that he left Cairo in 1943 that the Americans were our chief enemy: that the United States was fundamentally antipathetical to Britain as an imperial power, and committed in a sense by its very nature to the destruction of Britain as an imperial nation.[7] Powell's anti-Americanism was based upon his belief that the Americans were doing all they could to destroy the British Empire or the ties that bound it. He never pays any attention to all the other forces that were at work bringing pressures upon all empires and not just that of Britain. 'They [the Americans] were obsessed with NATO, as they were obsessed with their picture of America leading one half of a divided world.' According to Powell, Britain meekly fell in with American wishes, because 'we believed America had won the war for us—so massive was the input of the United States, so impressive was its effort, that we fell into the vulgar and common error of supposing that the Americans won the war, and therefore that we had to be on the side of America in any further conflict.'[8] When one examines Powell's anti-Americanism it should be judged in relation to the policies and actions taken by the Americans that assisted in weakening British power but also it should be seen in the second perspective of his resentment and anger at the declining power of Britain as the United States rose in its place. For an imperialist like Powell this changing scenario was very hard to take. As shadow defence secretary in the 1966 defence debate, Powell attacked Healey when he said he was, 'finding it rather curious that the Secretary for Defence has to go to the United States twice within three weeks in order to see if it is O.K. before decisions are taken and announced to the House of Commons'.[9] During the 1966 election Powell spoke at Falkirk and during his speech he said he feared there were contingency plans to send British troops to Vietnam. The American Administration have made no secret of desiring this, for reasons which are understandable from their point of view—he was attacking the Labour party record in office—and Powell concluded: 'Under the Labour government in the last eighteen months, Britain has behaved perfectly recognisably, as an American satellite.'[10] Powell repeatedly expressed his distress and anger at the way in which the United States was replacing British power round the world and in this respect he was an old-fashioned imperialist regretting the passing of empire. Apart from this, he wanted Britain to be strong and saw the United States as an enemy to that desire as it spread its hegemony round the world. Against this background, what he objected to most strongly was the way various British governments, some of which he served if only briefly, kowtowed to Washington and behaved as though the American Administration of the day had a right to oversee British policy making while successive British governments accepted without any apparent reservations some form of satellite status to America.

Anthony Nutting, a rising Tory politician whose interest was foreign affairs, was Parliamentary Under-Secretary of State for foreign affairs (1951–4) then Minister of State for foreign affairs (1954–6). He resigned from Eden's government over Suez. In 1960 his book, *Europe will not Wait* was published. Lord Boothby said of it: 'By far the best account of the failure of British leadership in Europe since the Second World War.' Nutting's first target is the special relationship. Apart from old prejudices, 'there existed also among the top echelons of the Government and their advisers an obsessive determination to preserve the Anglo-American Alliance as something exclusive. This school of thought feared that the closer we got to Europe, the more we should have to share America with Europe.'[11] When America moved away from the special relationship—for whatever reason—Britain worked desperately to get the US back into line. The obsession with the special relationship was partly a hangover from the war. As the European countries built their new, post-war futures Whitehall felt no need to associate them with the special relationship. 'Rather did it intensify the feeling that at all costs we must keep America to ourselves.' The American loan was the defining factor in the immediate post-war period. The terms 'made Great Britain even more dependent on America than she had become by the end of six exhausting years of war'. Apart from the financial provisions of the loan—which were unexceptionable—the obligations relating to commercial policy involved acceptance of free convertibility of sterling within a year and a promise to consider favourably the elimination of all our trade preferences. Nutting continues: 'Inevitably this dependence upon the United States in the immediate post-war years meant that the errors of judgement and the shortcomings of American foreign policy were reflected and repeated in the foreign policy of Great Britain.'[12]

What historically is most interesting about the immediate post-war period is that Britain (or more accurately Churchill) took the lead in organising the West to challenge the USSR in the Cold War. Until the March 1947 financial crisis that led Attlee to request Truman to undertake financial support for Greece and Turkey which led him to enunciate the Truman Doctrine, the United States had persisted in its belief in the Roosevelt myth of one world of international brotherhood, enshrined in the concept of the United Nations. When Churchill tried to rouse the Americans against the Russian menace with his Fulton, Missouri 'Iron Curtain' speech, Truman declined to make any comment, Dean Acheson pointedly excused himself from a dinner for Churchill in New York while Henry Wallace, US Secretary for Commerce, attacked the idea of 'getting tough with Russia' and warned against letting 'British balance-of-power manipulations determine whether and when America gets into war'.[13] Shortly thereafter there was to be a dramatic shift of American policy with the launch of the Marshall Plan and Churchill could not complain that his warnings conveyed in his 'Iron Curtain' speech had been ignored. The unintended consequence was that the United States eventually deployed its forces so thoroughly as to make the spread of American hegemony the mainspring of US policy and that included replacing British power with American power, which was not Churchill's intention at all.

Once Marshall aid had been applied to Europe as a whole Britain was bound to pay greater attention to what happened in continental Europe. Churchill had described Britain as 'geographically and historically a part of Europe—as having to play her full part as a member of the European family'. These immensely encouraging words were read with Churchill's earlier statement at Zurich in 1946 that 'the sovereign remedy' was to 'build a kind of United States of Europe'. Later, when Churchill made his speech in which he placed Britain at the centre of three inter-linking circles, it was clear that he was moving away from his earlier enthusiasm for a united Europe. The foreign secretary, Ernest Bevin, who in 1946 had insisted that Britain had its own bomb with the 'bloody union jack' on top of it, now became much more comfortable with the American Alliance as he saw the impact of Marshall aid upon Europe. A former under-secretary at the Foreign Office said of Bevin, 'he had constantly to fight off the assaults of the pathologically anti-American colleagues such as Aneurin Bevan who wanted above all things to detach Great Britain from the United States'.

Nutting was a passionate advocate of the European dream of unity but this was not promoted by Macmillan. In 1957 Britain withdrew from the Messina negotiations and in 1958 the Europe of 'The Six' came into being and Macmillan set about undermining it, first with his proposal of a free trade area, then with the formation of the EFTA or 'Outer Seven', and finally, admitting defeat, when he applied to join the Six in 1961. Nutting encapsulates the British reluctance (deviousness) over Europe as follows: 'The British proposal of a Free Trade Area suggested in paragraph after paragraph that what Great Britain was proposing was an alternative and not a supplement to the arrangements of the Six. Needless to say, this aroused all the old Continental suspicions that we were out to sabotage their plans for a merger of their resources by attempting to substitute a Free Trade Area for industrial goods which would benefit us in place of a Common Market which might threaten us.'[14] As he says later: 'When we could have led the European Community, we were content to observe, misguidedly believing that it would never work. Now [1960] that we want to get with it, we are told to stay outside. When we refused the leadership of Europe, we did not think we were letting down our friends. But they did, and now they have found both the will and the means to go it alone without us.' Although later Britain did join the European Community, this was the beginning of a long history of British half-heartedness over Europe. Nutting had the temerity to suggest that Britain should combine/share its nuclear know-how with France and Germany for Europe. Europe will win in the end: because it is there; because British history has always been intertwined with that of Europe; because it is our major trading partner; because the special relationship makes less and less sense as a policy; because the EU uses soft power; and because at the heart of the EU Britain would make a bigger impact than in any other situation.

19

THE UNITED STATES

A TURNING POINT?

Following the Anglo-American exercise to overthrow Mosadegh (1953), 'Washington encouraged Muslim fundamentalists as a presumed antidote to communism for the next four decades. It also encouraged the weakening of British power in the region and the rise of American influence—and oil interests—in the Middle East.'[1] Capitalism in crisis coincided with the end of the American century. It is the nature of international power politics that the dominant power of any age, sooner or later, will be challenged. From 1945 to 2000 the United States was the dominant power and though for a time it had been challenged by the Soviet Union, that challenge collapsed with the end of the Cold War and the United States sighed with triumph as its neo-conservatives plotted a new world order dominated by the United States. They had forgotten China. The extraordinary rise of China as a new economic power took off with the new century even as President George W. Bush was busy pushing NATO to Russia's borders, erecting a provocative defence screen in Poland and the Czech Republic, and as a consequence ensuring that post-Cold War Russia continued as an enemy of the West. Meanwhile, reversing the work of four decades in which it had encouraged Islamic fundamentalism including its support for the Taliban in Afghanistan, the United States targeted the Islamic world as its current enemy. This however was less than satisfactory, a messy process that without gaining any rewards had created chaos from Israel to Pakistan although it allowed the United States to target Iran as a core enemy. In the background, however, China rose to challenge US world hegemony. China possesses all the attributes that are necessary for superpower status. What to do with American power? 'A large part of the United States' problem, whether Republicans or Democrats are in power, is that it believes it has the right and obligation to intervene everywhere, in whatever form it chooses, and that its interests are global.'[2] Given the instability that the collapse of the Cold War order has left and the American fear that its predominant position is not only being challenged but also undermined, we are now entering a profoundly dangerous period in the world's history. Challenges to American power, sooner or later, meet retribution. Because it has preponderant military power the United States persuades itself that it can define political and moral behaviour for the rest of the world. In 1945 a triumphant United States established the United Nations, which for a time it treated as its preferred ally, while it saw the Western World as its sphere of influence so that its leadership began to speak of the American Century. The nineteenth century had belonged to Britain, the old enemy of the Thirteen Colonies, and this fact added spice to the new American hegemony, which in part at least was due to the downsizing of Britain.

When Barack Obama won the presidential election in 2008 many people, both inside America and beyond, allowed themselves to be deluded by his speeches and liberal airs into believing that there would be a fundamental change in US foreign policy. They were soon disabused as he demonstrated his determination to stand up to China. First, he demanded that China revalue its currency upwards by 20–25 per cent, or face a loss of patience by the international community. 'Loss of patience', in this context refers to American patience. Obama was speaking at the November 2011 APEC summit of Asia-Pacific powers held in Hawaii and his speech was seen as another increase in anti-China rhetoric. He followed this with proposals for a free trade bloc that would include the United States, Canada, Mexico, Japan and Australia but not China. Second, he announced on a fleeting visit to Australia that the United States was to station thousands of marines at a base in Darwin, northern Australia. This announcement was seen as a response to China's increasing belligerence in the Pacific. The marine task force would eventually consist of 2,500 men. This is the first time since the Second World War and the Japanese threat that the United States has deployed troops in Australia. China responded to the announcement by questioning whether it was 'in the interest of countries within this region' to intensify military alliances. Western analysts saw the move as a strategic US shift away from the Middle East and the war on terror to the Asia/Pacific region where China is now challenging US predominance, which it has maintained ever since 1945. Sidestepping questions as to whether the new security deal, as the marines were referred to, was a move to contain China, Obama said, ambiguously, that Beijing had to accept the responsibilities that came with being a world power, and 'play by the rules of the road', a statement that, if analysed, opened up huge questions about American behaviour. At a news conference in Canberra, Obama said: 'The notion that we fear China is mistaken. The notion that we are looking to exclude China is mistaken. We welcome a rising, peaceful China.'[3] His two decisions—to base US troops in Australia and to foster a regional free trade area that pointedly excluded China—belied his claims. This visit to Asia by the American president clearly signalled a change of emphasis in US world strategy. The signs were multiplying that the coming US 'war' would be with 'rising' China rather than either Islam or the war on terror.

The heavyweight US political figure Zbigniew Brezinski, formerly National Security Advisor to President Jimmy Carter, published a brief book in 2012—*Strategic Vision: America and the Crisis of Global Power*—which could well prove a blueprint for US policy in the coming decades. He describes the region west of China through to Egypt as having the greatest potential for violent upheaval. He poses the American problem in the following terms: 'How the American system performs at home, and how America conducts itself abroad will determine the place and role of the West in the new objective and subjective global context. Both issues are wide open today, and ultimately their constructive resolution is America's current and unique historical responsibility. Only by demonstrating the capacity for a superior performance of its social system can America restore its historical momentum, especially in the face of a China that is increasingly attractive to the third world.'[4] He examines the European allies of the United States: 'Great Britain seeking to manipulate a balance with the EU while continuing to preserve a special relationship with a declining United States.' He 'writes off' Europe (enmeshed in its recession and Eurozone crisis): 'The EU thus faces potential irrelevance as a model for other regions. Too rich to be relevant to the world's poor, it attracts immigration but cannot encourage imitation. Too passive regarding international security, it lacks the influence needed, to discourage America from pursuing policies that have intensified global cleavages, especially with the world of Islam. Too self-satisfied, it acts as if its central political goal is to become the world's most comfortable retirement home. Too set in its ways, it fears multicultural diversity. With one half of the geopolitical West thus disengaged from active participation in ensuring global geopolitical stability at a time when the world's new pecking order of power lacks coherence and a shared vision of the future, global turmoil and a rise in political extremism could become the West's unintended legacy ... Paradoxically, that makes the self-revitalisation of America more crucial than ever.'[5] Brezinski is perhaps a little too hard upon the EU, but aside from that he has scripted the perfect justification for US unilateral action wherever it judges the world needs it. Reform, yes, but don't change the system. He quotes President Bill Clinton on 20 January 1997: 'At the dawn of the 21st century—America stands alone as the world's indispensable nation,' and President George W. Bush on 28 August 2000: 'Our nation is chosen by God [but not Allah] and commissioned by history to be a model for the world.' A last quote from this *Strategic Vision* is a piece of Orwellian double-speak if ever there was one: 'to generate Chinese understanding that America's Pacific Ocean strategy is not meant to contain China but rather to engage it in a larger web of cooperative relationships.'

The point of the special relationship was to enhance British influence and power and if it did not achieve these ends there seems little point in it. Constantly using British power through the special relationship to support American policies made the United States stronger but it did not make Britain stronger. On the contrary, it drained Britain of the self-respect that is the essence of successful power. When a crisis arose or a new policy was put forward by Washington the world no longer asked where Britain stood on the issue because it was assumed that it would automatically echo and endorse the Americans so that it ceased to be a factor. When Bush determined to attack Iraq and sought allies it was assumed rightly that Britain would support the United States. France and Germany refused and were dubbed 'old Europe' by Donald Rumsfeld. Had Britain used its initiative as an independent country and joined with old Europe the combination of the three most power-ful European countries might just have led Bush to pause but even had he gone ahead unilaterally Britain could have held her head up and claimed to have done her best to prevent what turned into a disaster. The Tory MP Ian Gilmour makes a nice power parallel: 'Yet the gap between American and British power that Churchill had noted in 1945 widened to a gulf in the post-war years. If Britain was still one of the Big Three, she was at most, as one official wrote, "Lepidus in the tri-umvirate with Mark Antony and Augustus". Only if she was joined with Europe could she have become the equivalent of Mark Antony. That was in fact what the United States wanted, but Britain preferred to be Lepidus on her own. She was happier being a subsidiary partner, or rather a satellite of the United States.'[6]

The concept of quiescent allies, as Robert Cooper points out, suits the Americans very well. 'If America is not imperial in the usual sense it is certainly hegemonic: it does not want to rule, but it does aim to control foreign policy. The hegemony is essentially voluntary, part of a bargain in which America provides protection and allies offer bases and support. From an American point of view, countries can choose to be allies or they can be irrelevant, in which case they can be left alone. If they begin to be a threat then they become, potentially at least, a tar-get.'[7] Was the mesmeric attraction of remaining a great power the key to the insistence by the British political elite upon maintaining the American alliance, which they turned into the special relationship? Churchill, Eden and Macmillan (as well as Attlee) had each been at the centre of British power during the war and found it impossible to relin-quish the illusion of power that the special relationship provided. Only Attlee of these leaders was fundamentally determined to improve the lot of the British people by the introduction of a comprehensive social programme. Churchill, Eden and Macmillan loved foreign affairs as opposed to the more mundane home problems because in foreign affairs they were wielding power. Macmillan's biographer Alistair Horne claimed that his subject revelled in foreign affairs and the part Britain could play.

The Bush doctrine, first enunciated in the president's speech at West Point in June 2002 and then incorporated in the national security strat-egy in September 2002, is built on two pillars: First, the United States will do everything in its power to maintain its unquestioned military supremacy and, second, the United States arrogates (to itself) the right to pre-emptive action.[8] The same author wrote that the neocons 'regard the American model of national success as superior to all others and want the rest of the world to benefit from it. That is the origin of the quaint idea that we can introduce democracy to a country like Iraq by military force.' Surveys conducted in November 2002 revealed that fully one-third of all Britons viewed George Bush as a greater threat to world peace than Saddam Hussein. George Soros, best known for his financial manipulations, produced a short but effective polemic about American politics—*The Bubble of American Supremacy*—in which he examined the proponents of a 'New American Century' and saw the world as a struggle for survival and believed that the United States, having proved itself the fittest, had both the right and duty to impose its will on the world. If neocons really believe this they indeed represent a danger to the rest of the world for this principle of the 'right' of the fittest could have come straight out of the mouth of Hitler. Soros argues that the United States cannot do anything it wants, as it discovered in Iraq. But, little can be done in the way of international co-operation without American leadership or participation. Others can concern themselves with the well being of the world. 'Their attitude is not without consequence, but it is the United States that sets the agenda for the world, other countries have to respond to whatever policies the United States pursues.'[9] This brings us back to the special relationship. Britain could respond robustly to the policies the United States advances, it does not have to accept them without question. It does seem that under Obama the United States has at least accepted that it cannot solve the world's problems on its own even though it has downgraded action through the United Nations. The abuse of power worldwide by the United States was easy to pinpoint when George W. Bush was president and supported by his two hardline lieutenants, Dick Cheney and Donald Rumsfeld. Their attitude towards the rest of the world was one of contempt. Under them crude abuse of prisoners at Guantanamo Bay was paraded openly to do heavy damage to America's image with Bush being described outside America as the world's No. 1 terrorist. When Obama won the 2008 election, change was expected. He had committed himself to closing Guantanamo Bay and ending torture but had not done so by 2012 and this failure raised the question of how different the foreign policy of the two presidents was in reality. Obama clearly wanted to impress Americans that he would be, and was, tough on foreigners and one way to do this was to continue and increase the drone attacks upon al-Qaeda targets in Pakistan. In August 2012 the UN special rapporteur on human rights and counter-terrorism, Ben Emmerson QC, demanded that the US allow independent investigation over its use of unmanned drones or the UN would step in. Between 282 and 585 civilians had died in Pakistan as a result of their use. Pakistan's US ambassador Sherry Rehman said the drone war 'radicalises foot soldiers, tribes and entire villages in our region: Their use is armed aggression, pure and simple.' Whereas there had been fifty-two drone strikes in Pakistan during the eight years of Bush's presidency, there had been 280 over three and a half years of Obama's presidency. Former US President Jimmy Carter described drone attacks as a 'widespread abuse of human rights' which 'abets our enemies and alienates our friends'. Despite public condemnation of despotic regimes and claims to support human rights, in 2010 the United States concluded the biggest ever arms deal worth $60 billion with Saudi Arabia, seen as one of the most despotic regimes in the Gulf. These examples suggest that the rhetoric is not matched by the actions that are undertaken. On the contrary, unilateralist, hegemonic decisions that bypass the principles which the United States espouses, are as much a part of the Obama administration as they were of his predecessor's. Obama, it seems, had become a prisoner of the Pentagon and State Department in pursuing policies that extend the American hegemon and treat with contempt people who—unintended consequences—get in the way. American international policies are shaped round its military might.

'American military supremacy over the rest of the world is now as great as that exercised by the European powers collectively a century ago. It provides the unchallengeable basis for a new world order.' The US owes its primacy not only to size and resources, but to its readiness to accept and adequately reward scientists, technologists, engineers and entrepreneurs from throughout the world and turn them into Americans.[10] Britain, with its messy immigration policies, could learn from this.

In his book *False Dawn*, John Gray examines the delusions of global capitalism: 'In China, Malaysia and Singapore, in Egypt, Algeria and Iran, in post-communist Russia and parts of the Balkans, in Turkey and India, the end of the Cold War has released powerful political movements which reject all westernising ideologies. The future of this [twentieth century] oldest westernising regime, that of Attaturkist Turkey is uncertain, as Islamist movements arise within it to challenge its secular, westward-leaning institutions.'—'The re-emergence of ethnicity, territory and religion as deciding forces in war and politics makes a mockery of any diplomacy which rests on Enlightenment ideas of *homo economicus* and a universal civilisation.'[11] Gray recognised the basic ideological switch that was taking place and would under-mine and destroy the paramountcy of more than two centuries of Western dominance—despite the efforts of the Bush presidency and the aspirations of the neocons for American dominance. Such a changed world will open up many new avenues for diplomatic activity by medium or small powers. Such a change will be especially threatening to American interests and Washington may well see that a full-scale confrontation with China could be used as an instrument to rebuild old alliances to meet the threat of a new superpower. Old capitalism will be on trial as and when the United States and China begin to clash effectively. 'The dogma that free markets are the most effective means of wealth creation touches the world's actually existing capitalisms at virtually no point. In the world's most successful emerging economies modernisation has not meant adopting American-style free markets. It has meant continuous state intervention on a large scale.'[12] Social and other changes inside America will have a profound impact upon its external policies. Thus, by 2050 non-Hispanic whites will have declined from 73.1 per cent of the population in 1996 to 52.8 per cent. Why should we expect a population in which Americans of European descent are approaching a minority to accept European control and political traditions? In terms of the world system that has prevailed since 1945 all the major powers are having to reassess their positions: 'Any attempt to impose one's own will or values upon others or to unify the world (US hegemony) under a certain model of "civilisation" will definitely fail.—No one economic system is good for all countries. Each must follow its own path as China does.'[13] That represented an early warning from the awakening superpower. American policy mak-ers and politicians do not consider they are viewed from outside. In the case of Britain, its insistence upon being the indispensable ally of the United States has done its wider political standing enormous damage. We are now approaching the point when Britain must ask itself how much longer it is going to assist—or allow itself to be used—to spread American hegemony worldwide. When Britain was at the apex of its power in 1898, the prime minister Lord Salisbury's secre-tary of state George Hamilton, wrote in a memo: 'We are, I am afraid, universally detested.'

20

HOW TO RELATE TO THE BIG POWER LINE-UP

In the years 1900 to 1914 the Great Powers of Europe—Great Britain, France, Germany, Russia and the Austro-Hungarian Empire—manoeuvred themselves into inescapable blind alleys that could only end in war. During the Cold War the world divided into three: the 'free' West, the Communist bloc and the Non-Aligned. Today there is every indication that the world is splintering into a line-up comparable to that which ended in the First World War: the United States, China, Japan, India, Russia and the European Union. The participants may have changed but chessboard manoeuvres remain the same. Britain—half in and half out of the EU, slavishly addicted to the special relationship as a US satellite—could become an important middle-ranking power whose influence would be considerably greater than at present as long as it maintained its freedom of action.

Any attempt to map out a new foreign policy for Britain should take as its starting point that there is no special relationship to fall back upon. In other words, what could and should Britain do if acting on its own. Too often, almost de rigueur, the press carry a story (24 August 2012) such as the following: 'David Cameron joined Barack Obama yesterday in warning the Syrian regime that any use of chemical weapons would be "unacceptable" and hinted that it could prompt western military intervention.' Would Cameron have warned Syria of possible British action had the Americans not been involved? Or, to make the point even more plainly, would Prime Minister Blair, as a matter of

217

principle, have gone to war with Saddam Hussein's Iraq in 2003 if the United States had not been concerned to do so? If Britain is to escape the everlasting role of US satellite, always confirming that it will take the policy direction that Washington lays down, what alternative policies might it pursue and why should it pursue them? What policy, for example, ought Britain to pursue in relation to China, Japan, India, Russia, the EU, Israel and Iran?

Let us start with China. Any debate about China must begin by considering its present power and projections about its future. As Chinese officials asked at the time of Tiananmen Square and have continued to ask: 'What right does the US government have to—flagrantly interfere in China's internal affairs?'[1] The right, if there is such a right, is derived entirely from US power. As China emerges as the real challenge to US world hegemony so Britain should distance itself from giving slavish support to the United States and make plain its determination not to encourage a US confrontation with China for as this becomes more and more likely so will Washington work to draw former Cold War allies into a new alliance aimed at China. If, as seems almost certain, the United States adopts a policy of confrontation with the rising super power it should be left to do so on its own. This will not be easy. Writing in 1998, one year after the handover of Hong Kong to China, Chris Patten, the last British Governor, said: 'In short, the Chinese government may still be able to terrify its own people when necessary, but I see no reason why the rest of us should wake up in a sino-sweat in the middle of the night.'[2] A curious valedictory remark to make: half arrogant imperialist, half admission that the world must come to terms with the new power. His tone is both condemnatory and threatening and as such ignores reality. In the decade and a half since he wrote those words Chinese power, and still more its influence, have grown so that what it now does acts as a pervasive influence in half the world. Patten gives the impression that he is gearing up to take part (with the US) in a future confrontation. In 1997 US President Bill Clinton and China's Jiang Zemin declared that they wanted to build a strategic partnership and, assuming this meant more than summit rhetoric, where did it leave Japan, hitherto the principal ally of the United States in the region? China is all too well aware that the continuation of the Communist Party in control of China depends upon two policies: the pursuit of strong economic growth; and the assertion of Chinese power in Asia and the world. The huge expansion of China's trade has been founded on low labour costs as well as an under-valued currency but how long can these advantages last? China is the linchpin of trade in the Asia-Pacific region and accounts for 60 per cent of growth in regional trade over the past twenty years.[3] In order to impose itself as Asia's undisputed leader, China must supersede Japan as the dominant regional power and at the same time undermine American influence. In 1995 China formed the Shanghai Cooperation Organisation (SCO) with its permanent headquarters in Beijing. The SCO's other members were Russia, Kazakhstan, Kyrgyzstan, Uzbekistan and Tajikistan. Its aim is to encourage closer economic and strategic co-operation. China provides development assistance to the Central Asian members and hopes to lessen the influence of Islam in the region. It sees the SCO as a rampart against the expansion of US influence.

Mistrust between China and Japan has a long history while the aims of the two countries are incompatible. China aims at supremacy in Asia and Japan will not accept satellite status in relation to China. Until mid-2010 Japan was the world's second economy in size but that year it was pushed down into third place by China. Although apparently a close ally of the United States, with huge US bases on its soil, it will from now on exert itself as a great power and, it should be remembered, as an Asian great power and not a western country. Japan must wonder where it would stand if, for example, there were to be a truly dangerous confrontation between the United States and China because the latter unilaterally had invaded Taiwan. With US bases on its soil, would Japan become involved in such a confrontation whether it wanted to do so or not? While China concentrates upon replacing Japan as the top Asian power, Japan can rely upon another fifteen years of being ahead of China in terms of industrial efficiency and technological innovation—but certainly not more. Despite its economic weight, Japan is derided as a political pygmy and that must change if it is to stand up to China. Japan's economic growth must be subject to demographic factors. Its population is shrinking and if this is to be reversed Japan will have to offer huge incentives to the younger generation to increase the size of their families. It will also have to rethink—and alter—its attitude to immigration. Non-Japanese incomers account for only 1.6 per cent of the population. The Japanese population, in any case, is ageing at an alarming rate: the proportion of older people rose from 7 per cent in 1970 to 23 per cent in 2008. By 2030 the reduction of the working population will be 13 million fewer.[4]

The third Asian contender is India. Like Russia, Brazil and China (the other three BRICs), India has suddenly emerged as a major economy and increasingly as a world player that must be taken into account. India's strategic needs, like those of Japan, require a rapprochement between the two countries in the face of China's formidable rise. Even though well behind China in development terms, India has potentially massive economic potential, a young population, a long-working democratic tradition, formidable military resources—including substantial nuclear capacity—and is already regarded as a long-term counterweight to China. Like Japan it fears the formation of an Asia dominated by the one power—China. A number of geopolitical factors ought to draw India and Japan closer together into some form of strategic alliance but such speculations should be treated with caution. Similar arguments about German power led to the system of alliances and ententes that preceded the outbreak of war in 1914. Both India and Japan want permanent seats on the UN Security Council and think these are overdue as recognition of their Big Power status. Both Japan and the United States would like to foster India as a counterweight to China and India, which has its own agenda, should be wary of such ambitions on its behalf. In 2006 Japan proposed the creation of a vast Asia-Pacific free trade area. President Obama hijacked the idea and put it forward during the 2012 APEC summit in Hawaii but neither Japan nor the United States wanted China to be part of the free trade area, which was like having a European Union without Germany.

In a sweeping survey of Russia, Robert Kagan draws attention to its strategic position between China in the Far East and the European Union in the West.[5] Russia is a great power and its ability to act closely with Europe where energy is the key, or China through the SCO will ensure it has strategic weight in two main theatres of power and diplomacy. It is instructive to note that of the leading EU countries Britain has had more strained relations with Russia than any other EU country, almost as though it wished to maintain a continuation of the Cold War while the United States pushed NATO to Russia's borders. Between 1998 and 2006, the overall size of the Russian economy increased by more than 50 per cent, real income increased by 65 per cent and poverty rates were cut in half. Meanwhile, Russian businesses were buying up strategic assets across Europe, especially in the energy sectors. EU reliance upon Russian energy became greater than upon that of the Middle East. Russia remains a major military power. It has

16,000 nuclear warheads, an army of one million soldiers and is developing new jet fighters, new submarines and new aircraft carriers. Meanwhile, it has resumed long-range strategic bomber flights for the first time since the end of the Cold War. Russian military power has to be seen as an integral part of its foreign policy. It was fighting a war in Chechnya parallel with the Americans in Iraq, it has troops in Georgia and Moldova, and is the leading supplier of advanced weaponry to China. The Russians deeply resented the post-Cold War settlement as nothing more than a surrender imposed by the United States and Europe at a time of Russian weakness. What the Russians yearn for are the days when Russia is respected as a major power that is capable of influencing the world and that has certainly been a principal objective of Vladimir Putin. Russia's relations with the EU require careful handling both ways. When Poland joined the EU it brought into the Union a long history of enmity and suspicion of Russia and this was also the case with regard to the three Baltic states so that there is a great deal of baggage from the past that needs to be handled with care if the EU-Russian relationship is to improve. Russia is now the world's largest oil producer, pumping about 10 million barrels of oil a day, slightly more than Saudi Arabia. Of this, Russia exports 7 million barrels a day, mostly to Europe and Asia. 'Rising prices are a boon for every oil producer. But Russia has a particular advantage: the ability to direct more or less of its oil either eastwards or westward, to Europe and Asia. Also, the grade of Russia's main export oil, Ural Blend crude, is similar to Iran's and has already been in greater demand as an alternative to Iranian oil for European refineries.'[6] Russia's extensive pipeline network gives it enviable flexibility to direct its oil to wherever demand—and prices—are highest.

East Asia's international trade accounts for 26 per cent of world trade; NAFTA's for 16 per cent; while Europe accounts for 39 per cent. The EU controls huge wealth and has remarkable development potential for the future yet all through 2011 and into 2012 it has been in deep crisis triggered by the collapse of the Greek economy. Recession, greed, mismanagement and the threat of a Eurozone collapse have deprived the EU of any effective voice in world affairs and reduced it to seeking loans from China. This state of affairs has been a Godsend to British Eurosceptics and will continue to be so until the EU has overcome its problems. Britain, never a full participant in Europe's affairs but always on the sidelines has yet indicated a desire to have some form of special relationship with the EU. What it has chosen, ironically, is a military tie-up with France. The irony resides in the fact that a military choice is the one area that would spell danger to the United States. Prime Minister Blair and French President Chirac discussed the creation of an Anglo-French strike force. Economic stringency persuaded Britain's prime minister Cameron and French President Nicolas Sarkozy to build close military ties. At the beginning of November 2010 the French president arrived in London to sign two military treaties that covered a deal on the testing of nuclear warheads, the creation of a new Anglo-French 10,000 strong rapid reaction force, coordinating aircraft carriers so that a British or a French vessel is always available. French jets could fly from the UK carrier and vice versa. This last clause caused a rumpus. Cameron was warned by a senior Tory MP not to rely on a French aircraft carrier to defend Britain's interests. Liam Fox, the defence secretary said, 'We have the ability entirely to defend the Falklands.' What was at stake was the fact that Britain only had one aircraft carrier and the 'coordinating aircraft carriers' was an economy measure made necessary by financial constraints on the military. This Anglo-French problem illustrated the fact that France and Britain are two medium powers with global ambitions, but less than global budgets to support them. As a British general pointed out, 'The French and British armies are more similar in the way they go about things than they are to the Americans.'[7] Aircraft carriers underscored the fact that European unity—and not just that of Britain and France—would be required if the EU was to make the impression on international affairs that its leading members would like to see.

Israel is at the centre of half the confrontations that make the Middle East so dangerously volatile. Early in 2005, two years after the coalition invasion of Iraq, Tony Blair, with an election coming up, was trying desperately to produce some momentum on the Middle East question. He wanted a return from Bush after his 'shoulder to shoulder' support for the President's Iraq policy but as an EU diplomat put it, 'Blair has got nothing back for Iraq.' According to one of Blair's aides, 'Bush was never against having a go in the Middle East in principle; he was against failing. He felt he only had one shot at it.' This was an extraordinary excuse for inaction, one that could be used to put off any action indefinitely. A year later, in July 2006, the Hizbollah's rockets into northern Israel sparked a 34-day war in which massive Israeli bombardment of southern Lebanon failed to destroy the

Hizbollah and revealed major military weakness of the Israeli Defence Forces (IDF). In the House of Commons there were angry claims from both Labour and opposition benches that the government had given diplomatic cover to continued Israeli bombing by failing to call for an immediate ceasefire. Labour MPs attacked the government for its stance on Israeli attacks and Clare Short warned that 'massive killing of innocent Lebanese civilians and destruction of infrastructure' amounted to a war crime. Chris Mullin, a former Foreign Office minister said: 'Is it not just a tiny bit shameful that although we rightly condemn Hizbollah for what they have done, we can find nothing stronger than the word regret to describe the slaughter and misery and mayhem that Israel has unleashed on a fragile country like Lebanon.' The UN secretary-general Kofi Annan had called for an immediate ceasefire but this was delayed because neither the United States nor Britain would support it in the Security Council. Sir Menzies Campbell, the Liberal Democrat leader, said: 'Both myself and others have repeatedly asked for the Prime Minister to support an even-handed response. We all accept that the Hizbollah should be condemned. Tony Blair must now accept that Israel's actions are disproportionate and amount to collective punishment. There should be an immediate ceasefire.' By not agreeing to an immediate ceasefire the US administration (with Blair in full support) wanted to give Israel more time to destroy the Hizbollah which, despite these US tactics, it failed to do. Chris Mullen accused the US and British governments of standing by while the Israelis committed war crimes. An interesting comment on US and EU attitudes came as follows: 'Europeans do not understand why America refuses to resolve the Israeli-Palestinian question since it clearly has the power to do so. They are beginning to wonder if Washington might in fact be content to have a perpetual hot spot in the Middle East and to have Muslim countries express a growing hostility to the Western world.'[8]

Historically the state of Israel has always relied upon military superiority over its neighbours and would be enemies and like the ancient Spartans it came to believe it was invincible. The July 2006 war against the Hizbollah came as a major shock because it destroyed the myth of invincibility. As Israel discovered the Hizbollah were able to inflict immense damage on it and not be destroyed themselves.

Both Britain and the United States must bear responsibility for the state of Israel. The British, following the 1917 Balfour Declaration, created and took the Palestine Mandate in the carve-up of the Ottoman Empire and many pro-Zionist British politicians, including Churchill, saw a Jewish State as a means of consolidating British power in the Arab world. The Americans, on the other hand, under President Franklin D. Roosevelt between 1933 and 1945 allowed very few Jews to enter the United States and only became engaged with the Jewish question under President Harry S. Truman who exerted powerful pressures upon Britain to allow the emergence of the State of Israel. Thereafter the Americans behaved towards Israel in the way it had been suggested Britain wanted—the Jewish state as an instrument of British local power and influence. Thus, 'Nor will there ever be an administration in Washington ready to do diplomatically what none has ever dared do since 1947, namely compel Israel to make an equitable peace with the Arabs.'[9] The 34-day war in Lebanon, starting 12 July 2006, was a disastrous turning point for Israel. 'There are many reasons why the Israelis lost the war in Lebanon, but there is general agreement within Israel that the war ended in disaster and the deterrent value of the once unbeatable IDF has been gravely diminished in the entire Arab world for the first time since 1947.'[10] The American, and therefore the British policies towards Israel are likely to be determined by the way the Americans continue asymmetrically to pressure Iran over its nuclear programme while ignoring Israel's possession of eighty or more nuclear warheads.

The United States and Russia agreed a new nuclear arms treaty in April 2010 to be followed by a summit of forty world leaders in Washington DC on combating the threat of nuclear terrorism. The review said the United States would forswear the use of nuclear weapons against non-nuclear countries, which was a clear break from the policy of the Bush administration but made exceptions of countries not in full compliance with the Non-Proliferation Treaty, a statement that was aimed at Iran and North Korea. As US Defense Secretary Robert Gates pointed out: 'All options are on the table when it comes to countries in that category.' The United States accepted that the biggest nuclear threat to America came from rogue states and terrorist groups rather than established nuclear powers such as China or Russia. At the time of this conference the Obama administration was seeking tougher sanctions against Iran, which it saw as public enemy No. 1 in terms of rogue states with nuclear weapons ambitions. The Israeli prime minister, Benyamin Netanyahu did not attend the security summit in Washington because of his then poor relations with Obama, because of Israel's continued settlements expansion in East Jerusalem and also because he feared the conference would draw attention to Israel's undeclared nuclear arsenal of anything from eighty to 200 nuclear warheads. Both Turkey and Egypt want to ask why Israel will not subscribe to the 1970 Nuclear Non-Proliferation Treaty; both countries were leading a campaign for the Middle East to be declared a nuclear-free zone by the United Nations. They oppose the West's double standards in relation to Israel and its nuclear weapons while the entire Arab world is angry with the West for turning a blind eye to Israel's status as an undeclared nuclear power.

In November 2011 Israel was again threatening an attack upon Iran's nuclear plants even as it tested a long-range ballistic missile believed to be capable of reaching Iran. The Israeli defence minister, Ehud Barak, described the missile as an 'impressive technological achievement' and went on to claim: 'The successful experiment proves again that the engineers, technicians and staff of the Israeli defence industries are of the highest level.'[11] There were divisions in the Israeli cabinet as to the wisdom of any strike against Iran. Such a strike was a matter of public debate and, for example, though it was widely believed that such a strike would lead to wars on two fronts—in Gaza and Lebanon—public opinion was evenly divided as to whether or not such a strike should be launched. Discussion between Britain and Israel over Iran intensified with the visit to Tel Aviv of the British chief of defence staff General Sir David Richards. The Israeli defence minister Ehud Barak visited London where he was expected to meet Philip Hammond, the defence secretary and William Hague the foreign secretary. There are regular meetings between the British and Israeli defence chiefs. The NATO secretary–general Anders Fogh Rasmussen said they were in favour of diplomatic means to resolve the dispute with Iran. He added (possibly a veiled warning to Washington): 'Let me stress that NATO has no intention whatsoever to intervene in Iran, and NATO is not engaged as an alliance in the Iran question.' Half the Iran 'threat' has been created by persistent statements by Israel that it is 'threatened' though as yet Iran has no nuclear weapons; and partly because Israel keeps the tension high by public statements that it is about to take punitive action. 'The reality is that Iran's acquisition of nuclear weapons is seen as a threat for reasons partly of Israel's own making—foremost its absolute reliance on a policy of military supremacy and deterrence to underpin security. A nuclear-armed Iran would hole that policy below the waterline.'[12] Both China and Russia have been lukewarm about sanctions against Iran, in the case of China because it takes a large proportion of its imported oil from Iran and also has a great deal invested in the country. A Chinese foreign ministry spokesman said China was 'firmly opposed' to any use of force against Iran to prevent it acquiring an atomic weapon. 'China always holds that the Iranian nuclear issue should be properly solved through dialogue and cooperation.' A report by the International Atomic Energy Authority provided 'credible evidence' of Iran's pursuit of nuclear weapons. Israel's response to the report was to call on the international community to halt Iran's 'pursuit of nuclear weapons'. The Iran question has gone round a well-worn circuit of escalating tensions: Israeli threats to 'take out' Iran's nuclear plants; attempts by the United States to control Israel; the threat to increase sanctions; the opposition to any coercive action by China and Russia; a cooling-off period; then new Israeli threats of action, and the wheel revolves yet again. President Ahmadinejad, meanwhile, has perfected his brinkmanship. Commenting on the possibility of using force against Iran, Sir Malcolm Rifkind, Chair of the Commons Intelligence and Security Committee said a military strike 'might be the least bad option'. He said: 'There's a question of whether it is desirable and the answer is, well, you can't rule it out, but it would have to be at the very, very end of the day because of all the horrendous implications of military action.' He said: 'I don't think Obama wants to do it, I think it's the last thing Obama wants to do.'[13] Obama may not want to do it but in an election year Obama must not seem to be 'soft' on Iran and must be ready to assist America's special ally Israel. In any case, there is no guarantee that air strikes alone would be successful. To be certain the West would have to invade and occupy Iran. Bush's invasion of Iraq has left Iran as the dominant regional power. The Republicans say they would go to war rather than let Iran get nuclear weapons. Why is Iran seen as such a menace while India, which has not signed up to the Non-Proliferation Treaty, is now being wooed by the United States as a strategic partner to offset the growth of Chinese power; and Pakistan, which is one of the most unstable countries in the world, is not deemed to be a menace? Despite American military power, 'Iran will always exist in the region and the Gulf States must live with it. They increasingly want to and wish the United States would cease trying to change reality.'[14] Has the United States ever forgiven Iran for the 1979 seizure of American hostages? Never relaxing his pressures upon the West, but really upon the United States, Netanyahu said in early September 2012, that Iran's 'brutal regime' was rushing to a nuclear programme because it did not see a 'clear red line from the international community. And it doesn't see the necessary resolve and determination from the international community.' Perhaps, despite Netanyahu, the international community is quite right and should leave Iran to resolve its own position in the world.

21

NATO

NATO is a system of collective defence whereby member states agree mutual defence in response to an attack by an external party and that, in effect, meant the USSR. By 2012 NATO had twenty-eight members across North America and Europe. The last two countries to join—Albania and Croatia—did so in 2009. An additional twenty-two countries participate in NATO's Partnership for Peace and another fifteen are involved in institutionalised dialogue programmes. The combined spending on their military establishments by all NATO members is equivalent to 70 per cent of the world's defence spending. NATO came into being in April 1949 as the Cold War began to dominate international strategic thinking and it created an integrated structure in the latter half of 1950 after the Korean War had begun. In response to the Western creation of NATO the Soviet Union formed the Warsaw Pact of communist countries that included Hungary, Czechoslovakia, Poland, Bulgaria, Romania, Albania and East Germany in 1955 (although the USSR had suggested in 1954 that it should join NATO to preserve the peace in Europe, a proposal that the West rejected). NATO's first secretary-general, the British soldier Lord Ismay, famously claimed that the objective of NATO was 'to keep the Russians out, the Americans in, and the Germans down'. However, despite 'keeping the Germans down', on 9 May 1955 West Germany was incorporated in the Alliance which needed its additional manpower. The formation of the Warsaw Pact came a week later on 14 May. A recurring dilemma for NATO was the tension between the United States and Europe: the Americans urged their European partners to increase their defence budgets and deploy more troops on the 'frontline' facing the Soviet Union while the Europeans did not wish to be dominated by the United States. In 1966 France under de Gaulle withdrew from the NATO structure. In 1989 the Berlin Wall was pulled down as a prelude to the end of the Cold War. The years 1989–1992 represented one of those rare occasions when political courage could have changed the course of history. This could have been achieved by the immediate termination of NATO as a military alliance aimed at the USSR. The opportunity was not taken. Instead the United States saw the end of the Cold War offered the opportunity to spread US hegemonic power and entrench itself in Europe while NATO embarked upon a twenty-year period in which it sought justifications to remain in being. Between 1999 and 2004 several former Warsaw Pact countries joined NATO while the 9/11 terrorist attacks upon the United States led to the only occasion in NATO's history when Article 5 (that an attack upon one member should be treated as an attack upon them all) was invoked, leading to NATO participation in the war in Afghanistan.

On 4 April 1949 NATO was signed into being in Washington by the original twelve founder members: Britain, France, the Netherlands, Belgium and Luxembourg (which were already members of the Treaty of Brussels) plus the United States, Canada, Portugal, Italy, Norway, Denmark and Iceland. The fundamental principle of NATO was simple: that an attack either in North America or Europe upon one member was to be treated as an attack on every member. An alliance of NATO's size—Greece and Turkey joined in 1952, West Germany in 1955 to bring membership up to fifteen—was bound to face internal squabbles. A crisis came in 1958 after de Gaulle had come to power in France. He protested that the United States exercised too much control and objected to what he saw as the special relationship between Britain and the United States. On 17 September 1958 he sent a memorandum to President Eisenhower and Prime Minister Macmillan in which he suggested the creation of a tripartite directorate of NATO that would put France on an equal footing with the United States and Britain. The United States and Britain did not respond favourably to de Gaulle and so he set about creating an independent French defence force. De Gaulle wanted to give France—should East Germany backed by the USSR invade West Germany—the option of making a separate peace with the Eastern bloc instead of being drawn into a larger, NATO-Warsaw Pact war. (How France would have been able to keep out of such a war was another matter.) In February 1959 France withdrew its Mediterranean fleet from NATO command. Subsequently, he banned the stationing of foreign (US) nuclear weapons on French soil. The United States then transferred 200 military aircraft out of France and returned air bases that had operated in France since 1950 back to France by 1967. However, France remained a member of the Alliance. Secret agreements set out how French forces would be deployed in the event of war.

The build-up of Warsaw Pact nuclear capacity in Europe during 1979 led the Americans to deploy Cruise and Pershing II missiles in Europe on the assumption that they could strengthen the NATO negotiating position regarding nuclear disarmament. In its turn, this deployment led to the growth of anti-nuclear deployment peace movements. The invasion of northern Cyprus by Turkey in 1974 persuaded Greece to withdraw its forces from NATO command structures. Greece was readmitted in 1980 with Turkish concurrence. On 30 May 1982 Spain became the sixteenth member of NATO. Over the years 1989–92 the Berlin Wall came down, the two Germanys reunited, the Cold War came to an end and in 1991 the Warsaw Pact dissolved itself. These events removed the reasons for NATO's existence and it set about finding alternative reasons to continue in being rather than follow the logical course and dissolve itself. To secure Soviet approval of a united Germany remaining in NATO it was agreed that foreign troops and nuclear weapons should not be stationed in the east. This 'agreement' was later to be challenged by the West. In 2005 Stephen F. Cohen argued that a commitment had been given that NATO would never expand further east. Robert Zoellick, for the State Department, argued that this was a misperception and that no formal commitment had been made. In May 2008 Gorbachev repeated his view that such a commitment had been made and that 'the Americans promised that NATO would not move beyond the boundaries of Germany after the Cold War'. Whichever version was correct, the fact is NATO began its expansion eastwards in the 1990s. Wider forums such as the Partnership for Peace were set up between NATO and non-member countries. Then, on 8 July 1997 three former communist countries—Hungary, the Czech Republic and Poland—were invited to join NATO, which they did in 1999. The Prague Summit of 2002 inaugurated talks about membership with seven East European countries—Estonia, Latvia, Lithuania, Slovenia, Slovakia, Bulgaria and Romania—and they joined NATO on 29 March 2004. Also that March, NATO's Baltic Air Policing began when fighter planes were detailed to react to any unwanted aerial intrusions, which could only mean the Russians. In 2006 NATO held its annual summit in Riga, the first in a former Soviet territory. Whether or not the United States had agreed not to push NATO eastwards, in fact over these years it did so with what could only be described as unseemly haste. In April 2008 the summit in Bucharest agreed that Croatia and Albania could join NATO, which they did in April 2009 to bring total membership to twenty-eight. Also that year Ukraine and Georgia were told they could eventually become members. Although assurances were given to Russia that this expansion was not aimed at it, both President Medvedev and Prime Minister Putin said it was, since it was almost impossible to suggest any other target country. President Obama, who originally had appeared ready to cancel the Bush proposal to erect an anti-missile screen in Poland and the Czech Republic, now suggested using a ship-based Aegis Combat system although stations still had to be built in Turkey, Spain, Portugal, Romania and Poland. Obama wanted NATO to maintain the 'status quo' of its nuclear deterrent in Europe. Whatever had been agreed at the time the two sides declared the Cold War to be over and whatever hopes of a better two-way relationship had been aroused, this subsequent expansion of NATO represented a level of bad faith and vaunted hubris that made impossible any real détente between the West and Russia. There was no justification for it other than an American desire to expand its influence and control across Eastern Europe, which it could use to bring Western Europe into a US-dominated military system.

Britain was always a faithful supporter of the NATO concept. When Hugh Gaitskell died in 1963 and Harold Wilson became leader of the Labour Party, he made Denis Healy shadow defence secretary. As Healey records in his memoirs, 'I had worked hard to win support for NATO ever since my post-war years at Transport House. Now I had to consider how to reconcile Britain's role as the United States' main partner in NATO with her need to come to terms with our European allies in the Common Market. Fortunately I had already accumulated a wide range of friends on both sides of the Atlantic.' Meanwhile, he goes on, 'NATO's reliance on the American nuclear deterrent was beginning to impose severe strains on the unity of the alliance. Washington refused absolutely to give its allies any say in the use of its strategic forces. While it distributed some shorter-range nuclear weapons to its allies, they remained under European ownership and control; the allies had the right, in theory, to veto their use, but not to order their use if Washington disagreed.'[1] The first aim of British military policy in the early days of NATO, according to Healey, was still to strengthen the deterrent by increasing the probability of America's atomic response to aggression in Europe.

The threat posed by Russia was seen as real by Bevin, Britain's foreign secretary under Attlee, though this was not a view held by all members of the Labour Party. 'The intelligence material merely corroborated that. To have acted otherwise, not to have eased the United States back into Europe and to have kept them there by locking them into NATO, would have been to take an appalling risk.'[2] Moreover, the signing of the NATO Treaty by America—an alliance with eleven other countries—meant a major change of policy while for Britain it represented the acceptance that it could no longer fight a major war without American assistance: in other words that it was no longer a superpower. The right to wage war is a mark of national sovereignty. Commenting on this decades later, Andrew Marr said: 'And the surrender of British national authority on that issue during the Cold War, binding the country into a NATO command structure under the control of the US president, rather than the British Parliament, was an act which, for most politicians and citizens, seemed irreversible.'[3] Another comment, by Raymond Williams, a staunch member of the old Labour Party, was as follows: 'It was also clear that overshadowing and finally continuing these was the period of rearmament, the increasing involvement with the political economy of the United States, the movement towards NATO, the whole post-war military and political establishment in which the Labour government had taken an enthusiastic and leading part, and against which the protests of parts of the labour movement had been quite unavailing.'[4] At a later date Tony Benn voices a different kind of lament. In 1968 Britain faced financial difficulties and so had to make expenditure cuts that included shutting down the military base in Singapore. As Benn claims, 'We didn't even know what the American role in Europe would be.' But he suggested that the whole function of NATO as a worldwide rapid deployment force to control the world on behalf of the rich industrialised north is re-emerging.

Queries as to the purpose of maintaining NATO were to come from both sides of the Atlantic once the Cold War had come to an end. Thus, 'No matter that NATO was established in 1949 to confront a claimed Soviet threat to Europe, no matter that the presumed threat vanished in 1991, NATO has become its own vested interest. NATO receives the bulk of its operational funding from the US and many of its weapons systems are linked to American military corporations.—If the US is to be "globocop", then NATO should be its deputy.'[5] The same critic continues: 'If a resurgent and strengthened NATO is to emerge during the Obama administration then this will alienate Russia even more and cause her to do what it did when first confronted by this alliance. It will intensify its own arms build-up, improve its nuclear arsenal and the world will be back at five minutes to midnight.' George Soros, famous for his financial activities, became a critic of American foreign policies. He argued that: 'During the Cold War Western democracies banded together in NATO, which was clearly under US domination. But once the threat of Soviet Union invasion had been removed, the primary impulse for Western unity under American leadership disappeared (except for Britain). Other countries became far less motivated to submit to the will of a superpower. As a result NATO has changed its character.'[6] The United States needed to rethink its NATO strategies in the light of the Balkan problems of the 1990s. The United States had to continue treating Europe as a strategic priority and for that decade the NATO alliance appeared to have found a new post-Cold War mission in bringing peace to that part of the (European) continent still prone to violent ethnic conflict. One sarcastic view of Europe's attitude towards NATO comes from Robert Kagan: 'The enlargement of the NATO alliance to include former members of the Soviet bloc—the completion of the Cold War victory and the creation of a Europe "whole and free"— was another grand project of the West that kept Europe in the forefront of American political and strategic thinking.'[7] As early as 1991, as the new post-Cold War order began to emerge, the Americans gave their attention to a new role for NATO. 'There has been the consistent advance of the US-led and US-determined expansion of NATO, an organisation that has lost any discernible purpose except that defined by Bush Snr, who in remarks made in the Hague on 9 November 1991 saw this military alliance as the means to "enrich our peoples, create new opportunities and fuel growth"—in other words to fulfil the enduring underpinning of American foreign policy.'[8] Bush Snr did not have his NATO allies in mind except as instruments to be used in furthering American capitalist aims.

The expansion of NATO has been paralleled by the expansion of the EU and in the chaotic state of the Balkans during the 1990s one of the most powerful motives driving reform was the hope of joining the Euro-Atlantic community. However, for any thinking member of the EU its future must be separate from that of NATO and here the EU comes up against a dilemma borne out of the Cold War. Countries such as Poland and the Czech Republic wanted to join the EU in a negative sense because they wished to escape from Russian control rather than from a more positive appraisal of what EU membership might mean for them and for this reason they will also welcome the expansion of NATO. Why do the Americans build up NATO and push Russia as though it is still the enemy? If Russia is not the enemy then who is? The answer of course is Europe. The Americans do not wish to see a fully independent and economically viable Europe that is able to go its own way, have its own defence force and initiate policies without reference to Washington. It was the British who first brought the Americans into the Balkan conflict in 1992, despite the claim that Bosnia was a European problem. At the end of the decade NATO and the Americans were still involved but by that time against Serbia. 'According to the NATO Commander [Wesley Clark] "the really decisive impulse" propelling the NATO bombing campaign "was not Milosevic's human rights violations in Kosovo before March 1999"; nor was it his wholesale eviction after the bombing began. What mattered most was the need to impose NATO's will on a leader whose defiance, first in Bosnia and then in Kosovo, was undermining the credibility of American and European diplomacy and of NATO's will power.'[9] The intent of the NATO bombing was 'to provide an object lesson to any European state fancying that it was exempt from the rule of the post-Cold War era' established by Washington. What counted was 'affirming the dominant position of the United States in a Europe that was unified, integrated and open'. To accept such a status would be to accept straightforward imperial subordination.

Few judgements of NATO are other than hostile: either because it is seen as an institution whose purpose has disappeared; or because it is seen as a weapon of US domination. Throughout its history NATO has been used by the United States to impose its hegemony upon Western Europe during the days of the Cold War and subsequently to extend that control to all Eastern Europe. No matter what rhetoric of freedom the United States employed, in fact it was always opposed to Europe pursuing an independent policy—or policies—of its own. 'Washington replaced Western Europe's independent conception of itself with the fear of the USSR, in response to which "Atlanticism"—protection through unity behind an American shield—became the new ideology. But once the Soviet Union ceased to exist in 1991 NATO became an anomaly.'[10] The Americans were fully aware of the importance of NATO in maintaining their dominance over Europe. In the late 1990s, for example, the Clinton administration indicated that NATO could become a relic if the Europeans created a military organisation of their own whose decisions America could not control. Although 9/11 gave NATO a new role as it invoked Article 5 in support of the United States, since its allies had no voice in military decisions they resented being treated as no more than auxiliaries. Meanwhile, Europe wanted a different relationship with Russia, which supplied a substantial proportion of its total oil and gas needs and found it difficult to defend pushing NATO to its borders, a policy that was regarded as hostile. Germany in particular opposed setting up an anti-missile defence screen in Poland and the Czech Republic as well as pushing the enlargement of NATO to include Georgia and Ukraine. As it had been in the Cold War, Germany would still be in the front line should the US NATO policy provoke a war with Russia. Slowly, the idea of a European defence force is gathering support although it will only become a viable reality if agreement is reached between France, Germany and Britain. The expansion of NATO, however justified, threatens Russian security and has created a new Cold War between the United States and Russia and destroys all the possibilities of a different European-Russian relationship that was opened up at the conclusion of the Cold War. 'The United States will be more prudent, and the world will be far safer, only if it is constrained by a lack of allies and isolated. And that is happening.'[11]

Writing in 2006, Adrian Hamilton provided a wide appraisal of NATO in Afghanistan. He posed the question: 'What no one dares to ask, however, is what the hell NATO is doing there in the first place? Once the wall came down, NATO should have been downgraded to something much smaller and looser. Instead, it did the opposite, adding new members and developing a new policy of "out of theatre" operations and extending its remit from Europe to the world. Part of this extension was what any large bureaucracy would do. If the Russian threat no longer warranted a huge defence alliance, then they had to think up new challenges.' The questions still remain with regard to Afghanistan. At one level the NATO force is in the country to fight a war on behalf of the political centre, to break the power of the warlords and to overturn a major part of the economy by trying to eradicate the drug trade. In any case, NATO is an all-white western grouping led by the US (the Great Satan), which has regional aims of its own, supported by its sidekick Britain. As Hamilton's article is headlined, 'Afghanistan is a western intervention', under an agenda quite different from NATO's purpose.[12]

In a farewell speech to NATO in Brussels in June 2011, the US defense secretary, Robert Gates, described NATO as facing a 'dim if not dismal' future of 'military irrelevance'. He was expressing Washington's growing irritation with its European allies (something Washington did throughout the Cold War) for not doing more in Afghanistan and over Libya. 'If they didn't pull their socks up,' he said, 'it would all be over for NATO.' His European allies at this point ought to have cheered for if Gates' analysis was correct it meant that at last Europe would be rid of the incubus of NATO, which by 2011 had long passed its sell-by date. The revolt against Gaddafi in Libya was nothing to do with NATO. The intervention by Britain, France and the United States was about re-opening Libya to oil exploitation. Gates' speech implied that the United States was becoming tired of shouldering the burden (of world policing). 'Behind Gates's speech was the clear implication that the US itself is beginning to tire of shouldering the burden. "The blunt reality," he said, "is that there will be dwindling appetite and patience in the US Congress—and in the American body politic writ large—to expand increasingly precious funds on behalf of nations that are apparently unwilling to devote the necessary resources to make the necessary changes to be serious and capable partners in their own defence."' Gates did not tell his alliance partners against whom they had to defend themselves. The most important message conveyed by Gates—whether intentional or not—was that the transatlantic partnership, in so far as it was a military alliance based on mutual self-interest, has reached the end of its shelf-life. If that is both true and believed by the Americans it lifts a huge burden from the shoulders of Europe, one that has gone on far too long.

The killing of Osama bin Laden by the Navy Seals at his 'hideout' in Pakistan brought an end to the mission whose raison d'être was precisely that, although a decade of war in Afghanistan had to be endured first. Obama's success altered the whole perspective of the Afghanistan intervention but where did it leave Britain and what had it done to NATO? Writing in *The Independent* Mary Dejevsky said: 'Here in London the scene could not have been more different. The US and British experience of Afghanistan has furnished a salutary study in comparative power, and the 24 hours before Obama announced his "drawdown" found Britain scrambling, as so often, to catch up. Thus the Foreign Secretary, William Hague, suddenly turned up in Kabul; we also learnt that the British had been conducting their own talks with the Taliban—a week after confirmation from President Karzai and the Americans that they had as long rumoured, begun talks of their own. And now the Ministry of Defence is broaching the possibility that British forces—of whom a mere 400 [of 9,500] are due to be withdrawn this year—could return more quickly.' What ought to have been apparent for years—that the British in Afghanistan were a sideshow and that all the crucial decisions, good or bad, were taken by the Americans—was now revealed in all its stark absurdity as the foreign secretary rushed out to Kabul to give the impression that Britain was a part of the decision-making process. The special relationship may have persuaded Blair to send the largest auxiliary force to support the Americans when the original invasion took place—under NATO command—but once in place their role was a PR one, supporting an American policy that was irrelevant as far as British interests were concerned.

Meanwhile, Britain and France had become involved in the civil war in Libya that led to the demise of Gaddafi. Their motives were mixed: oil of course and seizing an opportunity to show that militarily they could act on their own, independently of the United States. Hailing the end of Gaddafi's rule, the secretary-general of NATO, Anders Fogh Rasmussen, praised the success of the military operation, which had been conducted with precision in a highly complex situation. But it also demonstrated that NATO was in deep trouble. Germany and Poland had refused to be involved. The United States was described as 'leading from the back'. Washington's low profile may have been dictated by home politics but it hardly demonstrated any US enthusiasm for NATO, even though US policy in Europe had been to expand NATO membership eastwards as fast as it could.

Zbigniew Brezinski looking to the future in 2012 claimed that all European countries were opting out of any serious commitment to their own, or even to NATO-based, collective security. Assuming that his judgement is correct why is the United States so much more concerned with security than anybody else? He argues as follows: 'However, through its cultural, ideological, and economic connections to America and more concretely through NATO, Europe remains a junior geopolitical partner to the United States in the semi-unified West.'[13] Except for Britain, which, in respect of the United States, positively seeks a junior role, European scepticism and wariness of American motives explains why it plays the junior partnership role so badly. The Cold War ended with dramatic suddenness in 1989 to leave a huge geopolitical vacuum to be filled. The United States knew what it wanted to do and proceeded to spread and enhance its worldwide hegemony wherever the opportunities arose. The European Union also knew what it wanted and set about the business of enlargement almost as surely as the Americans enlarged NATO. What the Americans also did was downgrade Europe as a military ally as they began to concentrate upon what they assumed was to be a confrontation with China. This was made clear by President Obama when he announced that US military deployment would be concentrated upon the Asia-Pacific region. The death-knell of NATO was sounded in 2012 when President Hamid Karzai of Afghanistan called upon NATO to withdraw its troops from villages. He insisted that his country's forces were able to provide security in the villages and NATO forces should be confined to their bases. There was widespread perception that once Western forces leave, large areas of the country would return into Taliban hands, a development that was already underway. In mid-March 2012 the Taliban issued a statement that it was breaking off talks with the US because, they argued, the Americans had failed to follow through on promises. A Taliban spokesman explained, 'We must categorically state that the real source of obstacle in talks was the shaky, erratic and vague standpoint of the Americans. Therefore all the responsibility for the halt also falls on their shoulders.'[14] The Americans wanted to leave as did the Europeans, the Karzai government took a strong line against NATO because it knew NATO wanted to leave, the violence and terrorist attacks continued and were not prevented by the Afghanistan police or military and the Taliban sat on the sidelines waiting to move back into power. The situation duplicated the chaos in Vietnam before the Americans left.

22

GREAT BRITAIN

AN EXIT STRATEGY

Much of this book has been about Britain's loss of power: her fall from being the centre of a worldwide Empire to being the principal satellite of her American successor. This does not mean that she lacks weight, although assisting the United States spread its hegemony was not the best way to use it. Britain can claim to be a substantial middle power. The question is one of degree: how best to use the weight and influence which she possesses in pursuit of her own interests. In the nineteenth century Britain was the world's leading trading nation but the Second World War set Britain back and it has only partly recovered its pre-eminence in this field, lying behind the United States, China, Japan and Germany as well as other contenders for a top ranking such as Brazil. In almost every aspect of foreign policy the demands of the special relationship have hampered the possibility of a distinctive British policy emerging. Polls over the years have revealed a changing public appraisal of the value to Britain of the special relationship. In 1942 a Gallup poll conducted after the Japanese attack upon Pearl Harbor showed the wartime Russian ally was more popular than the USA among 63 per cent of Britons. At that time only 6 per cent of Britons had ever visited the United States and only 35 per cent knew any Americans personally. In 1969 the United States and the Commonwealth tied as the most important overseas connections for the British while Europe came third. In 1984, a decade after becoming a member of the Common Market, Britons saw Europe as the most important of their overseas connections. Cold War considerations brought to the fore the military aspect of Britain's ties with other countries. Polls over the years revealed an up-and-down ambivalence towards the United States, mainly concerned with matters of defence. A 1998 ICM poll showed that 61 per cent of Britons had more in common with Americans than with the rest of Europe. A poll of the US public in 2006 showed that Britain as an ally in the 'war on terror' was viewed more positively than any other country, a showing that owed a good deal to the 'Blair' effect. A poll by Populus for *The Times* of June 2006 showed the number of Britons agreeing that it was important for Britain's long-term security to have a close and special relationship with America had fallen to 58 per cent (71 per cent in April) while 65 per cent of those polled believed that Britain's future lay more with Europe than America. Also, during the 2006 Israel-Lebanon conflict 63 per cent of Britons felt that Britain was too closely tied to the United States. An *Economist* poll of 2008 showed British views differed considerably from US views on religion, values and national interest and that Britons were more closely aligned with other Europeans, especially the Germans and Dutch. Tony Blair spoke of the 'blood price' that Britain should be prepared to pay in order to sustain the special relationship. Britain has always wanted a 'unique' special relationship with the United States while Americans use the term more widely, applying it also to Israel, Germany and South Korea. A You-Gov poll of May 2010 revealed that 66 per cent of Britons had a favourable view of the United States and that 62 per cent agreed that the United States was Britain's most important ally. However, the same poll also showed that 85 per cent of those polled believed that Britain had little or no influence on American policies and that 62 per cent thought that America did not consider British interests.[1] Polls reveal a mixture of sentiment and realism: thus, Americans are our best ally yet do not consider British interests.

Weaker allies who believe they are important always become sycophants. The special relationship did not enhance British influence but diminished it. In 1949 Britain's foreign secretary, Ernest Bevin, acted as an equal with his American counterpart General Marshall as the two statesmen worked to create NATO. Half a century later Britain's prime minister, Tony Blair, was seen as all but irrelevant, despite his posturing, when President George W. Bush made the decision to invade Iraq. Blair went along with him by which time the illusion of a special relationship with the United States had distorted Britain's image of itself to such an extent that its prime minister spent his time defending American policies instead of safeguarding British interests. 'So long as the future is to a large degree—to paraphrase Defense Secretary Donald Rumsfeld—"unknowable", it is not in the national interest of the traditional US allies to perpetuate the relationships created from 1945 to 1990.'[2] The Germans and the French—Rumsfeld's 'old Europe'—have largely managed to do this while the British have clung to the alliance as though it guaranteed Britain's place in the world. Kolko, quoted above, goes to the heart of American policy when he says that the USA 'has always believed, as well it should, that Europe and its control would determine the future of world power.' Stopping the United States controlling Europe to this end ought to be a leading British objective, as opposed to abetting such an outcome. The extent to which the special relationship has devitalised Britain as an independent power contributing to world events is equivalent to its contributions to holding up and backing American power. A break in this pattern must be achieved if Britain is to contribute to a fast-changing world in its own right rather than as a loyal American satellite. Such a change of role will itself be a huge challenge to a political leadership and civil service that appear to have been brainwashed over decades into a willing acceptance of their status as an auxiliary to the United States. If the Americans now embark upon a policy of confrontation with China they will expect Britain to continue providing loyal support in a policy likely to prove as sterile as the earlier US Cold War stance. In its foreign policy and the strategies it pursues, the United States has always been concerned to safeguard capitalism, and in this regard Britain is not far behind, which is the basis of its strength. Thus, at the end of the Second World War, Republican critics of Britain were appalled at the idea of using American aid and loans to build a welfare state, an attitude that resurfaced in the first decade of the twenty-first century when Obama tackled the issue of health care in America. With the world financial structures in chaos after the fall of 2008, does this mean the coming of an international trade war, which would end with a China-US standoff? It certainly stands as a threat to a much more ordered financial system. If this proves to be the case, Britain and the rest of Europe should stand aside, if they can, and let the Chinese and the

Americans fight it out between them. Above all, Britain should aim for economic, and therefore, trading stability.

American arrogance in relation to international institutions emerged over the question of using the International Criminal Court. 'Not only did the Bush Administration reject the International Criminal Court, but it embarked upon an active campaign to sabotage it.'[3] The question of reciprocal arrangements to extradite wanted individuals, usually in connection with terrorist activities, between Britain and the United States have led to many accusations that the procedures are one-sided in favour of the United States. Thus, for example, the United States harboured Provisional IRA terrorists in the 1970s and 1980s despite repeated British requests for them to be extradited. Following the 9/11 attacks in the United States in 2001 exchanges of terrorist suspects was agreed between the two countries but the measure was soon used by the United States to extradite and prosecute people who were not wanted on terrorist charges. An extradition treaty was agreed in 2003, which supposedly allowed for equal extradition between the two countries. However, critics were soon to argue that Britain was obligated to make a strong prima facie case to US courts before extradition would be granted while, by contrast, extradition from Britain to the United States was a matter of administrative decision alone, without prima facie evidence. The extradition issue became a running sore in Britain where the asymmetrical nature of the agreement was seen to work wholly in America's favour. Thus, 'Few British people can understand why our countrymen are being "extradited" to the US for a dubious trial when any crime that has been committed has been committed here in the UK, if at all.—There is no test of where the events took place, no protection afforded by the European Convention on Human Rights and Fundamental Freedoms, no protection from the Human Rights Act 1998, no *habeas corpus*, no Magna Carta, just nothing.'[4] In Britain, the people if not the government, have come to see the Anglo-American extradition treaty of 2003 as hideously imbalanced. Such imbalance raises the question: just why do successive British governments fail so dismally to insist upon equality of treatment between their subjects and American subjects?

William Hague became Britain's foreign secretary in the Tory-led coalition government that came to power following the May 2010 election. He wasted no time in visiting Washington in order to assure the United States of Britain's loyalty: Anglo-American ties will continue to be Britain's foreign policy priority he assured them. Talks with US Secretary of State Hillary Clinton covered Afghanistan and Iran and Hague reassured her, 'There will be a strong continuity of British policy on these matters.' Clinton insisted that she had 'no concern whatsoever' that the coalition would lead to problems in the transatlantic relationship. At a news conference Hague said: 'It is good for our relationship and good for world affairs when the UK is in support of the foreign policies of the Obama administration.' Hague's first call on assuming his office had not been to any of his counterparts in Europe but to Clinton to whom he suggested an immediate visit. His haste to run to Washington was in line with longstanding British policy and Cameron was expected to follow.[5] Despite these warm words there were differences over Afghanistan with British public opinion overwhelmingly in favour of withdrawal while the Americans wished to stay the course to 2015. Hague, however, insisted that Britain would stay the course in the Afghan war and that Iran must mend its ways or face the consequences. In August 2012 Hague was interviewed at length in the London *Evening Standard* and spoke of Britain's powerful new role in the world. Under his tenure new embassies were being opened up across Africa and in China, India and Latin America as part of the expansion of British presence in the world. He talked of an equal partnership with countries, some of which had been British colonies, but, he said, it was a world where networks defeat hierarchies and where the world is not in blocks. It is the networked world and Britain, he said, is a natural centre. He claimed that 80 per cent of foreign-born executives said that London is the place that is most open to business. 'We are a European nation and we are firm allies of the United States. But more than any of that, we are a natural centre in a global network.' He said, 'The Olympics should be the launch pad for Britain's global expansion and should also mark the end of our post-empire apologetic relations.' Hague did not spell out just what Britain's global expansion meant: simply concentrating upon more trade or what else? Harping upon post-colonial guilt, the foreign secretary said the British must, 'be confident in ourselves.' If he really meant it, the corollary to this greater self-confidence would be to ditch the special relationship, which would no longer be needed to bolster British self-confidence. The foreign secretary spoke of Britain supporting the opposition in Syria, providing support for refugees and being prepared to criticise Russia's human rights record. In the end he returned to the special relationship. Referring to the new embassies he is opening in the emerging economies of China, India and Brazil, he was firm that 'the world still relies a lot on American leadership'. He said, 'For the United Kingdom, it is the indispensable relationship.' Saying that he had no fear of a change in the (American) presidency, Hague in a giveaway sentence said, 'You don't have to be president for many days to realise that the United Kingdom is absolutely indispensable to them as well.' This was an extraordinary claim to make. In any case, indispensable for what reasons? At no point does Hague spell out why the special or indispensable relationship is so important. What does it actually do for Britain?[6]

As China attracts ever more attention from the United States so must America's allies take the China question into account. Quite suddenly, Australia has found itself to be a potential base for the deployment of American military power as Washington develops its new policy of concentrating the bulk of its military resources in the Pacific region. Australia is in the unenviable position of supporting its closest ally (the United States) on the one hand and not upsetting China, its largest trading partner, on the other. In 2011 the United States persuaded Australia to allow a small base for marines to be set up at Darwin as part of an agreement on increased military co-operation. China condemned the move as a return to Cold War practices. The proposal envisaged that up to 2,500 marines might eventually be based there. In August 2012 the United States took up a Pentagon proposal to relocate a carrier and its support fleet from the US east cost to HMAS Stirling, an Australian naval base south of Perth, as part of a new strategic focus on Asia. However, Stephen Smith, the Australian defence minister, said Australia would not host a US aircraft carrier group, which typically includes submarines, destroyers and fighter jets. Smith said, 'We have made it crystal clear from the first moment—we don't have US military bases in Australia, and we are not proposing to.' Australia does not want China to see it as part of a US military build-up in Asia. Hugh White, Head of the Australian National University's Strategic and Defence Studies Centre, said: 'The US, which has announced plans to shift the bulk of its naval fleet to the Pacific by 2020 has been forging closer military ties with countries in the region, in an effort to counter China's growing military strength. It already has a carrier strike group based in the Japanese port of Yokosuka.' The more the United States builds up its military capacity in the Western Pacific the greater the risk that the US-China relationship will become more competitive and adversarial. Australia does not want to be pushed into a situation in which it has to choose between China and the United States. The likelihood is that as the United States relocates its military strength to the Pacific region to confront China, the more it will put pressure upon Australia to provide base facilities. And if the confrontation becomes seriously menacing, as seems to be the logical outcome of this US policy, so will Washington seek other allies to bolster its position and that means Britain. This American policy of deploying massive military force against China is a sign of weakness rather than strength because it is afraid of China becoming a competitive superpower. As US power wanes relative to the rest of the world so will it seek to buttress its predominant position with allies in which case it may turn to the special relationship to support its interface with China, a renewal of the special relationship (if that turns out to be the case) that Britain should steadfastly refuse to countenance. Many signs now point to a new polarisation of the world led by China and the United States and in such circumstances it is essential that the EU, including an engaged Britain, stands aside and refuses to be drawn into a new alliance system to face China.

Reflections

During the war and in the immediate aftermath the United States, while treating Britain as an ally, also worked to downsize the British Empire and take its place while Britain sought alternative policies to membership of the Big Three. Bevin, for example, was keen to establish a block consisting of Britain, the Commonwealth and Western Europe though this was not to work out. The 1946 US loan in any case made Britain financially dependent upon the United States while, over the following years, various occasions presented Britain with the chance to break its heavy dependence upon the American alliance. Thus US hostility to Britain at the time of the Suez fiasco presented a real opportunity—in line with the British public's anger at the US attitude—to break the relationship and pursue a more independent policy. It was possible at that time, as the US ambassador informed Washington, that Britain might have told the US to remove its bases from Britain. Similarly, British anger at the US withdrawal of co-operation over nuclear matters again presented an issue over which a break could have occurred. At the same time, over this period, the special relationship was used by both Britain and the United States to prevent a full British commitment to the united Europe that was then emerging. What Britain should or should not do about Europe became a constant and uneasy consideration for British strategic thinking. Bevin, before his death in 1950, had assumed that over ten to twenty years Europe could become militarily independent of the United States. In fact, Britain consistently sidelined any major decisions in relation to Europe while the United States policy makers wanted to use Britain as a Trojan horse in Europe. Full British engagement at the centre of European developments was not then considered. Meanwhile, upholding her position as the centre of a worldwide empire cost Britain dear and lessened the expansion of trade that ought to have been the first priority. Throughout these years to the end of the Cold War and into the twenty-first century Britain as a US satellite helped to spread its hegemony when in terms of her own Realpolitik objectives she ought to have done nothing of the kind. Thatcher demonstrated a quite extraordinary devotion to the American alliance though why she did so is not clear. Blair, with his 'shoulder to shoulder' support for President Bush got nothing in return.

Always looming in the background is the question: how does the special relationship assist Britain which, increasingly, has come to be seen as a 'yes man' for the United States? What does Britain gain or get in return for playing the satellite role? Churchill always appeased the Americans though he could have stood up to them far more than he did. He famously said at a dinner with Acheson that the peace of the world depended upon the Anglo-American alliance. Did he really believe this or was it just a rhetorical flourish? Sometimes, as with President Johnson and Harold Wilson, the Americans clearly wanted Britain to support a particular policy, in this case by sending a token force of troops to join their huge military deployment in Vietnam. Such a token force would have been a PR exercise, but for once the US request was met with a 'no'. Even so, Wilson recognised that the special relationship meant a client relationship as far as Britain was concerned, so why did Britain keep it up? When Cameron became prime minister in 2010 he gave a few indications that he wanted to follow a more independent policy and then spoiled the effect by adding, 'We are the junior partner.' Was this the result of sixty-five years of brainwashing of successive British leadership elites? Britain appears to have bred generations of politicians who take the special relationship as a fixed policy as formerly they regarded the existence of the Empire. Trying to explain the special relationship, Timothy Garton Ash suggests that there is a strand of neurotic self-doubt at work and that Britain should stop talking about its role and instead consider its interests. 'We, the British, the public as well as the elites, need to define and redefine our interests.'—and that 'an enlightened definition of British interests should also include a decent respect and concern for the basic interests of others around the globe'.[7] The question that has never been satisfactorily answered is why politicians from Attlee to Macmillan toyed with alternative policies but never came down in favour of adopting them. What made the special relationship so attractive even when its obvious asymmetrical one-sidedness had been revealed? In his *Clash of Civilizations* Huntington posed a question that may become ever more important as China and the United States seem determined to confront one another. Is a civilisation-based world emerging, he asks, and if so will this lead the West to work more closely together with the result that it enhances US hegemony in the West and if so, where does that leave Britain? Will the West's universalist pretensions about democracy and freedom bring it increasingly into conflict with China and the Islamic world? The survival of the West, he claims, depends on Americans reaffirming their western identity and westerners accepting their civilisation as unique, not universal, and uniting to renew and preserve it against challenges from non-western societies.[8] These gloomy prognostications are a recipe for disaster, a world based on broad nationalist distinctions that we cannot and do not want to break down. An American-Chinese confrontation will be a calamity for the rest of the world. Huntington quotes Lee Kuan Yew of Singapore in 1994: 'The emergence of new great powers is always highly destabilising, and if it occurs, China's emergence as a major power will dwarf any comparable phenomenon during the last half of the second millennium. The size of China's displacement of the world is such that the world must find a new balance in 30 or 40 years. It is not possible to pretend that this is just another big player. This is the biggest player in the history of man.' What China does will dominate international politics for the next half century and, above all, will affect the United States, which at the present time is the world's only superpower and intends to retain that position for as long as it is possible to do so. That means a confrontation and that, in turn, will affect everyone else. As

China spreads its hegemony to rival that of the United States so the latter will demand support and, for example, is already exerting pressure upon Australia to allow American bases on its soil to face China. Such a confrontation would recreate an armed, nationalist Cold War that would see the United States seeking allies and dividing the world into friends and foes much as it did throughout the Cold War. It is a situation that the world should strive to prevent.

An alternative policy for Britain

The world is in a state of flux as the old order, dominated by the United States, faces the challenge of a new order based upon the shift of power from West to East. Policy adjustments are required first from the major powers—the United States, China, Russia, Japan, India and the EU—while on the periphery of world policy changes are Latin America led by Brazil, the world of Islam coming to terms with the dramatic challenge presented by the Arab Spring and an Africa that at last is beginning to feel it can break away from the aid and development tutelage that has bound it to the West since independence. Many questions need to be addressed. Are new political openings occurring as the leading countries revert to old-fashioned nationalist policies? What in this changing world are British interests? Should it continue to act as a US satellite, looking to Washington for guidance, or will it finally break the bonds that have enmeshed it ever since the beginning of the Cold War? The sheer tenacity with which Britain has clung to the special relationship is astonishing. Possibly, adherence to the Atlantic alliance is a form of racism, the British seeking comfort in an Anglo-Saxon world that is more comfortable than engagement elsewhere, though such an attitude goes against the grain of British history. Whatever the reason, the special relationship has become the shroud of the Empire. The American extension of bases around the world and its equivocal peace-keeping mission in the Middle East have weakened its power even as it has been extended. Like the British after the First World War acquiring mandates from the break-up of the Ottoman Empire to increase its imperial spread and becoming so involved in safeguarding the Empire that it neglected the basis of its strength, the economy, so the United States appears to be falling into the same trap. For Britain, the story of the special relationship revolves round diminishing British power because its economy could not support its world role and it would not cut its cloth according to its wealth. When the Americans talk about security they mean security from the challenge that now comes from the East—either Islam in one of its various manifestations or China. Security in this context is the American way of replacing the Cold War with an alternate 'enemy' to control or combat. The time is ripe in this changing world scene for Britain to re-examine its policies with regard to its participation (or lack of it) in the EU, NATO, US bases in Britain, asymmetrical arrangements between the two countries, Britain's military presence in the Middle East, its attitude to Iran and Israel and, above all, the choices it will face when US-China rivalries turn into confrontation.

The European Union

The one policy area where Britain could have made an impact commensurate with its strength—Europe—was the one to which she consistently avoided making a full commitment even when in the early post-war days Europe begged her to give a lead. As Gladstone said in the nineteenth century, 'We are part of the community of Europe and we must do our duty as such.' We have not done so. In the aftermath of the Second World War, Churchill called upon Europe to unite but did not intend that Britain should be part of the union. Neither Attlee nor Eden showed much interest in the European idea while Macmillan, with his alternatives, tried to kill the union at birth. The Americans encouraged European unity when they saw it as a barrier against the USSR or encouraged British membership of a united Europe when they believed Britain might act as a Trojan horse to safeguard American interests. The British objection to full participation in the European dream, where it could have had the most influence, was always paralleled by its adherence to the special relationship where it could have the least. The upheavals in the Western financial system that began with the collapse of 2008 and have had a profound impact upon the EU provide a new starting point for Europe and for Britain. Logically, Britain's future lies—and must lie—with Europe and not with the United States. A real British commitment to Europe must address two fundamental reservations: the first, whether a federation of twenty-eight countries (with more to come) is either possible or acceptable; the second, that all fundamental decisions must be voted upon by the peoples who make up the whole. Britain should re-engage with Europe and press for these two concerns to be dealt with honestly and at the top of an agenda, which should include giving real power to the Parliament at Strasbourg. Britain, advocating such an approach while at the same time making plain its readiness to be a full participant in building a united Europe, could alter the present scenario of suspicions about a centralised bureaucracy that wields all the levers of power. Full commitment to a Europe that is willing to rethink along such lines should be Britain's first concern for it is the only one that is both international and national. Finally, a word of warning provided by Vince Cable, the Liberal Democrat business secretary: the consequences of a collapse of the European project would be 'incalculable' and it is as much a British responsibility to prevent such an eventuality whether it is on the sidelines or deeply committed.

NATO

NATO was created in 1949 to enable the countries of Western Europe and North America to present a united front to the USSR, whose presumed hostility to the West was the raison d'être for the alliance. When thirty years later the two principals—the United States and the USSR—declared the Cold War to be over the justification for NATO disappeared and the organisation ought to have been dismantled, as was the Warsaw Pact. The end of the Cold War did bring a temporary sense of euphoria but this was not to last. The obvious outcome should have been for the West, led by the United States, to have welcomed Russia (as it emerged from the disintegration of the Soviet Union) as a friend as Europe probably would have done on its own. Instead, the United States pushed NATO to the borders of Russia and by doing so in a fit of hubris rubbed in the fact that they had won the Cold War and were determined to deploy their military power through NATO to ensure that Russia did not again become an effective opponent. This policy extended Cold War attitudes into the new world order and instead of subduing Russia ensured that old habits of suspicion and enmity were resurrected. 'By March 1994, the new American Defense Secretary, William Perry, had to admit publicly that it was possible Russia could emerge from her turbulence as an authoritarian, militaristic, imperialistic nation hostile to the West.'[9] By the simple expedient of moving NATO to the borders of Russia the United States had succeeded in destroying the opportunities for a genuine new relationship with

Russia that the end of the Cold War had made possible, instead extending old enmities into a new era. This was not to the advantage of Europe but such was the US grip on NATO that no objections were raised against a policy that perpetuated Cold War antagonisms. In any case, the EU was so determined to expand that it did not take into account the likely impact of its expansion (taking in countries such as Poland and Hungary) upon Russia. The net result was to destroy the chance of establishing good post-Cold War relations with Russia, instead raising fears that the West wanted to intimidate its former enemy, which is exactly what these moves achieved. Rather than subduing Russia they perpetuated old suspicions and ensured that Russia regards both NATO and the EU as enemies rather than as friends in the new world order. Moreover, if as the West has tried to suggest such expansion is not aimed at Russia then who is the target? From a British point of view Russia as a trading partner and ally would make more sense than a hostile Russia that is the outcome of these manoeuvres. If this is the case Britain should withdraw from NATO and urge its disestablishment since it is not in the interest of either the EU or Britain to create a hostile Russia to satisfy American hegemonic ambitions.

American bases in Britain

It is astonishing that sixty-five years after the end of the Second World War and twenty years after the end of the Cold War the United States still has military (air) bases including nuclear weapons in Britain. They do not serve any of the purposes for which they were originally established. Instead, they act as an extension of US hegemony and could be used to exert pressure upon the EU at some future date. It is not, and should not be, the business of Britain to assist in the extension of the US worldwide hegemony and Britain should request the US to remove all its bases from British territory.

Asymmetrical relations

If there is an alliance of unequals then asymmetrical relations must necessarily follow and that, unsurprisingly, has been a part of the special relationship. In recent years British public opinion has focused upon the extradition arrangements between the two countries and their apparent asymmetrical nature in favour of the United States. Central to the debate has been the case of Gary McKinnon, a computer hacker who had hacked into US military computers although he has argued that he was only searching for information on UFOs. McKinnon has Asperger's syndrome. He would have faced up to sixty years in prison had he been extradited to the United States and his mental state suggested that he might commit suicide. Finally, after ten years in which he was confined to his home and faced a series of appeals, the home secretary, Theresa May (16 October 2012), ruled that McKinnon should stay in Britain as his extradition would be incompatible with his human rights. 'Her decision is—the right one. Not because Mr. McKinnon's psychiatric issues obviate any crime he might have committed; nor even because the US legal system can reasonably be considered less judicious than our own; but because the hacking took place in this country, broke this country's laws, and should therefore be prosecuted here.'[10] The British director of public prosecutions must consider where McKinnon should be tried in Britain. A series of extradition disputes have created the impression that the system was tilted in favour of the United States and whether in fact justified or not, they eroded both public and parliamentary confidence in the system. The home secretary proposed to introduce a 'forum bar' under which British courts can block extradition in cases where the suspect could stand trial in UK instead. The issue is a complicated one but as far as its importance to the special relationship is concerned it has raised public anger against what is perceived to be an imbalanced relationship. After years of an asymmetrical relationship it is not surprising that a particular case relating to an individual has raised public anger to a level of anti-Americanism that may often be aroused just below the public surface. Given that only a few days earlier Abu Hamza and other terrorist suspects had been sent to the United States it was clear that the McKinnon case had not broken the general pattern of extradition between the two countries. The home secretary indicated that she would review the whole extradition procedure.

Involvement in the Middle East

British participation in the wars in Afghanistan and Iraq was clearly at the behest of the United States even though the Afghan war was mandated by the United Nations. If Britain is to break the special relationship so as to be free to judge if and when it is a British interest to become involved in an overseas war it must first break its habit of committing itself in advance to support American military adventures. Churchill envisaged a role for Britain as a mediator between the two superpowers though nothing came of it. What is envisaged here is a Britain free of entanglements like NATO that would inhibit it from proposing solutions to problems that would not be acceptable to the United States but urgently need somebody to voice them. If there is ever to be a resolution of the Palestine question a different approach to both Iran and Israel needs to be voiced where at present only hypocrisy prevails. Put simply we need to consider the following proposition: why are ever greater western sanctions applied to Iran to force it to abandon its nuclear programme (it hasn't got the bomb and has broken no NPT rules) while no sanctions or other pressures are applied to Israel to make it decommission its store of nuclear warheads and, despite some sixty-six UN resolutions since 1967 against illegal settlements in the West Bank, it continues to plant them with impunity, ignoring the United Nations and protected when necessary by the United States?

Confrontation: China and the United States

The natural outcome of great power status is confrontation and all the evidence of recent years suggests such a confrontation will develop between the United States and China. It is a confrontation that bodes ill for the world at large. As it takes shape so the rest of the world will have to consider where it stands in relation to it. China has few allies—though its alliance of convenience with Russia should not be forgotten—but a number of powerful enemies who fear its growing power, and most notably Japan and India. The United States under President Obama has given a number of indications that he regards China as a potential threat to US interests and wants to contain it by carrying out an eastward shift of military power to the Southeast Asia region. China's reaction has been to accuse the United States of trying to encircle China. In a contradictory statement at the end of September 2012, Kurt M. Campbell, assistant secretary for East Asia in the State Department, first said that the suggestion that the United States was pursuing a Cold-War style containment of China was not true but then added that, 'the Chinese respect strength, determination and strategy'. Meanwhile, Secretary of State Hillary Clinton, reporting on her visit to the region said: 'Time and again, I had leaders—I mean I am talking about the highest leaders—essentially say: "Thank goodness. Thank you. I'm so pleased you are here. We were worried about America."' If Clinton's statement is to be taken at face value then the United States is busy organising Asian allies against China even if their expressed concerns were in part diplomatic. As this confrontational build-up grows so must Britain decide where it stands. A new Cold War between China and the United States would be a disaster and it should be a British interest to do anything in its power to prevent such an outcome. Its contribution to a more peaceful world would be more effective if it resists any US attempts to persuade Britain to back its stand against China. In due course, as such a confrontation develops, the United States will almost certainly invoke the special relationship in order to draw upon British support. Such an approach should be resisted by Britain whose interests do not include a confrontation with China.

Changing course is never easy but power manoeuvres over the coming decades threaten to be as complex and dangerous as anything that occurred during the twentieth century. In simple terms the optimum British interest is peace rather than confrontation, soft power as opposed to military might. Changing course is not easy yet British interests lie in its membership of Europe, which it cannot escape, ending the special relationship that would otherwise bind Britain to American confrontations with Russia and still more with China; and using what influence it has to damp down incipient conflicts by working through the United Nations, the Commonwealth and the EU—a combination that represents massive soft power.

As Machiavelli writes in *The Prince*: 'One always ought to remember that there is nothing more difficult to undertake, nor more dangerous to administer, nor more unlikely to succeed, than to introduce a new political order.'

NOTES

1. INTRODUCTION: COLLAPSE OF POWER

1. Organski, A. F. K., *World Politics*, New York: Alfred A. Knopf, 1958, p. 311.
2. Gelber, Lionel, *America in Britain's Place*, New York: Frederik A. Praeger, 1961, p. 80.
3. Hayter, Sir William, *The Diplomacy of the Great Powers*, London: Hamish Hamilton, 1960, pp. 14, 42.
4. Shanks, Michael, *The Stagnant Society*, London: Penguin Special/Pelican, 1961, pp. 29, 214, 215.
5. Fowler, Norman, *Ministers Decide*, Edinburgh: Chapmans, 1991, p. 150.
6. Galbraith, John Kenneth, *The Culture of Contentment*, London: Sinclair-Stevenson, 1992, p. 50.
7. Benn, Tony, *Conflicts of Interest: Diaries 1977–80*, London: Hutchinson, 1990, p. 211.
8. Riddell, Peter, *Hug Them Close*, London: Politico's, 2003, p. 304.
9. *Our Global Neighbourhood*, The Commission on Global Governance, Oxford: OUP, 1995, p. 337.
10. Barnett, Corelli, *The Collapse of British Power*, London, Stroud: Eyre-Methuen, Sutton Publishing, 1972, 1997, p. 49.
11. Ibid., p. 254.
12. Ibid., p. 257.
13. Ibid., p. 410.
14. Ibid., p. 42.
15. Ibid., p. 267.

2. 1940–1945: US POLICIES, BRITISH RESPONSES

1. Amery, Leo, *The Empire at Bay: The Leo Amery Diaries 1929–1945*, Barnes John, and Nicholson, David, eds., London: Hutchinson, 1988, p. 352.
2. Ibid., p. 353.

3. Ibid., p. 705.

4. Ponting, Clive, *1940 Myth and Reality*, London: Hamish Hamilton, 1990, p. 178.

5. Ibid., pp. 198–9.

6. Ibid., p. 201.

7. Ibid., p. 209.

8. Ibid., p. 210.

9. Ibid., pp. 212–3.

10. Ibid., p. 226.

11. Hurd, Douglas, *Choose Your Weapons*, London: Weidenfeld & Nicolson, 2010, p. 310.

12. Ibid., pp. 317–8.

13. Hurd, Douglas, Choose Your Weapons, London: Weidenfield & Nicolson, 2010.

3. THE ATTLEE YEARS 1945–1951

1. Hennessy, Peter, *Having it so Good: Britain in the 1950s*, London: Penguin Books, 2006/2007, p. 137.

2. Castle, Barbara, *Fighting All the Way*, London: Macmillan, 1993, p. 137.

3. Ibid., p. 138.

4. Horne, Alistair, *Macmillan 1957–1986: The Official Biography*, London: Macmillan, 1989, p. 290.

5. Callaghan, James, *Time and Chance*, London: Collins, 1987, p. 72.

6. Clarke, Peter, *A Question of Leadership*, London: Hamish Hamilton, 1991, pp. 80–1.

7. Gilmour, Ian, *Whatever Happened to the Tories*, London: Fourth Estate, 1997, pp. 25–6.

8. Marr, Andrew, *Ruling Britannia*, London: Michael Joseph, 1995, p. 184.

9. Barnett, Corelli, *The Lost Victory*, London: Macmillan, 1995, p. 4.

10. Callaghan, op. cit. p. 74.

11. Walker, Martin, *The Cold War*, London: Fourth Estate, 1993, p. 22.

12. Clarke, Peter, *The Last 1000 Days of the British Empire*, London: Penguin: 2007, p. 395.

13. Healey, Denis, *When Shrimps Learn to Whistle*, London: Michael Joseph, 1990, p. 98.

14. Barnett, op. cit., p. 45.

15. Clarke, op. cit., p. 421.

16. Burridge, Trevor, *Clement Attlee*, London: Jonathan Cape, 1985, p. 236.

17. Ibid., p. 240.

18. Ibid., p. 257.

19. Clarke, op. cit., p. 87.

20. Acheson, Dean, *Present at the Creation*, New York: W. W. Norton, 1969, p. 173.

21. Healey, op. cit., p. 15.

22. *The Chicago Tribune*, 27 July 1945.

23. *Hansard* (23 January 1948), Vol. 466, Col. 566.

24. Shore, Peter, *Leading from the Left*, London: Weidenfeld & Nicolson, 1993, p. 8.

25. Quoted in *Power Politics and the Labour Party* from New Fabian essays, Turnstile Press, 1952.

26. Hennessy, Peter and Anthony Seldon, *Ruling Performance*, Oxford: Basil Blackwell, 1987, p. 39.

27. Hennessy, Peter, *Never Again: Britain, 1945–1951*, London: Jonathan Cape, 1992, pp. 216–8.

28. Castle, op. cit., p. 184.

29. Acheson, op. cit., p. 416.

30. Walker, op. cit., p. 26.

31. Gilmour, op. cit., pp. 29–30.

32. Burridge, op. cit., p. 203.

33. Bullock, Alan, *Ernest Bevin Foreign Secretary*, Portsmouth: Heineman, 1983, p. 5.

34. Ibid., pp. 184–5.

35. Hurd, Douglas, *Choose Your Weapons*, London: Weidenfeld & Nicolson, 2010, pp. 326, 330.

36. Ibid., p. 139.

37. Bullock, op. cit., p. 12.

38. Bevin to Cripps, 20 Sept, 1945. FO 800/512/US/45/25.

39. Quoted in Bullock, op. cit., p. 602.

4. CHURCHILL AND THE ATLANTIC ALLIANCE

1. Clarke, Peter, *The Last 1000 Days of the British Empire*, London: Penguin, 2007, p. 117.

2. Ignatieff, Michael, *Isaiah Berlin*, London: Chatto & Windus, 1998, p. 114.

3. Amery, Leo, *The Empire at Bay*, London: Hutchinson, 1988, p. 713.

4. Kolko, G., *The Politics of War: Allied Diplomacy and the World Crisis of 1943–45*, London: Weidenfeld & Nicolson, 1969, pp. 291–3.

5. Clarke, op. cit., p. 25.

6. Kagan, Robert, *Paradise and Power*, London: Atlantic Books, 2003, p. 71.

7. Gelber, Lionel, *America in Britain's Place*, New York: Frederik A. Praeger, 1961, p. 15–6.

8. Ibid.

9. Attwood, Paul L., *War and Empire: The American Way of Life*, London: Pluto Press, 2010, p. 60.

10. Ash, Timothy Garton, *Free World*, London: Allen Lane, 2004, p. 31.

11. Hennessy, Peter, *Never Again: Britain, 1945–1951*, London: Jonathan Cape, 1992, p. 368.

12. Cooper, Robert, *The Breaking of Nations*, London: Atlantic Books, 2003, p. 133.

13. Gelber, Lionel, *The Alliance of Necessity*, London: Robert Hale, 1966, p. 183.

14. Hennessy, op. cit., pp. 353, 355.

15. Hennessy, Peter, *The Secret State*, London: Allen Lane, The Penguin Press, 2002, pp. 26, 28.
16. Horne, Alistair, *Macmillan 1957–1986*, London: Macmillan, 1989, p. 330.
17. Acheson, Dean, *Present at the Creation*, New York: W. W. Norton, 1969, p. 73.
18. Horne, op. cit., p. 347.
19. Hennessy, Peter, *Having it so Good: Britain in the 1950s*, London: Penguin Books, 2006/2007, p. 413.
20. Gilmour, Ian, *Whatever Happened to the Tories*, London: Fourth Estate, 1997, p. 71.
21. Shanks, Michael, *The Stagnant Society*, London: Penguin Special, 1961, p. 222.
22. Quoted in Alistair Horne, *Macmillan 1957–1986*, London: Macmillan, 1989, pp. 451–2.
23. Denman, Roy, *Missed Chances*, London: Cassell, 1996, p. 292.
24. Attwood, op. cit., p. 163.
25. Clark, William, *Less than Kin*, Cambridge: The Riverside Press, 1957, p. 44 et seq.
26. Brivati, Brian, *Hugh Gaitskell*, London: Richard Cohen Books, 1996, p. 170.

5. EDEN AND SUEZ

1. Eden, Anthony, *Full Circle*, London: Cassell, 1960, p. 99.
2. Ibid., p. 133.
3. Ibid., pp. 135–6.
4. Ibid., p. 256.
5. Ibid., p. 337.
6. Ibid., p. 484.
7. Ibid., p. 540.
8. Cooper, Robert, *The Breaking of Nations*, London: Atlantic Books, 2003, p. 5.
9. Thorpe, D. R., *Selwyn Lloyd*, London: Jonathan Cape, 1989, p. 226.
10. Gilmour, Ian, *Whatever Happened to the Tories*, London: Fourth Estate, 1997, pp. 110–1.
11. Hennessy, Peter, *Having it so Good*, London: Penguin Books, 2006/07, p. 450.
12. Woollacott, Martin, *After Suez*, London, New York: I. B. Tauris, 2006, p. 31.
13. Kyle, Keith, *Suez*, London: Weidenfeld and Nicolson, 1991, p. 509.
14. Gilmour, op. cit., p. 124.
15. Drew Middleton, *The British*, London: Pan Books, 1972, p. 167, and *The Supreme Choice*, London: Secker and Warburg, 1963, p. 227.
16. Hennessy, op. cit., p. 442.
17. Strachey, John, *The End of Empire*, London: Victor Gollancz, 1959.

6. MACMILLAN

1. Kyle, Keith, *Suez*, London: Weidenfeld and Nicolson, 1991, p. 508.
2. Horne, Alistair, *Macmillan 1957–1986*, London: Macmillan, 1989, p. 16.

3. Barnes, John, *From Eden to Macmillan*, in Hennessy, Peter and Anthony Seldon, *eds.*, *Ruling Performance*, Oxford: Basil Blackwell, 1987, p. 99.

4. *The Supreme Choice*, London: Secker and Warburg, 1963, p. 217.

5. Gelber, Lionel, *The Alliance of Necessity*, London: Robert Hale, 1966, p. 207.

6. Horne, op. cit., p. 26.

7. Barnes, op. cit.

8. Horne, op. cit., p. 325.

9. Ibid., p. 46.

10. Thorpe, D. R., *Alec Douglas-Home*, London: Sinclair Stevenson, 1996, pp. 239–40, [For a detailed cover of the Cuban Crisis from the British point of view see Thorpe, *Alec Douglas-Home*, 'The Cuban Missile Crisis', London: Pimlico, 1999, pp. 231–52.]

11. Fursenko, Aleksandra and Timothy Naftali, *One Hell of a Gamble*, London: Pimlico, 1999, pp. 235–36, Chomsky, Noam, *Hegemon of Survival*, London: Hamish Hamilton, 2003, p. 79.

13. Horne, op. cit., For a detailed account of the Kennedy-Macmillan 'rapport' during the Cuban Crisis see Horne, *Macmillan 1957–1986*, 'A Trial of Wills', pp. 362–85.

14. Thorpe, op. cit., p. 215.

15. Riddell, Peter, *Hug Them Close*, London: Politico's, 2003, p. 57.

16. Acheson, Dean, *Present at the Creation*, New York: W. W. Norton, 1969, p. 323.

17. Acheson, op. cit., p. 387.

7. THE NUCLEAR QUESTION

1. Gowing, Margaret, *Independence and Deterrence: Britain and Atomic Energy 1945–1951, Vol. 1; Policy Making*, London: Macmillan, 1974, pp. 1–2.

2. Cooper, Robert, *The Breaking of Nations*, London: Atlantic Books, 2003, p. 128.

3. Hennessy, Peter, *Muddling Through*, London: Victor Gollancz, 1996, p. 101.

4. Williams, Raymond, *Resources of Hope*, London and New York: Verso, 1989, p. 196.

5. Hennessy, op. cit., p. 102.

6. Gilmour, Ian, *Whatever Happened to the Tories*, London: Fourth Estate, 1997, p. 40.

7. Hennessy, Peter, *Never Again: Britain, 1945–1951*, London: Jonathan Cape, 1992, pp. 313–4.

8. Cathcart, Brian, *Test of Greatness*, London: John Murray, 1994, p. 25.

9. Hennessy, Peter, *Having it so Good*, London: Penguin, 2006/07, p. 148.

10. Hennessy, Peter, *Muddling Through*, London: Victor Gollancz, 1996, p. 159.

11. Cathcart, op. cit., p. 273.

12. Hennessy, Peter, *The Secret State*, London: Allen Lane, the Penguin Press, 2002, p. 57.

13. Ibid., p. 57.

14. Shore, Peter, *Leading the Left*, London: Weidenfeld & Nicolson, 1993, p. 68.

15. Adams, Jad, *Tony Benn*, London: Macmillan, 1992, p. 133.

16. Adams, op. cit., pp. 223–4.

17. Peter, Carrington (Lord), *Reflections on Things Past*, London: Collins, 1988 p. 155.

18. Shore, op. cit., p. 9.

19. Hennessy, Peter, *Muddling Through*, London: Victor Gollancz, 1996, p. 110.

20. Dalyell, Tam, *Misrule*, London: Hamish Hamilton, 1987, p. 76.

21. Shukman, David, *The Sorcerers Apprentice*, London: Hodder & Stoughton, 1995, pp. 96–8.

22. Devjensky, Mary, *The Independent*, 2 June 2010.

8. WILSON AND VIETNAM

1. Pimlott, Ben, *Harold Wilson*, London: Harper Collins, 1992, p. 365.

2. Ibid., p. 384.

3. Goodman George, ed., *The State of the Nation*, London: Victor Gollancz, 1997, p. 60.

4. Pimlott, op. cit., p. 185.

5. Shore, Peter, *Leading the Left*, London: Weidenfeld & Nicolson, 1993, p. 94.

6. Mark Curtis, *Web of Deceit*, London: Vintage, 2003, pp. 104–5.

7. Pimlott, op. cit., p. 433.

8. Pearse, Edward, *The Lost Leaders*, London: Little Brown, 1997, p. 165 et seq.

9. Ibid., p. 167.

10. Gilmour, Ian, *Whatever Happened to the Tories*, London: Fourth Estate, 1997, p. 281.

11. Curtis, op. cit., p. 107.

12. Ponting, Clive, *Breach of Promise*, London: Hamish Hamilton, 1989, p. 235.

13. Ibid., p. 237.

14. *The Independent*, 30 March 2006.

15. Russell, Ben, *The Independent*, 24 May 2007.

16. *The Independent*, 2 April 2010.

17. Evans, Rob and Richard Norton-Taylor, *The Observer*, 5 December 2012.

9. HEATH TAKES BRITAIN INTO THE EEC

1. Kissinger, Henry, *White House Years*, New York: Simon & Schuster, 1979, p. 933.

2. Ibid., p. 933.

3. Ibid., p. 932.

4. Heath, Edward, *Edward Heath: The Course of My Life*, London: Hodder & Stoughton, 1998, p. 472.

5. Ibid., p. 473.

6. Kissinger, op. cit., pp. 964–5.

7. Kissinger, op. cit., p. 425.

8. Riddell, Peter, *Hug Them Close*, London: Politico's, 2003, p. 45.

9. Kissinger, Henry, *Years of Renewal*, London: Simon & Schuster, 1999, p. 603.

10. Heath, op. cit., p. 492.

11. Riddell, op. cit., p. 45.

12. Muller, Rory, *Inglorious Disarray*, London: Hurst, 2011, p. 41.

13. *International Herald Tribune*, 14 November 1973.

14. Dimbleby, David and David Reynolds, *An Ocean Apart: The Relationship Between Britain and America in the Twentieth Century*, London: BBC Books, Hodder & Stoughton, 1988, p. 266.

15. Muller, op. cit., p. 25.

16. Callaghan, James, *Time and Chance*, London: Collins, 1987, p. 75.

17. Ibid., p. 76.

18. Ibid., p. 81.

19. Ibid., p. 90.

20. Riddell, op. cit., p. 46.

21. Ibid., p. 295.

22. Ibid., p. 296.

23. Callaghan, op. cit., pp. 319–20.

24. Riddell, op. cit., p. 47.

10. MARGARET THATCHER

1. Thatcher, Margaret, *The Path to Power*, London: Harper Collins, 1995, p. 91.

2. Young, Hugo, *One of Us*, London: Macmillan, 1989, p. 120.

3. Thatcher, op. cit., p. 86.

4. Thomson, Andrew, *Margaret Thatcher The Woman Within*, London: W H Allen, 1989, p. 160.

5. Vincent, John, 'The Thatcher Governments, 1979–1987', in *Ruling Performance*, Hennessy, Peter and Anthony Seldon, eds., Oxford: Basil Blackwell, 1987, p. 282.

6. Cradock, Sir Percy, *In Pursuit of British Interests: Reflections on Foreign Policy under Margaret Thatcher and John Major*, London: John Murray, 1997, p. 54. Quoted in Riddell, Peter, *Hug Them Close*, London: Politico's, 2003, p. 48.

7. Thatcher, op. cit., p. 810.

8. Ibid., p. 472.

9. Howe, Geoffrey, *Conflict of Loyalty*, London: Macmillan, 1994, p. 508.

10. Thomson, op. cit., p. 167.

11. Young, op. cit., p. 399.

12. Thomson, op. cit., pp. 106–7.

13. Thatcher, Margaret, *Downing Street Years*, London: Harper Collins, 1993, p. 157.

14. Cradock, Sir Percy, op. cit., 1997, p. 125, London: John Murray, 2002.

15. Thatcher, *Downing Street Years*, p. 320.

16. Hennessy, Peter, *Having it so Good*, London: Penguin Books, 2007, p. 614.

17. Thatcher, *Downing Street Years*, p. 227.
18. Healey, Denis, *The Time of My Life*, London: Michael Joseph, 1989, p. 507.
19. Thatcher, *Downing Street Years*, p. 268.
20. Dalyell, Tam, *Misrule*, London: Hamish Hamilton, 1987, p. 31.
21. Thatcher, *Downing Street Years*, p. 769.
22. Thatcher, *Downing Street Years*, p. 783.
23. Heseltine, Michael, *Where There's A Will*, London: Hutchinson 1987, p. 275.
24. Ibid., p. 283.
25. Cooper, Robert, *The Breaking of Nations: Order and Chaos in the Twenty-First Century*, London: Atlantic Books, 2003, p. 99.
26. Thomson, op. cit., p. 141.
27. Haig, Alexander, *Caveat*, London: Weidenfeld & Nicolson, 1984, p. 280.
28. Henderson, Sir Nicholas, *Channels and Tunnels*, London: Weidenfeld & Nicolson, 1987, p. 14.
29. Freedman, Lawrence and Virginia Gamba-Stonehouse, *Signals of War*, London: Faber and Faber, 1990, p. 189.
30. Gilmour, Ian, *Whatever Happened to the Tories*, London: Fourth Estate, 1997, p. 252.
31. Thatcher, *Downing Street Years*, pp. 331–2.
32. Howe, op. cit., p. 331.
33. Young, op. cit., p. 347.
34. Thatcher, *Downing Street Years*, p. 442.
35. Harris, Kenneth, *Thatcher*, London: Weidenfeld & Nicolson, 1988, p. 202.
36. Dalyell, op. cit., p. 61 et seq.
37. Gilmour, op. cit., pp. 256–7.
38. Benn, Tony, *The End of an Era, Diaries 1980–1990*, London: Hutchinson, 1992, p. 433.
39. Dalyell, op. cit., p. 65.
40. Howe, op. cit., p. 505.
41. Young, op. cit., p. 470.
42. Ibid., p. 478.
43. Tebbit, Norman, *Upwardly Mobile*, London: Weidenfeld & Nicolson, 1988, p. 59.
44. Ibid., p. 83.

11. JOHN MAJOR

1. Major, John, *John Major, the Autobiography*, London; Harper Collins, 1999, p. 225.
2. Ibid., p. 244.
3. Ibid., p. 496.
4. Ibid., p. 578.
5. Riddell, Peter, *Hug Them Close*, London: Politico's, 2003, p. 56.

12. TONY BLAIR

1. Riddell, Peter, *Hug Them Close*, London: Politico's, 2003, p. 61.
2. Ibid., p. 136.
3. Ibid., p. 172.
4. Ibid., p. 248.
5. Ibid., p. 303.
6. Ibid., p. 15.
7. Ibid., p. 168.
8. Byers, Michael, *War Law*, London: Atlantic Books, 2005, p. 68.
9. Ibid., p. 68.
10. Richards, Steve, *The Independent*, 21 October 2004.
11. Richards, Steve, *The Independent*, 21 October 2004.
12. *The Independent*, 17 November 2004.
13. Hamilton, Adrian, *The Independent*, 10 February 2005.
14. *The Independent*, 6 July 2006.
15. *The Independent*, 22 July 2006.
16. *The Independent*, 7 February 2007.
17. *The independent*, 10 October 2006.
18. Grice, Andrew, *The Independent*, 24 July 2007.
19. Cockburn, Patrick, *The Independent*, 8 July 2010.
20. Devji, Faisal, *The Terrorist in Search of Humanity*, London: Hurst, 2008, p. 81.
21. Brezinski, Zbigniew, *Strategic Vision*, New York: Basic Books, 2012, p. 66.
22. *The Independent*, 12 January 2006.
23. *The Independent*, 31 March 2006.
24. Richards, Steve, *The Independent*, 27 November 2009.
25. *The Independent*, 23 November 2009.
26. Sardar, Ziauddin and Meryl Wyn Davies, *Will America Change?*, Cambridge: Icon Books, 2008, pp. 39–44.
27. Sardar, op. cit., p. 65.
28. Riddell, op. cit., p. 19.
29. Perry, Mark, *How to Lose the War on Terror*, London: Hurst, 2010, p. 119.
30. Soros, George, *The Bubble of American Supremacy*, London; Phoenix, 2004, pp. 19, 25.

13. BRITAIN AND EUROPE

1. *Hansard*, 30 April 1944, col. 401.
2. Denman, Roy, *Missed Chances Britain and Europe in the Twentieth Century*, London: Cassell, 1996, p. 184.
3. W. S. Churchill, 14 May 1947, Albert Hall.
4. Kagan, Robert, *Paradise and Power*, London: Atlantic Books, 2003, p. 5.
5. Hennessy, Peter, *Never Again: Britain, 1945–1951*, London; Jonathan Cape, 1992, p. 293, Cooper, Robert, *The Breaking of Nations*, London: Atlantic Books, 2003, p. 96.

7. Quoted in Bullock, Alan, *Ernest Bevin Foreign Secretary*, London: Heinemann, 1983, p. 703.
8. Ibid., pp. 722–3.
9. Ibid., p. 723.
10. Acheson, Dean, *Present at the Creation*, New York; W. W. Norton, 1969, p. 385.
11. Ibid., p. 38.
12. Walker, Martin, *The Cold War*, London: Fourth Estate, 1993, p. 87.
13. Denman, op. cit., p. 206.
14. Gelber, Lionel, *The Alliance of Necessity*, London: Robert Hale, 1966, p. 38.
15. Ibid., p. 131.
16. Kissinger, Henry, *White House Years*, New York: Simon & Schuster, 1979, pp. 87–8.
17. Benn, Tony, *Office Without Power*, London: Hutchinson, 1988, p. 149.
18. Denman, op. cit., pp. 223–4.
19. Ash, Timothy Garton, *Free World*, London: Allen Lane, 2004, p. 28.
20. Ibid., p. 34.
21. Kagan, op. cit., p. 40.
22. Riddell, Peter, *Hug Them Close*, London: Politico's, 2003, pp. 176–7.
23. Ibid., p. 56.
24. Middleton, Drew, *The Supreme Choice*, London: Secker & Warburg, 1963, p. 228.
25. Shanks, Michael and John Lambert, *Britain and the New Europe*, London: Chatto & Windus, 1962, p. 34.
26. *The Times*, 7 August 1962.
27. See Paterson, Peter, *The Life of Lord George Brown*, London: Chatto & Windus, 1993.
28. Kissinger, Henry, *The Troubled Partnership: A Reappraisal f the Atlantic Alliance*, New York: McGraw Hill, 1965, p. 40.
29. Pimlott, Ben, *Harold Wilson*, London: Harper Collins, 1992, p. 441.
30. Walker, Martin, *The Cold War*, London: Fourth Estate, 1993, p. 129, Gilmour, Ian, *Whatever Happened to the Tories*, London: Fourth Estate, 1997, pp. 285–7.
32. Marquand, David, *The Unprincipled Society*, London: Jonathan Cape, 1988, p. 9.
33. Leonard, Mark, *Why Europe Will Run the 21st Century*, London: Fourth Estate, 2005, pp. 61–4, 82.
34. McRae, Hamish, *The World in 2020*, London: Harper Collins, 1994, p. 231.
35. Riddell, op. cit., p. 224.
36. Leonard, op. cit., p. 33.
37. Quoted in Ash, op. cit., p. 32.
38. *The Observer*, 20 December 2010.
39. Leonard, op. cit., p. 33
40. Kagan, op. cit., p. 21 et seq.
41. Cooper, op. cit., pp. 169–71.

42. Todd, Emmanuel, *After the Empire*, New York; Columbia University Press, 2003, p. 182.

14. CAMERON AND OBAMA

1. Stephen, Phillip, *The Financial Times*, 6 October 2010.
2. Usborne, David, *The Independent*, 19 July 2009.
3. *The Independent*, 4 December 2012.
4. *The Independent*, 4 December 2012.
5. Helm, Toby and Jamie Doward, *The Observer*, 16 October 2011.
6. McSmith, Andy and Kim Sengupta, *The Independent*, 20 October 2011.
7. Martin Woollacott, *After Suez*, London and New York: I. B. Tauris, 2006, p. 108.
8. Woollacott, op. cit., p. 119.
9. Healey, Denis, *When Shrimps Begin to Whistle*, London: Michael Joseph, 1990, p. 18.
10. Doyle, Leonard, *The Independent*, 4 February 2009.
11. *The Telegraph*, 17 January 2009.
12. *The Evening Standard*, 20 May 2011.
13. *The Evening Standard*, 12 March 2012.
14. *The Independent*, 13 March 2012.

15. PROBLEMS

1. Kyle, Keith, *Suez*, London: Weidenfeld & Nicolson, 1991, pp. 43–4.
2. Healey, Denis, *The Time of My Life*, London: Michael Joseph, 1989, p. 194.
3. Healey, op. cit., p. 205.
4. Ash, Timothy Garton, *Free World*, London: Allen Lane, 2004.
5. Patten, Chris, *East and West*, London: Macmillan, 1998, p. 5.
6. Ibid., p. 111.
7. Riddell, Peter, *Hug Them Close*, London: Politico's, 2003, p. 57.
8. Conquest, Robert, *Reflections on a Ravaged Century*, London: John Murray, 1999, p. 271.

16. DIFFERENT PERSPECTIVES

1. Kissinger, Henry, *White House Years*, New York: Simon & Schuster, 1979, p. 90.
2. Ibid., p. 91.
3. Soros, George, *The Bubble of American Supremacy*, London: Phoenix, 2004, p. 169.
4. Curtis, Mark, *Web of Deceit*, London: Vintage, 2003, p. 104.
5. Ibid., pp. 211–2.
6. Ibid., p. 114.
7. Harris, Kenneth, *Thatcher*, London: Weidenfeld & Nicolson, 1986, p. 123.

8. Hennessy, Peter and Anthony Seldon, *Ruling Performance*, Oxford: Basil Blackwell, 1987, p. 34.

9. Marquand, David, *The Unprincipled Society*, London: Jonathan Cape, 1988, p. 11.

10. Horne, Alistair, *Macmillan 1957–1986*, London: Macmillan, 1989, p. 289.

11. Ponting, Clive, *Breach of Promise*, London: Hamish Hamilton, 1989, pp. 105–6.

12. Walker, Martin, *The Cold War*, London: Fourth Estate, 1993, p. 47.

13. Shore, Peter, *Leading from the Left*, London: Weidenfeld & Nicolson, 1993, pp. 52–3.

14. Ferguson, Niall, *Colossus*, London: Allen Lane, 2004, p. 25.

15. Ibid., p. 162.

16. Walker, op. cit., p. 80.

17. Amery, Leo, *The Empire at Bay*, London: Hutchinson, 1988, p. 826.

18. Riddell, op. cit., p. 304.

19. Blum, William, *Killing Hope*, London: Zed Books, 2003, p. 108.

20. Ibid., p. 108 et seq.

17. THE GROWING AMERICAN IMPERIUM

1. Hennessy, Peter, *Muddling Through*, London; Victor Gollancz, 1996, pp. 55–6.

2. Attwood, Paul L., *War and Empire*, London: Pluto Press, 2010, p. 15.

3. Ibid., p. 137.

4. *Foreign Relations of the United States*, Washington D.C.: US Government Printing office, 1947, Vol. Viii, 54.

5. *The Independent*, 24 February 2007.

6. See Lutz, Catherine, ed., *The Bases of Empire*, London: Pluto Press, 2009, pp. 97, 98, 108, 109.

7. Todd, Emmanuel, *After the Empire*, 'The Breakdown of the American Order', New York: Columbia University Press, 2002, p. 170.

8. Kagan, Robert, *Paradise and Power*, London: Atlantic Books, 2003, pp. 85–6.

9. Ponting, Clive, *Breach of Promise*, London: Hamish Hamilton, 1989, p. 44.

10. Ibid., p. 46.

11. Ibid., p. 47.

12. Ibid., p. 58.

13. Ibid., p. 60.

18. BRITISH OPTIONS AND MISSED OPPORTUNITIES

1. Seldon, Anthony, *Ruling Performance*, Oxford: Basil Blackwell, 1987, p. 87.

2. King-Hall, Stephen, *Power Politics in the Nuclear Age*, London: Victor Gollancz, 1962, p. 35.

3. Ibid., p. 170.

4. Heffer, Simon, *Like the Roman*, London: Weidenfeld & Nicolson, 1998, p. 187.

5. Ibid., p. 400.

6. Ibid., p. 864.
7. Shepherd, Robert, *Enoch Powell A Biography*, London: Hutchinson, 1990, pp. 67–8.
8. Ibid., p. 20.
9. Cosgrave, Patrick, *The Lives of Enoch Powell*, London: The Bodley Head, 1989, p. 217.
10. Ibid., p. 219.
11. Nutting, Anthony, *Europe Will Not Wait*, London: Hollis & Carter, 1960, p. 5.
12. Ibid., p. 7.
13. Ibid., p. 11.
14. Ibid., p. 91.

19. THE UNITED STATES: A TURNING POINT?

1. Kolko, Gabriel, *World in Crisis: The End of the American Century*, London: Pluto Press, 2009, p. 7.
2. Ibid., p. 51.
3. Marks, Kathy, *The Independent*, 17 November 2012.
4. Brezinski, Zbigniew, *Strategic Vision*, New York: Basic Books, 2012, p. 35.
5. Ibid., p. 30.
6. Gilmour, Ian, *Whatever Happened to the Tories*, London: Fourth Estate, 1997, p. 72.
7. Cooper, Robert, *The Breaking of Nations*, London: Atlantic Books, 2003, p. 48.
8. Soros, George, *The Bubble of American Supremacy*, London: Phoenix, 2004, p. 11.
9. Ibid., p. 79.
10. Howard, Michael, *The Invention of Peace*, London: Profile Books, 1998, pp. 101, 108.
11. Gray, John, *False Dawn*, London: Granta Books, 1998, pp. 101–2.
12. Ibid., p. 105.
13. Shi, Qiag, 'Chinese Poliburo—interview', *New Perspectives*, Quarterly, vol. 14, no. 3, Summer 1997, pp. 9–10.

20. HOW TO RELATE TO THE BIG POWER LINE-UP

1. Kagan, Robert, *The Return of History and the End of Dreams*, London: Atlantic Books, 2008, p. 66.
2. Patten, Chris, *East and West*, London: Macmillan, 1998, p. 293.
3. Meyer, Claude, *China or Japan*, London: Hurst, 2011, p. 83.
4. Ibid., p. 37.
5. Kagan, op. cit., pp. 13–6.
6. *New York Times*, 4 February 2012.
7. *The Independent*, 2 November 2010.
8. Todd, Emmanuel, *After the Empire*, New York: Columbia University Press, 2002, p. 3.
9. Kolko, Gabriel, *World in Crisis*, London: Pluto Press, 2009, p. 90.

10. Ibid., p. 101.
11. MacIntyre, Donald, *The Independent*, 3 November 2011.
12. *The Independent*, 6 November 2011.
13. *The Independent*, 10 November 2011.
14. Kolko, op. cit., p. 119.

21. NATO

1. Healey, Denis, *When Shrimps Learn to Whistle*, London: Michael Joseph, 1990, pp. 193–4.
2. Hennessy, Peter, *Never Again: Britain, 1945–1951*, London: Jonathan Cape, 1992, p. 252.
3. Marr, Andrew, *Ruling Britannia*, London: Michael Joseph, 1995, p. 215.
4. Williams, Raymond, *Resources of Hope*, London: Verso, 1989, p. 68.
5. Attwood, Paul, *War and Empire: The American Way of Life*, London: Pluto Press, 2010, p. 236.
6. Soros, George, *The Bubble of American Supremacy*, London: Phoenix, 2004, p. 167.
7. Kagan, op. cit., p. 20.
8. Sardar, Ziauddin and Meryl Wyn Davies, *Will America Change?*, Cambridge: Icon Books, 2008, p. 231.
9. Chomsky, Noam, *Hegemon of Survival*, London: Hamish Hamilton, 2003, p. 57.
10. Kolko, op. cit., p. 67.
12. Hamilton, Adrian, *The Independent*, 10 September 2006.
13. Brezinski, Zbigniew, *Strategic Vision: America and the Crisis of Global Power*, New York: Basic Books, 2012, p. 22.
14. Gutcher, Lianne and Andrew Buncombe, *The Independent*, 16 March 2012.

22. GREAT BRITAIN: AN EXIT STRATEGY

1. These poll figures have been extracted from a *Wikipedia* appraisal of the special relationship.
2. Kolko, Gabriel, *World in Crisis*, London: Pluto Press, 2009, p. 75.
3. Soros, George, *The Bubble of American Supremacy*, London: Phoenix, 2004, p. 34.
4. *The Independent*, 28 February 2012.
5. *The Independent*, 15 May 2010.
6. *The Evening Standard*, 31 August 2012.
7. Ash, Timothy Garton, *The Observer*, 18 July 2010.
8. Huntington, Samuel P., *The Clash of Civilizations and the Remaking of World Order*, New York: Touchstone Books, 1997, pp. 20–1.
9. Shukman, David, *The Sorcerer's Apprentice*, London: Hodder & Stoughton, 1995, pp. 3–4.
10. *The Independent*, (editorial comment), 17 October 2012.

BIBLIOGRAPHY

Acheson, Dean, *Present at the Creation: My Years in the State Department*, London and New York: W. W. Norton, 1969.

Adams, Jad, *Tony Benn A Biography*, London: Macmillan, 1992.

Amory, Leo, *The Empire at Bay: The Leo Amery Diaries 1929–1945*, Barnes, John and David Nicholson, eds, London: Hutchinson, 1988.

Arnold, Guy, *The Maverick State: Gaddafi and the New World Order*, London: Cassell, 1996.

Arnold, Guy, *Towards Peace and a Multiracial Commonwealth*, London: Chapman and Hall, 1964.

Ash, Timothy Garton, *Free World*, London: Allen Lane, 2004.

Atwood, Paul L., *War and Empire: The American Way of Life*, London: Pluto Press, 2010.

Barnett, Correlli, *The Collapse of British Power*, Eyre Methuen [Sutton Publishing]. 1972, 1997.

——*The Lost Victory: British Dreams, British Realities 1945–1950*, London: Macmillan, 1995.

Benn, Tony, *Office Without Power Diaries 1968–72*, London: Hutchinson, 1988.

——*Conflicts of Interest: Diaries 1977–80*, London: Hutchinson, 1990.

——*The End of an Era: Diaries 1980–90*, London: Hutchinson, 1992.

Blum, William, *Killing Hope*, London: Zed Books, 2003.

Boggs, Carl, *The Crimes of Empire*, London: Pluto Press, 2010.

Brezinski, Zbigniew, *Strategic Vision: America and the Crisis of Global Power*, New York: Basic Books, 2012.

Brivati, Brian, *Hugh Gaitskell*, London: Richard Cohen Books, 1996.

Bullock, Alan, *Ernest Bevin Foreign Secretary*, London: Heineman, 1983.

Burridge, Trevor, *Clement Attlee*, London: Jonathan Cape, 1985.

Byers, Michael, *War Law*, London: Atlantic Books, 2005.

Callaghan, James, *Time and Chance*, London: Collins, 1987.

Carrington, Peter (Lord), *Reflections on Things Past*, London: Collins, 1988.

Castle, Barbara, *Fighting All The Way*, London: Macmillan, 1993.

Cathcart, Brian, *Test of Greatness: Britain's Struggle for the Atom Bomb*, London: John Murray, 1994.

Chomsky, Noam, *Hegemony of Survival: America's Quest for Global Dominance*, London: Hamish Hamilton, 2003.

Churchill, Winston Spencer, *Europe Unite Speeches 1947–1948*, London: Cassell, 1950.

Churchill, Winston Spencer, *The Unwritten Alliance Speeches 1953–1959*, London: Cassell, 1961.

Clark, William, *Less Than Kin*, Cambridge: The Riverside Press, 1957.

Clarke, Peter, *A Question of Leadership*, London: Hamish Hamilton, 1991.

Clarke, Peter, *The Last Thousand Days of the British Empire*, London: Penguin Books, 2007.

Cockerell, Michael, *Live from No 10: The Inside Story of Prime Ministers and Television*, London: Faber and Faber, 1988.

The Commission on Global Governance, *Our Global Neighbourhood*, Oxford: Oxford University Press, 1995.

Conquest, Robert, *Reflections on a Ravaged Century*, London: John Murray, 1999.

Cooper, Robert, *The Breaking of Nations: Order and Chaos in the Twenty-First Century*, London: Atlantic Books, 2003.

Cosgrave, Patrick, *The Lives of Enoch Powell*, London: The Bodley Head, 1989.

Curtis, Mark, *Web of Deceit: Britain's Real Role in the World*, London: Vintage, 2003.

Dayell, Tam, *Misrule*, London: Hamish Hamilton, 1987.

Denman, Roy, *Missed Chances, Britain and Europe in the Twentieth Century*, London: Cassell, 1996.

Devji, Faisal, *The Terrorist in Search of Humanity*, London: Hurst & Co., 2008.

Eden, Anthony, The Rt. Hon., The Earl of Avon, *Memoirs: Facing the Dictators*, London: Cassell, 1962.

Eden, Anthony, *Full Circle*, London: Cassell, 1960.

Ferguson, Niall, *Colossus: The Rise and Fall of the American Empire*, London: Allen Lane, 2004.

Fisher, Nigel, *Iain Macleod*, London: Andre Deutsch, 1973.

Fowler, Norman, *Ministers Decide*, London: Chapman, 1991.

Freedman, Lawrence and Virginia Gamba-Stonehouse, *Signals of War: The Falklands Conflict of 1982*, London: Faber and Faber, 1990.

Freedman, Lawrence and Efraim Karsh, *The Gulf Conflict 1990–1991*, London: Faber and Faber, 1993.

Fukuyama, Francis, *The End of History and the Last Man*, London: Hamish Hamilton, 1992.

Fursenko, Aleksandra and Timothy Naftali, *One Hell of a Gamble*, London: Pimlico, 1999.

Galbraith, John Kenneth, *The Culture of Contentment*, London: Sinclair-Stevenson, 1997.

Gelber, Lionel, *America in Britain's Place*, New York: Frederick A. Praeger, 1961.

Gelber, Lionel, *The Alliance of Necessity*, London: Robert Hale, 1966.

Gilmour, Ian, *Dancing with Dogma: Britain under Thatcherism*, London: Simon and Schuster, 1992.

——*Whatever Happened to the Tories*, London: Fourth Estate, 1997.

Goodman, Geoffrey, ed., *The State of the Nation: The Political Legacy of Aneuran Bevan*, London: Victor Gollancz, 1997.

Gray, John, *False Dawn The Delusions of Global Capitalism*, London: Granta Books, 1998.

Harris, Kenneth, *Thatcher*, London: Weidenfeld and Nicolson, 1988.

Hayter, Sir William, *The Diplomacy of the Great Powers*, London: Hamish Hamilton, 1960.

Healey, Denis, *The Time of My Life*, London: Michael Joseph, 1989.

——*When Shrimps Learn to Whistle*, London: Michael Joseph, 1990.

Heath, Edward, *Edward Heath: The Course of my Life*, London: Hodder & Stoughton, 1998.

Heffer, Simon, *Like the Roman: The Life of Enoch Powell*, London: Weidenfeld & Nicolson, 1998.

Hennessy, Peter, *Having it so Good: Britain in the Fifties*, London: Penguin Books, 2006/2007.

——*Muddling Through*, London: Victor Gollancz, 1996.

——and Anthony Seldon, *Ruling Performance: British Governments from Attlee to Thatcher*, Oxford; Basil Blackwell, 1987.

——*The Secret State: Whitehall and the Cold War*, London: Allen Lane, The Penguin Press, 2002.

Hennessy, Peter, *Never Again: Britain, 1945–1951*, London: Jonathan Cape, 1992.

Heseltine, Michael, *The Challenge of Europe: Can Britain Win?*, London: Weidenfeld and Nicolson, 1989.

Heseltine, Michael, *Where there's a Will*, London: Hutchinson, 1987.

Horne, Alistair, *Macmillan 1894–1956*, *Volume I of the Official Biography*, London: Macmillan, 1988.

——*Macmillan 1957–1986*, *Volume II of the Official Biography*, London: Macmillan, 1989.

Howard, Anthony, *Crossman: The Pursuit of Power*, London: Jonathan Cape, 1990.

Howard, Michael, *The Invention of Peace: Reflections on War and International Order*, London: Profile Books, 2000.

Howe, Geoffrey, *Conflict of Loyalty*, London: Macmillan, 1994.

Huntington, Samuel P., *The Clash of Civilisations and the Remaking of World Order*, New York: Touchstone Books, 1997.

Hurd, Douglas, *Choose Your Weapons*, London: Weidenfeld and Nicolson, 2010.

Ignatieff, Michael, *Isaiah Berlin*, London: Chatto & Windus, 1998.

Kagan, Robert, *Paradise and Power: Americac and Europe in the New World Order*, London: Atlantic Books, 2003.

Kagan, Robert, *The Return of History and the End of Dreams*, London: Atlantic Books, 2008.

King-Hall, Stephen, *Power Politics in the Nuclear Age*, London: Victor Gollancz, 1962.

Kissinger, Henry, *White House Years*, New York: Simon and Schuster, 1979.

——*Years of Renewal*, New York: Simon and Schuster, 1999.

Kolko, Gabriel, *World in Crisis: The End of the American Century*, London: Pluto Press, 2009.

Kyle, Keith, *Suez*, London: Weidenfeld and Nicolson, 1991.

Leonard, Mark, *Why Europe Will Run the 21st Century*, London: Fourth Estate, 2005.

Lewis, Geoffrey, *Lord Hailsham: A Life*, London: Pimlico, 1997.

Lutz, Catherine, ed., *The Bases of Empire*, London: Pluto Press, 2009.

Major, John, *John Major: The Autobiography*, London: Harper Collins, 1999.

Marquand, David, *The Unprincipled Society*, London: Jonathan Cape, 1988.

Marr, Andrew, *Ruling Britain: The Failure and Future of British Democracy*, London: Michael Joseph, 1995.

McCrae, Hamish, *The World in 2000: Power, Culture and Prosperity and a Vision of the Future*, London: Harper Collins, 1994.

Mercer, Derek, Geoff Mungham and Kevin Williams, *The Fog of War*, London: Heinemann, 1987.

Meyer, Claude, *China or Japan*, London: Hurst, 2011.

Middleton, Drew, *The British*, London: Pan Books, 1957.

——*The Supreme Choice—Britain and the European Community*, London: Secker & Warburg, 1963.

Muller, Rory, *Inglorious Disarray: Europe, Israel and the Palestinians Since 1967*, London: Hurst, 2011.

Nutting, Anthony, *Europe Will Not Wait*, London: Hollis & Carter, 1960.

Organski, A. F. K., *World Politics*, New York: Alfred A. Knopf, 1958.

Paterson, Peter, *The Life of Lord George Brown*, London: Chatto & Windus, 1993.

Patten, Chris, *East and West*, London: Macmillan, 1998.

Pearce, Edward, *The Lost Leaders: The Best Prime Ministers We Never Had*, London: Little, Brown and Co., 1997.

Perry, Mark, *How to Lose the War on Terror*, London: Hurst, 2010.

Pimlott, Ben, *Harold Wilson*, London: Harper Collins, 1992.

Ponting, Clive, *Breach of Promise: Labour in Power 1964–1970*, London: Hamish Hamilton, 1989.

Ponting, Clive, *1940: Myth and Reality*, London: Hamish Hamilton, 1990.

Porter, Bernard, *Empire and Super Empire Britain, America and the World*, New Haven, CT: Yale University Press, 2006.

Riddell, Peter, *Hug Them Close*, London: Politico's, 2003.

Sampson, Anthony, *The New Anatomy of Britain*, London: Hodder & Stoughton, 1971.

Sardar, Ziauddin and Merryl Wyn Davies, *Will America Change*, Cambridge: Icon Books, 2008.

Saul, John Ralston, *The Collapse of Globalism*, London: Atlantic Books, 2005.

Seldon, Anthony (ed.) and Peter Hennessy, *Ruling Performance*, Oxford: Basil Blackwell, 1987.

Shanks, Michael, *The Stagnant Society*, London: Penguin Special, 1961.

Shanks, Michael and John Lambert, *Britain and the New Europe: The Future of the Common Market*, London: Chatto & Windus, 1962.

Shepherd, Robert, *Enoch Powell: A Biography*, London: Hutchinson, 1996.

Shore, Peter, *Leading the Left*, London: Weidenfeld & Nicolson, 1993.

Shukman, David, *The Sorcerer's Apprentice*, London: Hodder & Stoughton, 1995.

Snow, C. P., *The Two Cultures and the Scientific Revolution* (The Rede Lecture 1959), Cambridge: Cambridge University Press, 1961.

Soros, George, *The Bubble of American Supremacy*, London: Phoenix, 2004.

Strachey, John, *The End of Empire*, London: Victor Gollancz, 1959.

Stafford, David, *Roosevelt and Churchill, 'Men of Secrets'*, London: Little, Brown and Company, 1999.

Tebbit, Norman, *Upwardly Mobile: An Autobiography*, London: Weidenfeld & Nicolson, 1988.

Thatcher, Margaret, *The Downing Street Years*, London: Harper Collins, 1993.

——*The Path to Power*, London: Harper Collins, 1995.

Thomson, Andrew, *Margaret Thatcher: The Woman Within*, London: W H Allen, 1989.

Thorpe, D. R., *Selwyn Lloyd*, London: Jonathan Cape, 1989.

Thorpe, D. R., *Alec Douglas-Home*, London: Sinclair-Stevenson, 1996.

Todd, Emmanuel, *After the Empire the Breakdown of the American Order*, New York: Columbia University Press, 2002 (translation 2003).

Toffler, Alvin and Heidi, *War and Anti-War*, New York: Warner Books, 1993.

Walker, Martin, *The Cold War*, London: Fourth Estate, 1993.

Williams, Raymond, *Resources of Hope*, London: Verso, 1989.

Woollacott, Martin, *After Suez*, London, New York: I. B. Tauris, 2006.

Young, Hugo, *One of Us*, London: Macmillan, 1989.

INDEX